UNEQUAL BARGAINING

A Study of Vitiating Factors
in the Formation of Contracts

JOHN CARTWRIGHT

CLARENDON PRESS · OXFORD
1991

Oxford University Press, Walton Street, Oxford OX2 6DP

Oxford New York Toronto
Delhi Bombay Calcutta Madras Karachi
Petaling Jaya Singapore Hong Kong Tokyo
Nairobi Dar es Salaam Cape Town
Melbourne Auckland
and associated companies in
Berlin Ibadan

Oxford is a trade mark of Oxford University Press

Published in the United States
by Oxford University Press, New York

British Library Cataloguing in Publication Data
data available

Library of Congress Cataloging in Publication Data
Cartwright, John, MA.
Unequal bargaining: a study of vitiating factors in the formation
of contracts/John Cartwright.
Includes index.
1. Contracts—Great Britain.   I. Title.
KD1559.C37   1991   346.41'02—dc20   [344.1062]   91-17336
ISBN 0–19–825243–9
ISBN 0–19–825750–3 (pbk.)

Typeset by Cotswold Typesetting Ltd, Cheltenham
Printed in Great Britain by
Biddles Ltd
Guildford & King's Lynn

Preface

Why does one write a book of this kind? I suppose that it begins with a dissatisfaction with the treatment of the subject-matter in the existing books. And there may be a particular desire to set down on paper one's own perspective on the subject-matter. In the case of my decision to write this book, both of these reasons are true. It will become apparent to the reader that, in a number of areas, my treatment is different from that found in the standard textbooks on contract; and I have chosen the topics which are contained in this book—certain aspects of the formation of contracts, together with misrepresentation, duress, undue influence, and unconscionable bargains—because there seems to be a link between them, based on the inequality of bargaining between the parties. From my own teaching, I know that some of the material covered in this book is often found difficult by students of contract law—particularly when they approach it for the first time in the first year of their course. So I have attempted to deal with the topics in a straightforward way, whilst still keeping the perspective throughout the book which I wish to emphasize: the common link of the inequality of bargaining.

I should give thanks where they are due. In writing the book I was given much encouragement by my former colleague at Christ Church, Edward Burn, who also read the whole manuscript in draft and made many valuable comments. I am also most grateful to Jack Beatson, who read Part III in draft, and saved me from many errors. I owe a particular debt to my colleague Edwin Simpson, who read the whole book in draft and made numerous suggestions which improved the substance and style of the text; helped me with the checking of the final manuscript; and assisted in correcting the proofs.

I should also acknowledge the encouragement which I received from Richard Hart in writing this book, and the friendly assistance which I have had at every stage from the production team at the Oxford University Press.

I know that it is customary for an author to thank his family for their tolerance during the preparation of the book; and now I know why. My wife has given much direct help in preparing the table of cases and in checking the proofs. But thanks are mainly due to her and my two daughters for not complaining when I wrecked the family Christmas in 1990 in order to meet my deadline to complete the manuscript.

Some of the material which I have used in relation to misrepresentation and mistake has appeared before, in articles published by Sweet & Maxwell in *The Law Quarterly Review* and *The Conveyancer and Property Lawyer*. Where appropriate, I have referred in the text to these earlier publications, and I am grateful to Sweet & Maxwell for allowing me to use the material again.

The book attempts to state the law as at 1 January 1991, but further developments have been incorporated where space permitted.

Christ Church,   J.C.
Oxford,
June 1991

Contents

Contents

Table of Cases

Table of Statutes

Principal Authorities Referred To

Anson   Anson's *Law of Contract*, 26th edn., 1984

Chitty   *Chitty on Contracts*, 26th edn., 1989

CFF   Cheshire, Fifoot and Furmston's *Law of Contract*, 11th edn., 1986

Goff and Jones   Goff and Jones, *The Law of Restitution*, 3rd edn., 1986

Restatement   American Law Institute, *Restatement of the Law, Second: Contracts 2d.* (1979)

Treitel   Treitel, *The Law of Contract*, 7th edn., 1987

Introduction

It is customary—and, indeed, it is analytically helpful to the student of Contract Law—to keep separate the questions:

(1) Is there a contract?
(2) On which terms is it formed?
(3) Are there any inherent defects in the contract arising out of the circumstances of its formation?

The purpose of this book is to look in some detail at these questions, and ultimately to consider whether there are any common themes or ideas which link them.

Part I will consider questions (1) and (2), by looking at the circumstances surrounding the formation of a contract—the way in which the courts establish whether the parties can be said to be sufficiently in agreement for a contract to come into existence, by reference to the words and conduct of each leading up to the moment of contracting. Parts II and III will consider question (3), by discussing vitiating factors which may be present in a contract from the moment of its formation: misrepresentation, duress, undue influence, and unconscionable bargains. These will be considered separately, under their traditional headings, to enable a full account of the relevant law to be given. However, it is hoped that general themes which unite the vitiating factors will be seen. Part IV will consider briefly the common ideas which emerge from the earlier parts, and will contrast another situation where a contract may be vitiated—a mistake shared by both parties ('common' mistake)—but which depends upon different principles.

The reader may find it helpful to bear in mind from the outset that a key to the unity of the vitiating factors in the formation of a contract is the responsibility to be borne by each party at the moment of contracting; and this responsibility may arise by virtue of what a party has taken upon himself to say, or simply by virtue of a position of strength in which he finds himself *vis-à-vis* the other. In short, the responsibility arises out of an inequality in the bargaining between the parties. How this responsibility operates in relation to each vitiating factor will be discussed in the following chapters.

I
CONTRACT FORMATION
AND TERMS

1

Formation of the Contract

1. FORMATION AND 'MISTAKE': INTRODUCTION

Textbooks on the law of contract have tended to treat separately the formation of the contract and the rules relating to mistakes in contract.[1] This can, however, be misleading, since certain mistakes—in particular, mistakes about the terms of the contract[2]—cannot be resolved without a consideration of the principles concerning the formation of contracts. Consider the following example:

A and B agree that B shall buy A's car for £1,000. However, A has two cars. A thinks that B has contracted to buy his red car; but B intends to buy A's blue car.

There is clearly a 'mistake' here; A and B are not actually in agreement about the subject-matter of the contract. And if either of the parties thinks that the identity of the car was a term of the contract (that is, that B had promised to buy either the red car or the blue car), it means that they are not in agreement about the terms of the contract. But as soon as one analyses the problem in this way, it becomes clear that the issue is about the formation of the contract. Is there a contract at all? If so, on which set of terms is it concluded? Clearly, the principles relevant to resolving the 'mistake' will need to be harmonized with (if not identical to) the principles to be applied in deciding when a contract is formed. Indeed, it is sometimes not easy to use the word 'mistake' in this context, since the word presupposes that one party is right and the other party is wrong. But they are simply in disagreement—at cross-purposes—about the terms, and the rules for the formation of a contract have to be

---

[1] See e.g. Treitel, chs. 2, 8 (although the two areas are mentioned as linked on p. 1); Anson, chs. 1, 8; CFF, chs. 3, 8; *Chitty*, chs. 2, 5.

[2] For mistakes about the identity of the contracting parties, see pp. 24 ff., below; and for mistakes about the subject-matter (or a quality of the subject-matter), pp. 6 ff. and Ch. 11, below.

applied to ascertain which party's understanding of the contract is to prevail.

It should be noted that only those mistakes which involve the parties being at cross-purposes[3] are in reality part of the issue of the formation of the contract. A quite separate area is that where the parties make the *same* mistake: that is, they are in agreement about the existence and the terms of the contract, but they have made the same mistake about (usually) the subject-matter of the contract. Such mistakes[4] raise quite separate issues, and are rightly dealt with separately from the rules relating to formation.[5]

Part I will consider the rules for the formation of contracts, and will draw upon cases which are often categorized as cases of mistake. The purpose is to consider whether there is any underlying principle in relation to formation of contracts which can assist us in understanding the vitiating factors, which will be discussed in detail in later chapters.

2. RULES FOR THE FORMATION OF A CONTRACT: OFFER AND ACCEPTANCE

A contract may be characterized in various ways. It may be seen as a promise or a set of promises;[6] or as a bargain; or as an agreement.[7] In each of these different aspects, however, there is a common element: that there must be some *communication between the parties of the common intention to contract*. Therefore, anything in the mind of one party which is not disclosed to the other cannot be part of the contract.[8] And even if the two parties have a desire to contract on similar terms, and each has communicated that desire to the other, there is not necessarily a contract, since one party's communication must be referable to the other's: cross-offers do not make a contract.[9]

---

[3] Called in the textbooks variously 'mutual' (CFF, p. 234) or 'unilateral' (Anson, pp. 253–4) mistakes or 'mistakes which negative consent' (Treitel, p. 223). In this book such cross-purposes mistakes will be called 'unilateral'.

[4] Called 'common' (CFF, p. 219) or 'mutual' (Anson, p. 253); or 'mistakes which nullify consent' (Treitel, p. 213). In this book such shared mistakes will be called 'common'.

[5] See Ch. 11, below.   [6] *Chitty*, §1; *Restatement*, §1.

[7] *Chitty*, §3; *Restatement*, §3.   [8] *Wood* v. *Scarth* (1858) 1 F. & F. 293.

[9] *Tinn* v. *Hoffmann & Co.* (1873) 29 LT 271 (*obiter*): 'there must be an offer which the person accepting has had an opportunity of considering, and which when he accepts he knows will form a binding contract': Grove J at p. 277.

In order to ascertain whether the parties to a supposed contract have actually agreed to the contract, it is conventional[10] to begin by looking for an offer by one party, containing a proposal of terms, followed by an unqualified acceptance of that offer by the other party. The offer and the acceptance may be by words (written[11] or oral[12]) or implied from conduct[13]—and sometimes may even be implied from silence.[14] It is obviously crucial, therefore, to analyse closely what each party wrote, said, and did at the time that the contract was alleged to have been concluded, so as to ascertain the existence and extent of the obligations contained in the contract. It is not proposed to discuss in detail here all the particular rules of offer and acceptance.[15] What is important, however, is to consider how the communications between the parties are to be interpreted. This will assist us to ascertain whether a contract exists, and (in cases of disagreement between the parties) on which party's terms it has been formed.

3. THE BASIC TEST

The test whether there has been correspondence between offer and acceptance is not subjective, but objective.[16] Therefore, it is not simply a question of whether both parties actually understood that there would be a contract and that it would contain a particular set of terms. There may still be a contract if, objectively tested, the parties can be said to have agreed (even though they did not in fact agree).

How, though, is the 'objective test' to be formulated? The most recent authoritative statements are to be found in the judgments of the House of Lords in *The Hannah Blumenthal*.[17] These judgments have, however, been subjected to discussion and interpretation in

[10] Indeed, it is the *rule* that there must be such an offer and acceptance before a contract can be found. Only in exceptional cases need there not be any offer and acceptance—and a case where the two parties are negotiating by correspondence is not such an exceptional case: *Gibson* v. *Manchester City Council* [1979] 1 WLR 294, 297.

[11] e.g. *Storer* v. *Manchester City Council* [1974] 1 WLR 1403.

[12] e.g. *Leroux* v. *Brown* (1852) 12 CB 801. Note, however, that a contract for the sale or other disposition of an interest in land can now only be made in writing: Law of Property (Miscellaneous Provisions) Act 1989, s. 2.

[13] e.g. *Brogden* v. *Metropolitan Railway Co.* (1877) 2 App. Cas. 666.

[14] See n. 33, below.

[15] See Treitel, pp. 7–40.

[16] *Whittaker* v. *Campbell* [1984] QB 318, 326.

[17] *Paal Wilson & Co. A/S* v. *Partenreederei Hannah Blumenthal* [1983] 1 AC 854.

later cases; and it will be seen that the tests stated in *The Hannah Blumenthal* are themselves built on earlier decisions, notably that in *Smith* v. *Hughes*.[18]

(a) Smith v. Hughes

Smith v. *Hughes* is generally categorized as a case dealing with mistake, rather than formation of a contract,[19] since the issue was not whether there was a contract, but only which party's terms were contained within the contract. However, the two questions are interdependent.[20]

In *Smith* v. *Hughes*, the defendant, an owner and trainer of racehorses, agreed to buy oats from the plaintiff, a farmer. The sale was by sample. The oats which the plaintiff supplied were *new* oats; the defendant refused to accept them, since he claimed that he was entitled to receive *old* oats under the contract. It was clear that both parties thought that they had entered into a contract; but the dispute was about what obligations were contained in that contract.

All turned on what had been said by the parties at the time that they had apparently agreed to the contract. On this, there was a conflict of evidence. The plaintiff claimed that, when he showed the defendant the sample of the oats which he had for sale, he had said simply that he had 'good oats for sale'; and that he did not realize that the defendant wanted to buy only old oats. The defendant, however, alleged that the plaintiff had said that he had 'good *old* oats for sale'.

The judge directed the jury that the defendant should have judgment if either (1) the word 'old' had been used by either party at the time of making the contract; or (2) the plaintiff believed that the defendant thought he was buying old oats. The jury found for the defendant, but did not state whether it was on ground (1) or (2). On appeal, the Court of Queen's Bench decided that the judge's direction (2) had been wrong. It had failed to distinguish between the plaintiff's belief

  (*a*) that the defendant thought he was buying oats which *as a matter of fact* were old (that is, the age was simply a factual quality of the agreed subject-matter of the contract); and

---

[18] (1871) LR 6 QB 597.
[19] In *Chitty*, for example, it is cited only in the chapters on misrepresentation and mistake; not in the chapters dealing with the formation of the contract.
[20] See p. 3, above.

(b) that the defendant thought that the plaintiff was *warranting* that the oats were old (that is, the age of the oats was a *term* of the contract).

If (a) were true, then the plaintiff could force the defendant to take the oats. Only if (b) were true—and so the plaintiff knew that the defendant was at cross-purposes with him concerning the terms of the contract—could the defendant escape the contract. Since it was not clear on which basis the jury had found for the defendant, the Court sent the case back for a new trial.

The Court was here drawing some clear lines about the validity of contracts. One party to a supposed contract cannot hold the other to terms to which he knows that the other does not intend to agree. But the fact that one party is under a misapprehension about the factual details of the subject-matter of the contract—its quality—does not enable that party to escape from the contract. This is so, even if the other party knows of the misapprehension.[21] Blackburn J summed up these points as follows:[22]

> on the sale of a specific article, unless there be a warranty making it part of the bargain that it possesses some particular quality, the purchaser must take the article he has bought though it does not possess that quality. And I agree that even if the vendor was aware that the purchaser thought that the article possessed that quality, and would not have entered into the contract unless he had so thought, still the purchaser is bound, unless the vendor was guilty of some fraud or deceit upon him, and that a mere abstinence from disabusing the purchaser of that impression is not fraud or deceit; for, whatever may be the case in a court of morals, there is no legal obligation on the vendor to inform the purchaser that he is under a mistake, not induced by the act of the vendor.

Blackburn J went on to state a general test for the formation of a contract—and this is the crucial passage for our purposes:[23]

> I apprehend that if one of the parties intends to make a contract on one set of

---

[21] However, it is different if he has *induced* the misapprehension: (1871) LR 6 QB 597, 603, 605 (Cockburn CJ), 607 (Blackburn J), 610–11 (Hannen J). Remedies for misrepresentation would then be available: see Part II, below. Note that Cockburn CJ at p. 605 thought that, in some circumstances, the silence of the seller, if designed to mislead, might amount to 'fraudulent concealment'.

[22] (1871) LR 6 QB 597, 606–7.

[23] Ibid., at p. 607. See also Hannen J at pp. 609–10. Howarth ('The Meaning of Objectivity in Contract' (1984) 100 LQR 265, 267–8, 271–2) maintains that Hannen J was stating a principle different from that of Blackburn J. See, however, Vorster, 'A Comment on the Meaning of Objectivity in Contract' (1987) 103 LQR 274.

terms, and the other intends to make a contract on another set of terms, or, as it is sometimes expressed, if the parties are not ad idem, there is no contract, unless the circumstances are such as to preclude one of the parties from denying that he has agreed to the terms of the other. The rule of law is that stated in *Freeman* v. *Cooke*.[24] If, whatever a man's real intention may be, he so conducts himself that a reasonable man would believe that he was assenting to the terms proposed by the other party, and that other party upon that belief enters into the contract with him, the man thus conducting himself would be equally bound as if he had intended to agree to the other party's terms.

Blackburn J's principle amounts to this: first consider whether the parties, say A and B, were *actually* in agreement.[25] If they were, there is a contract on those agreed terms. But if A and B were *not* in agreement about the terms on which they intended to contract, then there will only be a contract if

(1) a reasonable man would have believed, and
(2) A did in fact believe

that B was agreeing to A's terms. In that case, there will be a contract on A's terms. This is the so-called 'objective test'. It is not, of course, wholly objective[26] in that A's actual belief is required to be considered before he can hold B to the contract. But it is objective in that the belief of B, who is being held to a term which he did not intend, is not relevant. What the test involves, in essence, is that, in cases where the parties are not in agreement about the terms of their contract, one party's actual intention is overridden by the fact that he has caused the other to misunderstand his intention.

(b) *Freeman* v. *Cooke*

Blackburn J relied on *Freeman* v. *Cooke*[27] for his statement of principle. That case was concerned with estoppel by representation: that is, the rule of evidence by which a person who has (by words or conduct)

---

[24] (1848) 2 Ex. 654, 663.
[25] The orthodox view is that two parties will not be held to a contract which *neither* of them intended: such a contract can be the result of applying a different theory—'detached objectivity'—whereby the terms are those which a reasonable observer of both parties would conclude; see pp. 21–4, below.
[26] *The Hannah Blumenthal* [1983] 1 AC 854, 924 (Lord Brightman).
[27] (1848) 2 Ex. 654.

made a representation of fact to another, which that other has relied upon to his detriment, is estopped—or stopped[28]—from adducing evidence to show that the stated fact was untrue.[29] In effect, therefore, Blackburn J was using a form of estoppel to create a contract.

However, Blackburn J did not explicitly use the language of estoppel; and whether it ought to be strictly necessary to find an estoppel will be discussed below. However, the idea of an estoppel being used to create a contract in this way has been taken up in later cases. For example, in *Pearl Mill Co. Ltd.* v. *Ivy Tannery Co. Ltd.*,[30] the Divisional Court held that a contract to sell certain goods, 'delivery as required', had been abandoned where the buyers had not requested delivery for several years. McCardie J said that the lapse of time was so great that the proper inference to draw was that the parties had mutually abandoned the contract: that is, they had both in fact decided to abandon it. However, there was also another ground: that the conduct of the buyers was such as reasonably to lead the defendants to the conclusion that the buyers had regarded the contract as at an end; this was an estoppel.[31]

(c) *The Hannah Blumenthal*

The idea of estoppel is also reflected in the speeches of the House of Lords in *The Hannah Blumenthal*[32]—which concerned an alleged contract to abandon an arbitration. The case is complicated by the fact that the contract of abandonment was claimed to have been

---

[28] 'The word "estoppel" only means "stopped". You will find it explained by Coke in his *Commentaries on Littleton*. . . . It was brought over by the Normans. They used the old French "estoupail". That meant a bung or cork by which you stopped something from coming out': *McIlkenny* v. *Chief Constable of the West Midlands* [1980] QB 283, 316–17 (Lord Denning MR).

[29] See also *Pickard* v. *Sears* (1837) 6 Ad. & E. 469, 474; *Cornish* v. *Abington* (1859) 4 H. & N. 549, 555–6; and, generally, Spencer Bower and Turner, *The Law Relating to Estoppel by Representation*, 3rd edn., 1977.

[30] [1919] 1 KB 78; said, however, by the Court of Appeal in *Allied Marine Transport Ltd.* v. *Vale do Rio Doce Navegacao SA, The Leonidas D* [1985] 1 WLR 925, 939 to be a decision not on the formation of a contract but on repudiation. See also *Scriven Bros. & Co.* v. *Hindley & Co.* [1913] 3 KB 564, where A. T. Lawrence J decided that, on the facts, there was *not* a 'contract by estoppel'; *Colonial Investment Co. of Winnipeg, Man.* v. *Borland* (1911) 1 WWR 171, 187 (Supreme Court of Alberta).

[31] [1919] 1 KB 78, 83–4; relying on *Pickard* v. *Sears* and *Cornish* v. *Abington*, above, n. 29.

[32] [1983] 1 AC 854.

formed by the silence of both parties;[33] but there are general statements about the test for the formation of contracts in three of the
judgments. Unfortunately, the three are not consonant, which has
led to some discussion and interpretation in later cases.

The main judgment was given by Lord Brandon.[34] His statement is
as follows:[35]

Where A seeks to prove that he and B have abandoned a contract in this
way, there are two ways in which A can put his case. The first way is by
showing that the conduct of each party, as evinced to the other party and
acted on by him, leads necessarily to the inference of an implied agreement
between them to abandon the contract. The second method is by showing
that the conduct of B, as evinced towards A, has been such as to lead A
reasonably to believe that B has abandoned the contract, even though it has
not in fact been B's intention to do so, and that A has significantly altered his
position in reliance on that belief. The first method involves actual
abandonment by both A and B. The second method involves the creation by
B of a situation in which he is estopped from asserting, as against A, that he,
B, has not abandoned the contract: *Pearl Mill Co. Ltd.* v. *Ivy Tannery Co. Ltd.*[36]

Lord Brandon's approach seems to be similar to that of Blackburn J
in *Smith* v. *Hughes*: a contract is formed either by both parties in fact
agreeing to enter into the contract; or by one party being estopped
from denying that he intended to contract. It is clear, however, that
Lord Brandon thought that this latter test involved a true estoppel by
representation: he not only used the language of estoppel, but he
also required the representee, A, to have 'significantly altered his
position in reliance'.[37]

Lord Diplock,[38] by contrast, spoke of the objective test for the

---

[33] Silence is always likely to be difficult to interpret: and for a contract to be formed,
it will be necessary for the parties to have *communicated* with each other on the terms:
p. 4, above; *Allied Marine Transport Ltd.* v. *Vale do Rio Doce Navegacao SA* [1985] 1 WLR
925, 937; *MSC Mediterranean Shipping Co. SA* v. *B.R.E.-Metro Ltd.* [1985] 2 Lloyd's Rep.
239, 241–2; *Cie. Française d'Importation et de Distribution SA* v. *Deutsche Continental
Handelsgesellschaft* [1985] 2 Lloyd's Rep. 592, 598–9. However, a contract of abandonment of an arbitration *has* been formed by the silence of both parties: *Excomm Ltd.* v.
Guan Guan Shipping (Pte) Ltd., The Golden Bear [1987] 1 Lloyd's Rep. 330; *Tankrederei
Ahrenkeil GmbH* v. *Frahuil SA, The Multitank Holsatia* [1988] 2 Lloyd's Rep. 486.
[34] Lord Diplock, [1983] 1 AC 854, 900, made clear that the other judgments were
intended only to be 'supplementary to and in amplification of some parts of' Lord
Brandon's judgment.
[35] [1983] 1 AC 854, 914.
[36] [1919] 1 KB 78; p. 9, above.
[37] For the requirement of detrimental reliance, see pp. 13–15, below.
[38] [1983] 1 AC 854, 915–16.

formation of a contract being based on 'injurious reliance', rather than 'estoppel' as such. However, his formulation has caused some difficulty of interpretation:

To create a contract by exchange of promises between two parties where the promise of each party constitutes the consideration for the promise of the other, what is necessary is that the intention of each *as it has been communicated to and understood by the other* (even though that which has been communicated does not represent the actual state of mind of the communicator) should coincide. That is what English lawyers mean when they resort to the Latin phrase consensus ad idem and the words that I have italicised are essential to the concept of consensus ad idem, the lack of which prevents the formation of a binding contract in English law.

So far, so good. This makes clear that there is no requirement of actual—subjective—agreement between the parties to a contract; it is what they have caused each other (reasonably) to believe that binds them. However, Lord Diplock went on to give an example, which can be read as suggesting that his test will be satisfied only if the parties are actually in agreement:

Thus if A (the offeror) makes a communication to B (the offeree) whether in writing, orally or by conduct, which, in the circumstances at the time the communication was received, (1) B, if he were a reasonable man, would understand as stating A's intention to act or refrain from acting in some specified manner if B will promise on his part to act or refrain from acting in some manner also specified in the offer, and (2) B does in fact understand A's communication to mean this, and in his turn makes to A a communication conveying his willingness so to act or to refrain from acting which mutatis mutandis satisfies the same two conditions as respects A, the consensus ad idem essential to the formation of a contract in English law is complete.

It is the requirement that this test be satisfied on the part of both offeror and offeree—'mutatis mutandis'—which makes it appear that this might require both parties in fact to have the same intention. Moreover, Lord Diplock[39] gave a more specific example which may have just this outcome:

Where the inference that a reasonable man would draw from the prolonged failure by the claimant in an arbitration procedure is that the claimant is willing to consent to the abandonment of the agreement to submit the dispute to arbitration and *the respondent did in fact draw such inference* and by

---

[39] Ibid., at p. 916 (italics added).

his own inaction thereafter indicated his own consent to its abandonment in similar fashion to the claimant *and was so understood by the claimant*, the court would be right in treating the arbitration agreement as having been terminated by abandonment.

All that this example actually says is that each party (actually and on reasonable grounds) thinks that the other is consenting to abandonment. It does not require either party necessarily to intend to abandon the contract. However, the Court of Appeal in *Allied Marine Transport Ltd.* v. *Vale do Rio Doce Navegacao SA*[40] said (without explaining their reasons) that Lord Diplock's formulation involved the requirement that the actual intentions of both parties should in fact coincide; that is, the parties are subjectively in agreement. In *The Agrabele*,[41] Neill LJ, referring to this passage of Lord Diplock's judgment, left open the question whether the offeror, whose conduct is being held to override his actual intention, must believe that the other party had accepted his offer. It may be that the offeror must believe that the offeree is accepting *an* offer—but not that he needs to realize what the offeree thinks the offer was; that is, he must actually realize that the other party intends to contract, but not necessarily the terms on which he thinks the contract is made.

In the whole context of Lord Diplock's judgment, however, it is clear that he did not intend a subjective test.[42] Moreover, because of this difficulty of interpretation, Lord Diplock's test has in later cases[43] generally been disregarded, in favour of the third test stated in *The Hannah Blumenthal*, that of Lord Brightman.

Lord Brightman,[44] emphasizing that the test involves both subjective and objective elements, stated it simply, in terms which are very similar to the language of Blackburn J in *Smith* v. *Hughes*:[45]

[40] [1985] 1 WLR 925, 936.

[41] *Gebr. Van Weelde Scheepvaartkantor BV* v. *Compania Naviera Sea Orient SA, The Agrabele* [1987] 2 Lloyd's Rep. 223, 235. See also *Food Corporation of India* v. *Antclizo Shipping Corporation, The Antclizo* [1987] 2 Lloyd's Rep. 130, 138 (Bingham LJ), 145–6 (Nicholls LJ).

[42] Vorster, (1987) 103 LQR 274, 284–6. And see *Harvela Investments Ltd.* v. *Royal Trust Company of Canada (CI) Ltd.* [1986] AC 207, 225D–E (Lord Diplock). For a different view, however, see de Moor, (1990) 106 LQR 632, 649 ff.

[43] e.g. *Allied Marine Transport Ltd.* v. *Vale do Rio Doce Navegacao SA* [1985] 1 WLR 925, 936 (Court of Appeal), followed in *The Agrabele* [1985] 2 Lloyd's Rep. 496, 509 (Evans J); *The Golden Bear* [1987] 1 Lloyd's Rep. 330, 338 (Staughton J); *The Antclizo* [1987] 2 Lloyd's Rep. 130 (Court of Appeal); *The Multitank Holsatia* [1988] 2 Lloyd's Rep. 486, 492 (Phillips J). In *Collin* v. *Duke of Westminster* [1985] QB 581, 596 Oliver LJ applied Lord Diplock's test.

[44] [1983] 1 AC 854, 924.   [45] (1871) LR 6 QB 597, 607.

To entitle the sellers to rely on abandonment, they must show that the buyers so conducted themselves as to entitle the sellers to assume, *and that the sellers did assume*, that the contract was agreed to be abandoned sub silentio.

(*d*) Estoppel

We have seen[46] that the concept of estoppel has been used in some of the cases in conjunction with the objective test. The idea is that, if one party did not in fact mean to agree to the other party's terms, he might yet be estopped from denying that he had agreed because of the impact which his words and conduct had on the other party.

However, a true estoppel by representation requires that the representee should have relied upon the representation to his detriment. This means that the representee must show 'a change in [his] practical or business affairs or condition' which results in 'actual and temporal damage,—some loss of money or money's worth, which admits of quantification and assessment'.[47] If one were to look for detrimental reliance in *Smith* v. *Hughes*, however, it seems that the only place to find it would be in the fact that the party who (reasonably) misunderstands the other's intentions acts upon that misunderstanding by agreeing to enter into the contract; and, for example, he may thereby be induced not to enter into other contracts. Indeed, in a later case,[48] Blackburn J again applied *Freeman* v. *Cooke*[49] in the formation of a contract; and he made clear there that what constituted the reliance by the other party was his agreeing to enter into the contract. It is certainly sufficient to constitute detriment in an estoppel by representation if the representee assumes liabilities to which he would not otherwise be subject;[50] however, the liabilities arise under the *Smith* v. *Hughes* test only on the assumption that the estoppel is itself binding. The argument can appear rather circular.[51]

The confusion over whether this area involves true estoppel, and

---

[46] pp. 8–10, above.

[47] Spencer Bower and Turner, *The Law Relating to Estoppel by Representation*, §110.

[48] *Harris* v. *Great Western Railway Co.* (1876) 1 QBD 515, 530 (quoted at p. 39, below).

[49] (1848) 2 Ex. 654; pp. 8–9, above.

[50] Spencer Bower and Turner, *The Law Relating to Estoppel by Representation*, §112.

[51] But no more circular than the rule that mutual promises are consideration for each other in a wholly executory contract: Treitel, p. 55.

so whether there needs to be detrimental reliance, can also be seen in other cases. For example, Eveleigh LJ said in *The Splendid Sun*:[52]

they must be taken to intend that which any reasonable man would conclude that they intended, *particularly when* the other party has acted to his detriment in consequence.

Similarly, Leggatt J in *Tracomin SA* v. *Anton C. Nielsen A/S*[53] took the view that an arbitration had been abandoned by estoppel and found that there was injurious reliance[54] by the plaintiff on the offer which it supposed (wrongly) had been intended by the defendants.

Other judges have kept estoppel distinct from the objective test. For example, Phillips J in *The Multitank Holsatia*[55] clearly thought that estoppel (in its true form, requiring detrimental reliance on the other party's (implied) representation) was a separate issue from the formation of a contract of abandonment pursuant to the objective test. He held that the objective test of *The Hannah Blumenthal* had been satisfied, and so the parties had contracted to abandon their arbitration; but he also held that there was no estoppel, since there was no sufficient detriment.

It is the test set out by Lord Brightman in *The Hannah Blumenthal*[56] which has most consistently been followed in later cases.[57] Lord Brightman did not describe his formulation of the test as an estoppel; nor does it actually involve the elements of an estoppel by representation, since one party is bound simply by what the other party reasonably could, and in fact did, understand the agreement to contain. There is no specific stated requirement of detrimental

[52] *André & Cie. SA* v. *Marine Transocean Ltd.* [1981] QB 694, 706 (italics added). The case involved the abandonment of an arbitration by the silence of both parties. Eveleigh LJ found that there *had* been detrimental reliance on the facts, in that the defendants believed that the plaintiffs intended to abandon their claim, and made no further preparations for their defence, so that as time went on evidence ceased to be available to them.

[53] [1984] 2 Lloyd's Rep. 195.

[54] In that the plaintiffs had refrained from seeking evidence for the arbitration, and disposed of relevant files and documents.

[55] [1988] 2 Lloyd's Rep. 486, 493. And in *Collin* v. *Duke of Westminster* [1985] QB 581, 595 Oliver LJ appears to have thought that estoppel was a separate issue from the objective test as applied by Lord Diplock in *The Hannah Blumenthal*. See, however, Atiyah, (1986) 102 LQR 363, who thinks that the speeches of Lord Brandon and Lord Diplock in *The Hannah Blumenthal* show that the rationale of the objective test is that an *unrelied-upon* misleading communication of intention should not normally be held to have legal consequences.

[56] See pp. 12–13, above.

[57] See the cases cited in n. 43, above.

reliance. And this seems to be right.[58] Although, as we have seen, some of the earlier cases[59] had expressly used estoppel by representation to create the contract, others have used a more general concept, that a person's outward expressions are to be taken as proof of what he intends. The language of estoppel was not used in *Falck* v. *Williams*:[60]

If there was no contract in fact, was the proposal made on [the plaintiff's] behalf so clear and unambiguous that [the defendant] cannot be heard to say that he misunderstood it?

Moreover, it is often difficult to find any real detrimental reliance; and it is better to regard the so-called objective test for formation of a contract not as an application of the strict doctrine of estoppel, but simply as a rule whereby one party is entitled to rely on what he honestly and reasonably believes the other party to be agreeing—it is simply a rule of interpretation of communication.[61]

What is important here, however, is that the objective test shows the responsibility which the law attaches to the parties at the time of formation of the contract. It is the fact that one party has said something or done something, which—however innocently—has misled[62] the other party, which justifies that other party's interpretation of the contract being preferred. We shall see other situations in the formation of contracts where a similar principle is applied.

4. APPLICATION OF THE OBJECTIVE TEST OF FORMATION

We have seen that the objective test provides that, if A and B are not in actual agreement on the existence and terms of their contract, A

[58] Cf. *Centrovincial Estates plc* v. *Merchant Investors Assurance Company Ltd.* [1983] Com. L.R. 158.

[59] See n. 30, above.

[60] [1900] AC 176, 178–9.

[61] See also de Moor, (1990) 106 LQR 632, 641–2.

[62] It was even suggested by Staughton J in *The Golden Bear* [1987] 1 Lloyd's Rep. 330, 341 that the other party need not actually be misled: that he need not have addressed his mind to it—it is enough that he would have made the wrong assumption *if* he had thought about it. The Court of Appeal in *The Antclizo* [1987] 2 Lloyd's Rep. 130 were ambivalent about this: see pp. 138, 143 (Bingham LJ); 146–7 (Nicholls LJ). This may, however, be a particular problem relating to contracts of *abandonment by inactivity*; after all, it is in that situation that the parties are likely not actually to address their minds to the supposed offer or acceptance of the other: see *The Multitank Holsatia* [1988] 2 Lloyd's Rep. 486, 492–3 (Phillips J).

may still be able to assert that there is a contract, on his terms, if he can show that:

(1) B's conduct was such that a reasonable man would think that B was consenting to A's terms; and
(2) A in fact so understood B's conduct.

Certain points remain to be discussed. What if B could show that he too was honest and reasonable in his belief that the contract contained different terms? What if one party knows of the other's mistake? And what is the relevance of each party's fault in creating the mistake?

(a) Ambiguity Incapable of Resolution

The situation may arise whereby both A and B can assert that they honestly believed that their own terms were being adopted; and that it was reasonable for each of them so to believe, given the words and conduct of the other. In such a case, it is clear that there can be no contract, since the ambiguity in the terms of the contract is wholly incapable of resolution—the absence of actual agreement cannot be overridden by the objective test.[63] The statements of the objective test by Blackburn J in *Smith* v. *Hughes*[64] and Lord Brightman in *The Hannah Blumenthal*[65] do not consider this two-sided aspect of the objective test, probably because in most cases it is not raised. If A sues B for breach of a particular term of a contract, he must simply show that he has a contract with B which contains that term. What either party's understandings were of any *other* terms of the contract will not be relevant (unless they impact directly on A's claim or B's defences). Moreover, when A shows that he actually and reasonably believed B to have agreed to the relevant term, it will often be implicit that B's different understanding was unreasonable. Rarely, it seems, will there in practice be such an ambiguity, incapable of resolution.[66]

Such an ambiguity did however arise in *Falck* v. *Williams*.[67] The plaintiff and defendant attempted to contract using coded telegrams. However, there was a mistake in the messages, with the result that each party thought that the contract was on different terms: the

---

[63] Vorster, (1987) 103 LQR 274, 284, 286.
[64] (1871) LR 6 QB 597, 607.   [65] [1983] 1 AC 854, 924.
[66] Vorster, (1987) 103 LQR 274, 283–4.   [67] [1900] AC 176.

plaintiff thought there was a contract to carry copra from Fiji to the United Kingdom or Europe; the defendant to carry shale from Sydney to Barcelona. The Privy Council held that the parties were not in actual agreement; and that the objective test could not override the absence of agreement:[68]

It is not for their Lordships to determine what is the true construction of [the] telegram. It was the duty of [the plaintiff] to make out that the construction which he put upon it was the true one. In that he must fail if the message was ambiguous, as their Lordships hold it to be. If [the defendant] had been maintaining his construction as plaintiff he would equally have failed.

There may have been a similar ambiguity in *Raffles* v. *Wichelhaus*,[69] in which the plaintiff contracted to sell cotton to the defendant 'to arrive ex Peerless from Bombay'. There were, however, two ships of the same name, both sailing from Bombay: the defendant understood the contract to refer to the ship sailing in October; the plaintiff to the ship sailing in December. The plaintiff failed in its claim for the purchase price, thereby proving *at least* that there was no contract on the plaintiff's terms. It does not necessarily prove whether (1) there was no contract; or (2) there *was* a contract on the *defendant's* terms; but although no reason was given by the court for its decision, it seems likely that there was no contract because of the latent ambiguity which could not be resolved.[70]

(b) Known Mistakes

Under the objective test, for A to be able to hold B to his (A's) understanding of the terms of the contract, he must show that he reasonably could so have understood the contract, *and that he did in fact so understand it.*[71] Thus, the test has built into it the rule that a party cannot take advantage of the other's mistake—reasonable or unreasonable—about the terms of the contract of which he is

---

[68] Ibid., at p. 181.

[69] (1864) 2 H. & C. 906.

[70] Counsel for the defendant was arguing that there was no contract when he was stopped by the court; and this was the understanding of Hannen J in *Smith* v. *Hughes* (1871) LR 6 QB 597, 609. Contrast, however, *Van Praagh* v. *Everidge* [1902] 2 Ch. 266, 269, where Kekewich J thought that there had been a contract on the defendant's terms in *Raffles* v. *Wichelhaus*.

[71] This is the 'subjective' aspect of the so-called objective test: see p. 8, above.

actually aware. This was made very clear in the judgment of Hannen J in *Smith* v. *Hughes*:[72]

The rule of law applicable to such a case is a corollary from the rule of morality which Mr. Pollock cited from Paley,[73] that a promise is to be performed 'in the sense in which the promiser apprehended at the time the promisee received it,' and may be thus expressed: 'The promiser is not bound to fulfil a promise in a sense in which the promisee knew at the time the promiser did not intend it.' And in considering the question, in what sense a promisee is entitled to enforce a promise, it matters not in what way the knowledge of the meaning in which the promiser made it is brought to the mind of the promisee, whether by express words, or by conduct, or previous dealings, or other circumstances. If by any means he knows that there was no real agreement between him and the promiser, he is not entitled to insist that the promise shall be fulfilled in a sense to which the mind of the promiser did not assent.

For example, in *London Holeproof Hosiery Company Ltd.* v. *Padmore*,[74] the plaintiffs had an option to purchase from the defendant a factory of which they were tenants. The factory had been burnt down, and the plaintiffs, in exercising their option, thought that the defendant had undertaken to reinstate the building. The defendant knew that the plaintiffs were mistaken. When the defendant refused to reinstate the building, the plaintiffs were allowed by the Court of Appeal to escape from the contract to purchase, on the basis that the defendant's knowledge of the plaintiffs' mistake meant that there was no contract, because the parties were not *ad idem*.

It should be noted that the plaintiffs only sought to escape from the *defendant's* version of the contract; they did not seek to enforce *their own* version—that is, they did not claim that the defendant was obliged to reinstate the building and sell it to them. It appears that they could have so claimed, had they wished.[75] The objective test is therefore only to be applied if the party who wishes to rely upon it invokes it. This emphasizes that it is a one-sided principle, whereby one party can rely on the other's words and conduct as creating

---

[72] (1871) LR 6 QB 597, 610. This is a passage on which Howarth ((1984) 100 LQR 265, 266 ff.) relies to show a divergence of opinion on the objective test between the different judges in *Smith* v. *Hughes*. However, for a convincing counter-argument, see Vorster, (1987) 103 LQR 274. See also Hughes, (1938) 54 LQR 370, 375.

[73] *Moral and Political Philosophy*, book III, ch. v.

[74] (1928) 44 TLR 499.

[75] Ibid., at p. 501.

obligations in his favour, but the other party cannot so rely on his own words and conduct.[76]

One party cannot rely on the other's mistake of which he knows. Even if he does not know of the other's mistake, and so he is subjectively honest, he must also be reasonable in his belief before he can enforce the contract which he thinks has been concluded. However, the line between actual and reasonable belief can be fine— and of course the reasonableness of a person's belief will generally be evidence of whether he is to be trusted in his claims about what he actually believed. This fine line, between actual and reasonable belief, was illustrated by *Hartog* v. *Colin & Shields*,[77] where the parties to a contract for the sale of Argentine hareskins had throughout their negotiations referred to prices 'per piece'. However, the defendant seller, by mistake, produced an offer letter which gave a price 'per lb.'—which was much more favourable to the plaintiff. The plaintiff purported to accept, but Singleton J held that there was no contract. He said,[78]

I am satisfied . . . from the evidence given to me, that the plaintiff must have realised, and did in fact know, that a mistake had occurred. . . . The offer was wrongly expressed, and the defendants by their evidence, and by the correspondence, have satisfied me that the plaintiff could not reasonably have supposed that that offer contained the offeror's real intention. Indeed, I am satisfied to the contrary.

(c) Fault

Since a party can rely on what is communicated by the words and conduct of the other, and since he can only so rely if his own interpretation of those words and that conduct is reasonable, it is natural that the respective fault of the two parties should come under scrutiny in cases which have applied the objective test. One might expect that the party whose fault (in causing or contributing to the divergence of opinion over the terms of the contract) is less, will be more likely to succeed in his claim that it is his interpretation which constitutes the contract; for it will be easier for him to assert that he is reasonable in his interpretation.

This is, indeed, what can be seen in the cases. For example, in *Scriven Bros. & Co.* v. *Hindley & Co.*,[79] both parties to a contract were

---

[76] Hughes, (1938) 54 LQR 370, 376.   [77] [1939] 3 All ER 566.
[78] Ibid., at p. 568.   [79] [1913] 3 KB 564.

to some degree at fault in their mistake; but the party whose fault was the more serious was unable to enforce the contract which he claimed had been entered into.

In that case, there was an auction sale, at which the auctioneer offered tow for sale, and the defendants put in a successful bid, thinking that they were offering to buy hemp. The jury found, *inter alia*, that:

(1) hemp and tow are different commodities in commerce;
(2) the form of the catalogue, and the conduct of the foreman in charge of the showroom, had contributed to the mistake. The foreman had shown the defendants a sample of hemp, but had failed to draw attention to the fact that the shipping marks of the hemp and the tow which were being auctioned were similar; and the catalogue referred to the shipping marks without saying that they represented different commodities;
(3) the defendants' manager had been 'negligent' in not taking his catalogue when he had inspected the samples before the auction, and in not examining the samples more closely.

Since the parties were not actually in agreement about the subject-matter of the contract, A. T. Lawrence J applied the objective test: he said that the plaintiffs, who were seeking to enforce the contract, could recover from the defendants only if they could show that the defendants were 'estopped'[80] from relying upon what was the truth—that is, that they were actually bidding for tow. However, there was no such estoppel: it was unreasonable to expect the purchaser to discover the truth of misleading chalk marks on the floor, by which the samples were identified. The finding relating to the fault of the sellers in the misleading catalogue and marking of samples was enough to prevent their claiming a contract by estoppel. 'Such a contract cannot arise when the person seeking to enforce it has by his own negligence or by that of those for whom he is responsible caused, or contributed to cause, the mistake.'[81]

Moreover, a party who is at fault will not be able to resist the other party's claim to enforce the latter's understanding of the contract

---

[80] For estoppel in this context, see pp. 13 ff., above.

[81] [1913] 3 KB 564, 569. See also *Denny* v. *Hancock* (1870) LR 6 Ch. App. 1, where a bidder at an auction of property was not bound by his contract after being misled into thinking that he was purchasing a larger plot by the *crassa negligentia* of the sellers in their drawing of a plan.

against him, provided that the objective test is satisfied. For example, where a person agreed to purchase a plot of land thinking that it was larger than it really was—and where the vendor had given the purchaser the opportunity of checking the plans of the land, without in any way misleading him—the purchaser was held to be bound.[82] James LJ said,[83]

The vendors did nothing tending to mislead. . . . If a man will not take reasonable care to ascertain what he is buying, he must take the consequences. . . . It is not enough for a purchaser to swear, 'I thought the farm sold contained twelve fields which I knew, and I find it does not include them all,' or, 'I thought it contained 100 acres and it only contains eighty.' It would open the door to fraud if such a defence was to be allowed.

5. AN ALTERNATIVE APPROACH

Account must be taken of an alternative approach to the formation of a contract, which has been adopted in some cases. We have so far described the test for formation as 'objective', although we have seen that it is in fact partly subjective and partly objective: a person who wishes to enforce a term in a contract must show that he actually (subjectively) believed the contract to contain such a term, as well as being (objectively) reasonable in that belief.[84]

Another view is that the test is—or ought to be—wholly objective, in that the actual intentions of both parties are entirely irrelevant, and the terms of the contract are ascertained simply by asking what a reasonable observer of both parties would conclude. This is sometimes known as 'detached objectivity'.[85] In England this approach

---

[82] *Tamplin* v. *James* (1880) 15 Ch. D. 215. See also *Goddard* v. *Jeffreys* (1882) 30 WR 269; *Van Praagh* v. *Everidge* [1902] 2 Ch. 266; *Scott* v. *Littledale* (1858) 8 El. & Bl. 815. Note that in the earlier case of *Malins* v. *Freeman* (1837) 2 Keen 25, in which specific performance was refused against a purchaser who (by his own fault) misunderstood for which property he had bid, no decision was taken whether there was a contract— only whether specific performance was available as a remedy: see Lord Langdale at pp. 34–5. See also *Webster* v. *Cecil* (1861) 30 Beav. 62, where specific performance was similarly refused, without any decision on the validity of the contract at law; *Williams on Vendor and Purchaser*, 4th edn., 1936, vol. ii, pp. 752–3.

[83] (1880) 15 Ch. D. 215, 220–1.

[84] p. 8, above.

[85] Howarth, (1984) 100 LQR 265, esp. at pp. 275 ff., who supports detached objectivity; *contra*, Vorster, (1987) 104 LQR 274; Spencer, [1973] CLJ 104, 108–113.

has been adopted most notably by Lord Denning MR. In *Solle* v. *Butcher*[86] he said (as Denning LJ):

once a contract has been made, that is to say, once the parties, whatever their inmost states of mind, have to all outward appearances agreed with sufficient certainty in the same terms on the same subject matter, then the contract is good unless and until it is set aside for failure of some condition on which the existence of the contract depends, or for fraud, or on some equitable ground. Neither party can rely on his own mistake to say it was a nullity from the beginning, no matter that it was a mistake which to his mind was fundamental, and no matter that the other party knew that he was under a mistake.

This is a radically different approach. Denning LJ's test would not look to what either party thought, to determine whether there is a contract and what terms it contains: it is simply what they said and did, as interpreted by a reasonable observer. This is not to say, however, that the parties' actual knowledge is irrelevant. Denning LJ went on to say that once his test for the formation of the contract has been satisfied—that is, there is at common law a valid contract— *equity* might yet make that contract voidable on a number of separate grounds:[87]

It is now clear that a contract will be set aside if the mistake of the one party has been induced by a material misrepresentation of the other, even though it was not fraudulent or fundamental; or if one party, knowing that the other is mistaken about the terms of an offer, or the identity of the person by whom it is made, lets him remain under his delusion and concludes a contract on the mistaken terms instead of pointing out the mistake. . . .

    A contract is also liable in equity to be set aside if the parties were under a common misapprehension either as to facts or as to their relative and respective rights, provided that the misapprehension was fundamental and that the party seeking to set it aside was not himself at fault.

Denning LJ would therefore allow a contract between A and B, valid at common law according to his objective test of formation, none the less to be voidable in equity by A on three grounds:

---

[86] [1950] 1 KB 671, 691. See also, for example, *Frederick E. Rose (London) Ltd.* v. *William H. Pim Jnr. & Co. Ltd.* [1953] 2 QB 450, 460; *Oscar Chess Ltd.* v. *Williams* [1957] 1 WLR 370, 373–4; *Leaf* v. *International Galleries* [1950] 2 KB 86, 89. A case which may have applied detached objectivity is *Upton-on-Severn Rural District Council* v. *Powell* [1942] 1 All ER 220; this might, however, be explained as a case of restitution: *William Lacey (Hounslow) Ltd.* v. *Davis* [1957] 1 WLR 932, 938; Spencer, [1973] CLJ 104, 112 n. 46.

[87] [1950] 1 KB 671, 692–3.

(1) that B induced A to make a mistake by a material misrepresentation;

(2) that B knew that A was mistaken about the terms on which B intended to contract, or about B's identity;

(3) that A and B made the same, fundamental mistake of fact.

The first category—misrepresentation—is a clearly accepted area of equitable jurisdiction;[88] and the third category—'common' mistake—has also been applied in cases subsequent to *Solle* v. *Butcher*, although it appears to have been a novel principle at the time.[89] However, the second category—mistake known to the other party—was certainly a novel approach in 1950, and has not so far been applied in England.[90] The orthodox English approach has been to say that this area is a matter for the common law; a contract is valid (if the objective test of *Smith* v. *Hughes*[91] is satisfied); or it is void (if the test is not satisfied). Lord Denning's approach, however, is to say that as long as an observer would conclude that there is a contract, then there is such a contract; at most, it is voidable (not void) in equity. Indeed, in *Solle* v. *Butcher*[92] Denning LJ went so far as to say that *Smith* v. *Hughes* would nowadays be decided in equity, rather than at common law. The significance of the contract being voidable, rather than void, is that it may[93] give the court discretion over whether to avoid the contract; and a voidable contract will not be capable of avoidance if bona fide third parties have for value acquired rights in the subject-matter of the contract.[94]

However, in Australia, Lord Denning's approach appears to be gaining ground. The High Court of Australia in *Taylor* v. *Johnson*[95]

---

[88] See Ch. 4, below.

[89] Cartwright, '*Solle* v. *Butcher* and the Doctrine of Mistake in Contract' (1987) 103 LQR 594; *Associated Japanese Bank (International) Ltd.* v. *Crédit du Nord SA* [1989] 1 WLR 255. For more detail on common mistake, see Ch. 11, below.

[90] The *idea* of this category may underlie the equitable remedy of rectification for unilateral mistake; but this is not what Denning LJ appears to have meant in *Solle* v. *Butcher*; Cartwright, (1987) 103 LQR 594, 619–20; pp. 52 ff., below.

[91] (1871) LR 6 QB 597.

[92] [1950] 1 KB 671, 692–3.

[93] As in the case of *Solle* v. *Butcher* itself, dealing with a contract voidable for common mistake. Note, however, that (apart from the statutory discretion given by s. 2(2) Misrepresentation Act 1967), the court has no discretion whether to allow rescission for misrepresentation: see p. 101, below.

[94] See pp. 98–9, below. Indeed, it seems that one of Lord Denning MR's major concerns in ensuring that contracts were voidable, rather than void, was to protect third parties: see e.g. *Lewis* v. *Averay* [1972] 1 QB 198, 207.

[95] (1982–3) 151 CLR 423.

reviewed the conflict between the orthodox objective test of *Smith* v. *Hughes* and that of Lord Denning, and preferred the latter. They therefore awarded rescission in equity of a written contract, where one party knew that the other was mistaken about a fundamental term, and deliberately ensured that the mistaken party did not discover the mistake. In England, however, we have seen that the common law approach of *Smith* v. *Hughes* has dominated, and continues to dominate, the law relating to the formation of contracts.

6. MISTAKES OF IDENTITY

A final area which must be considered in this chapter is that relating to mistakes about the identity of the contracting parties. This is the appropriate place to consider such mistakes since they raise an issue concerning the formation of the contract. The question is: if A appears to enter into a contract with B, but on the assumption that B is in fact C (or, at least, on the assumption that B *is not B*), is there a valid contract?

(a) The Identity Must be Material

It must be noted at the outset that there can be no doubt about the validity of the contract unless there is some particular reason why B's identity matters to A. If A purchases a bar of chocolate at a supermarket, not knowing that the supermarket proprietor has just sold the business to another person, it is unlikely that A can claim that his contract was void on the ground of his mistake about the identity of the proprietor of the business. He wanted a bar of chocolate; it did not really matter who sold it to him. But it may be that, on the facts, the identity of the proprietor is important to A. In *Boulton* v. *Jones*[96] Jones sent an order for goods to the shop of one Brocklehurst, who had (unknown to Jones) just sold the business to Boulton. Jones did not learn of the transfer of the business until the invoice arrived—by which time it was too late to return the goods because they had been 'consumed'.[97] The Court of Exchequer held

---

[96] (1857) 27 LJ Ex. 117. Cf. *Fawcett* v. *Star Car Sales Ltd.* [1960] NZLR 406, 419–20 (Gresson P, dissenting), 426, 431; *Dennant* v. *Skinner and Collom* [1948] 2 KB 164, 168. It was emphasized in *Citibank NA* v. *Brown Shipley & Co. Ltd* [1991] 2 All ER 690, 699–700 that the identity must be a matter of crucial importance.

[97] It emerges from the report at (1857) 2 H. & N. 564 that the goods were in fact three 50-foot leather hose-pipes.

that the contract was void because of Jones's mistake about the identity of the proprietor of the business. The crucial fact was that Jones had a running account with Brocklehurst, under which the net balance was due from Brocklehurst to Jones. Jones was therefore entitled to set off the balance against purchases from Brocklehurst— but the set-off was not available against Boulton. Bramwell B said,[98]

> when any one makes a contract in which the personality, so to speak, of the particular party contracted with is important, for any reason, whether because it is to write a book or paint a picture, or do any work of personal skill, or whether because there is a set-off due from that party, no one else is at liberty to step in and maintain that he is the party contracted with.

However, this test is to be applied quite narrowly. In some early cases[99] the judges relied upon a statement of principle by Pothier:[100]

> Does error in regard to the person with whom I contract destroy the consent and annul the agreement? I think that this question ought to be decided by a distinction. Whenever the consideration of the person with whom I am willing to contract enters as an element into the contract which I am willing to make, error with regard to the person destroys my consent and consequently annuls the contract. . . . On the contrary, when the consideration of the person with whom I thought I was contracting does not enter at all into the contract, and I should have been equally willing to make the contract with any person whatever as with him with whom I thought I was contracting, the contract ought to stand.

However, to say that a contract will be void if 'the consideration of the person with whom I am willing to contract enters as an element into the contract which I am willing to make' can be interpreted much too widely, and can (contrary to the general approach taken by English law to the formation of a contract) be viewed as importing a *subjective* test to the issue of identity mistakes; in consequence, the statement of principle set out by Pothier has been rejected in later

---

[98] (1857) 27 LJ Ex. 117, 119. The ideas used here are similar to those determining whether an obligation is one the benefit of which can be assigned without the consent of the obligor: Treitel, pp. 517–19; and whether a valid contract has been concluded through an agent with an undisclosed principal: *Dyster* v. *Randall and Sons* [1926] Ch. 932, 938–9.

[99] *Smith* v. *Wheatcroft* (1878) 9 Ch. D. 223, 230; *Gordon* v. *Street* [1899] 2 QB 641, 647; *Lake* v. *Simmons* [1927] AC 487, 501; *Sowler* v. *Potter* [1940] 1 KB 271, 274.

[100] *Traité des Obligations*, s. 19.

cases.[101] The identity should be a determining factor of the validity of the contract only if the party who is mistaken about the identity of the other intends—or can be taken (objectively) to intend—his communications to be addressed to (and capable of being answered by) only the person with whom he wrongly assumes he is dealing.[102]

(*b*) Identity Mistakes and the Formation of Contract

If a mistake about the identity of one of the contracting parties is operative, the consequence must be that the contract is void. This is the position which has been taken consistently by the common law;[103] and it follows from seeing identity mistakes as being an issue concerning the formation of a contract. The communications (discussions and negotiations, and ultimately the offer and acceptance) are made between A and B, but B has no right to take part in those communications, since A addresses himself to C. As Pollock CB said in *Boulton* v. *Jones*,[104]

Now the rule of law is clear, that if you propose to make a contract with [C], then B cannot substitute himself for [C] without your consent and to your disadvantage, securing to himself all the benefit of the contract.

The typical situation in which the issue of identity has arisen is where A has sold goods to B, under the impression that B is C; but by the time A realizes the mistake, B has already sold the goods to D. The contracts may be represented as follows:

$$A \xrightarrow{\quad(1)\quad} B \xrightarrow{\quad(2)\quad} D$$

---

[101] *Gallie* v. *Lee* [1969] 2 Ch. 17, 33 (Lord Denning MR), 45 (Salmon LJ); notice, however, that both of these judges took a particularly strict line on identity mistakes, going so far as to suggest that identity mistakes ought *never* to make a contract void, but only voidable. See also *Lewis* v. *Averay* [1972] 1 QB 198, 206–7 (Lord Denning MR); *Solle* v. *Butcher* [1950] 1 KB 671, 691–2 (Denning LJ). And, on the danger of viewing Pothier's test as being subjective, rather than objective, see Goodhart, 'Mistake as to Identity in the Law of Contract' (1941) 57 LQR 228, 236; *Ingram* v. *Little* [1961] 1 QB 31, 54–6.

[102] This formulation covers the typical case, where A contracts with B on the mistaken assumption that B is C. Another case, such as occurred in *Sowler* v. *Potter* [1940] 1 KB 271, is where A contracts with B on the assumption that B *is not B*—that is, A would have been happy to contract with anyone *except* B. In such a situation the mistake should not vitiate the contract unless A regarded B's identity as so crucial that he was not prepared to allow his communications to be answered by B.

[103] *Cundy* v. *Lindsay* (1878) 3 App. Cas. 459. See, however, Lord Denning MR in *Lewis* v. *Averay* [1972] 1 QB 198, 206–7; pp. 34–5, below.

[104] (1857) 27 LJ Ex. 117, 118–19.

The issue in such cases is about the ownership of the goods. D has the goods, but A claims that he is still the owner and so may bring (for example) a claim in the tort of conversion against D. The validity of the two contracts is crucial to the question who owns the goods, and therefore whether the tort has been committed. If contract 1 is *void*, then B acquired no right to the goods; B therefore[105] had no property to pass to D under contract 2. However, if contract 1 was not void—that is, it was either valid or voidable[106]—the contract was effective to pass the property in the goods to B, and so D[107] acquired the property under contract 2.

This logic was applied with full force in *Cundy* v. *Lindsay*,[108] where Lindsays had sold goods to one Alfred Blenkarn, under the impression that they were dealing with a highly respectable firm called Blenkiron & Co. Blenkarn had sold some of the goods—250 dozen cambric handkerchiefs—to Cundys, who had no notice of the defect in the first contract. The House of Lords held that the contract between Lindsays and Blenkarn was void because of Lindsays' mistake as to Blenkarn's identity; Lindsays therefore still owned the handkerchiefs, and succeeded in their tort action against Cundys.

All turned on what Lindsays had intended when entering into their contract. The parties never met; everything was done in writing. The conclusion from that writing was that Lindsays did intend to deal with Blenkiron & Co., and did *not* intend to deal with Blenkarn. Blenkarn had used an address which was similar to Blenkiron & Co.: he was writing from 37 Wood Street, Cheapside, whereas Blenkiron & Co. traded from 123 Wood Street; and he always signed his letters to Lindsays so as to appear 'Blenkiron & Co.' It was therefore held[109] that Blenkarn

led, and intended to lead, [Lindsays] to believe, and they did believe, that the

---

[105] Assuming that the facts were not within any exception to the general rule that a seller can give no better title than he himself has: *nemo dat quod non habet*. For an example of such an exception, see Sale of Goods Act 1979, s. 22 (market overt).

[106] That is, valid for the time being, but capable of being avoided *ab initio* by A—for example, by reason of a misrepresentation. A voidable contract is incapable of avoidance once a third party has, without notice of the defect, acquired for value rights in the subject-matter of the contract. See p. 23, above. In cases of identity mistakes, the contract will almost always be voidable by reason of a misrepresentation of identity; in the reported cases, the mistake of identity rarely arises spontaneously.

[107] Provided, in the case of contract 1 being voidable, that he had no notice of the defect, and he gave value: see n. 106, above.

[108] (1878) 3 App. Cas. 459.   [109] Ibid., at p. 465 (Lord Cairns LC).

person with whom they were communicating was not Blenkarn, the dishonest and irresponsible man, but was a well known and solvent house of Blenkiron & Co., doing business in the same street.

The contract between Lindsays and Blenkarn was void, because Lindsays had never heard of Blenkarn and could not have intended to deal with him; there was therefore no *consensus* of mind between them to give rise to a contract. And there could of course be no contract between Lindsays and the real Blenkiron & Co., since Blenkiron & Co. knew nothing of the circumstances.[110]

(c) Examples of Identity Mistakes

The approach taken by *Cundy* v. *Lindsay* is consistent with an application of the general test for formation of a contract. The question is always: has A shown clearly that his intention was only to deal with C? We have seen that the basic test for the creation of a contract is:[111] has A so conducted himself that a reasonable man would think that he was agreeing to B's terms, and did B so think? The answer to both of these questions must be 'yes' for there to be a contract on B's terms. It is clear, therefore, that under the test of formation, B can never hold A to terms to which he knows A did not intend to agree.

If one considers this approach in relation to mistakes of identity, then one would expect the courts to ask: did B know—or ought he reasonably to have realized—that A was prepared to contract only with C?[112] If so, the natural conclusion would be that there is no contract between A and B. In practice, there is little difficulty in the cases in showing that B knew that A thought he was contracting with a person by the name of C, since in most of the reported decisions B has made a specific statement that he is C. However, that

[110] Ibid., at pp. 465–6. See also *Hardman* v. *Booth* (1863) 1 H. & C. 803.

[111] *Smith* v. *Hughes* (1871) LR 6 QB 597; p. 8, above.

[112] Goodhart, (1941) 57 LQR 228, 235. However, Goodhart took the view that the objective test applied here because the parties' identity was a term of the contract: ibid., at p. 231. It is difficult to accept this; it would lead to the conclusion that the mistaken party could in some circumstances sue the other for breach of contract in failing to be the person whom he claimed to be. However, the identity of the parties is certainly analogous to the terms of the contract, in that they both relate to the formation of the contract, and that similar rules relating to the objective interpretation of the terms of the contract and the identity of the parties ought to be applied. See also Chitty, §356.

does not go far enough: it must be shown that it was really C's *identity* that matters. This means, in effect, that B—even though he may know that A thinks that B is C—will be able to hold A to the contract as long as B actually thought, and it was reasonable for him to think, that C's identity was not crucial to A's decision to enter into the contract; and so B actually and reasonably thought that the communications put out by A could be taken as being capable of response by B. For example, in *Dennant* v. *Skinner and Collom*[113] Hallett J held that a bidder at auction who had misrepresented his identity had none the less contracted to purchase items for which he had bid:

At an auction sale, apart from any question of the reserve price, the lot is knocked down to the highest bidder, whoever he may be. When it comes to the question whether he shall be allowed to remove the lot without paying cash for it other questions arise, but as far as the contract is concerned, and the passing of the property in the object sold, the identity of the buyer does not usually enter into the question. I do not think it enters into the question any more than it ordinarily does on the sale of an article in a retail shop. In normal times a shopkeeper is not usually concerned with the identity of the customer when deciding whether he is willing to sell his goods to him, although he may be concerned with that matter when deciding whether, having effected the sale, he should give the purchaser credit.

Some examples of specific situations may help to understand the courts' approach.

(1) C is an identifiable, separate person from B; A and B communicate at a distance.

The first situation is where A deals with B without ever seeing him— for example, by post; and he knows of another, identifiable person, C, with whom he intends to deal.

This is of course what happened in *Cundy* v. *Lindsay*.[114] The facts of each case must be examined carefully to establish that the identity is sufficiently material to the contract, but it is perhaps in this situation that the courts are most likely to be able to say that the mistake about identity is operative. If the contract is concluded by correspondence, A is relying heavily on the name by which he identifies his correspondent; if there is another particular person with whom he thinks he is corresponding, he can more readily be heard to say that he is not directing his correspondence at B.

[113] [1948] 2 KB 164, 168.   [114] (1878) 3 App. Cas. 459; above.

(2) C is not an identifiable, separate person from B, but is simply the name used as an alias by B; A and B communicate at a distance.

Here, it may be more difficult for A to show that he is intending to deal with only C—because he cannot show that there is a person, C, who is physically distinct from B. Such was the case in *King's Norton Metal Co. Ltd.* v. *Edridge, Merrett and Co. Ltd.*[115] King's Norton sold a quantity of brass rivet wire to Hallam & Co., who then sold the wire to the defendants, Edridge, Merrett. King's Norton claimed that the wire was still their property, on the ground that their contract with Hallam & Co. was void for a mistake of identity. It emerged that 'Hallam & Co.' was simply an alias of a man called Wallis; there was no separate entity called Hallam & Co., but Wallis had used the name to make himself sound more respectable. He used printed notepaper, which included a statement that Hallam & Co. had agencies at Belfast, Lille, and Ghent, as well as in Sheffield.

The Court of Appeal held that, on the true construction of the transaction, King's Norton had intended to contract with the writer of the letters—by whatever name he called himself. It was explicitly stated by A. L. Smith LJ[116] that, if it could have been shown that there was a separate entity called 'Hallam & Co.', then the case might have come within the decision in *Cundy* v. *Lindsay*.[117]

(3) The parties deal face-to-face.

It is not easy for A to show that he did not intend to deal with B when B is the person physically present at the time the contract is concluded. In effect, he is attempting to say that he addressed his communications not to the person standing before him, but to the identity behind the name (either of another existing person, or simply an alias) by which the person physically present introduced himself.

Some cases have held that the mistake of a person in A's position was operative to prevent a contract coming into existence. In *Sowler* v. *Potter*,[118] for example, a person calling herself Ann Potter took a lease of a room from the plaintiff. In fact, Ann Potter was an

---

[115] (1897) 14 TLR 98.

[116] Ibid., at p. 99.

[117] (1878) 3 App. Cas. 459; above.

[118] [1940] 1 KB 271, relying on the statement of Pothier for the test for mistakes of identity: see p. 25, above. See also, however, *Hardman* v. *Booth* (1863) 1 H. & C. 803.

assumed name of Anna May Robinson, who had only three months earlier been convicted of permitting disorderly conduct in a café. The plaintiff claimed that she would not have entered into the contract had she known of Ann Potter's true identity. This was therefore an unusual case. The party alleged to have been mistaken was claiming that she thought B was C, and that her communications were addressed to C. However, the importance of the identity was not—as in the usual case—that she intended to deal *only with* C; instead, she alleged that she was happy to deal with C (or, presumably, anyone else) *but not with* B. Nevertheless, Tucker J held that the mistake was sufficient to render the contract void *ab initio*.

Tucker J relied upon *Lake* v. *Simmons*,[119] in which one Esmé Ellison was living with a Mr Van der Borgh as if she were his wife. She made a number of small purchases of jewellery from Lake's shop, calling herself Mrs Van der Borgh, paying on each occasion by a cheque which was met by the bank. On a later occasion, she induced Lake to allow her to take away on approval two valuable pearl necklets, on her representing that her 'husband', Mr Van der Borgh (who existed, but was not her husband, and knew nothing of the transaction) and one Commander Digby (who did not in fact exist) wished to see them with a view to buying them. Holding that Lake did not give consent to the property or possession being take by Esmé Ellison, and so no property passed to her, Viscount Haldane said,[120]

[Lake] thought that he was dealing with a different person, the wife of Van der Borgh, and it was on that footing alone that he parted with the goods. He never intended to contract with the woman in question. . . . There was not the agreement of her mind with that of the seller that was required in order to establish any contractual right at all. . . . Nothing short of a belief in her identity as a wife who was transacting for her husband as the real customer would have induced [Lake] to act as he did.

However, this case is not the most solid foundation on which to base a plea of a mistake of identity. First, the mistake made by Lake

[119] [1927] AC 487.

[120] Ibid., at pp. 500, 502–3. The issue arose in an action by Lake to recover in respect of the lost necklets under his insurance policy; the insurers pleaded that they were exempted from paying because the policy contained an exception where there was 'loss by theft or dishonesty committed by . . . any customer . . . in respect of goods entrusted to them by the assured'. The House of Lords held that the mistake of identity meant that Lake had not 'entrusted' the necklets to Esmé Ellison as a 'customer'; the exception in the policy did not therefore apply.

may really have been one relating to the *capacity* in which Esmé Ellison was contracting—as an agent, or for herself.[121] Second, although the language of Viscount Haldane is clear and can be applied generally to cases of mistaken identity where the parties deal face to face, the various judgments in the House of Lords were not unanimous in their approach.[122]

Moreover, *Sowler* v. *Potter* has been criticized heavily in the Court of Appeal,[123] and the cases have more readily held that where the contract has been concluded face to face, a mistake of identity has not been sufficient to prevent the contract coming into existence.

In *Phillips* v. *Brooks Ltd.*,[124] for example, Phillips contracted to sell some jewellery to one North, who said[125] he was Sir George Bullough. Phillips knew of Sir George Bullough, and checked the address given by North. He then allowed North to take the jewellery away. Horridge J held that the contract was valid. Even though Phillips said that he did not intend to contract with anyone except Sir George Bullough, he had still in fact intended to contract with the person physically present. Of course he had no one in mind as the purchaser except Sir George Bullough, and he would not have contracted with North had the misrepresentation of identity not been made; but that did not mean that the identity of the purchaser was so important as to be the determining factor of the validity of the contract.

Two more recent cases have shown a consistent approach to the question of identity mistakes in contracts concluded face to face. The approach is to say that, where there is such a situation, there is a *presumption* that the persons physically present are the intended parties.

In *Ingram* v. *Little*[126] the Court of Appeal employed such a presumption, but a majority found that the presumption had been rebutted. The case involved a sale of a car by the three plaintiffs to a man calling himself P. G. M. Hutchinson of Stanstead House,

---

[121] Treitel, p. 227.

[122] *Ingram* v. *Little* [1961] 1 QB 31, 70–3.

[123] n. 101, above.

[124] [1919] 2 KB 243.

[125] There is a possible argument that the representation of identity was made only *after* the contract had been concluded, and on that ground alone could not have been determinative of the validity of the contract: *Lake* v. *Simmons* [1927] AC 487, 501; *Ingram* v. *Little* [1961] 1 QB 31, 51, 60. This was, however, not accepted by Lord Denning MR in *Lewis* v. *Averay* [1972] 1 QB 198, 206; Treitel, p. 225.

[126] [1961] 1 QB 31.

Stanstead Road, Caterham. 'Hutchinson' called at the plaintiffs' house in response to a newspaper advertisement, and agreed to buy the car; but he wished to pay by cheque. One of the plaintiffs then slipped out of the house and went to check the name and address of P. G. M. Hutchinson in the telephone directory at the local post office. There was in fact such a name and address; but the man physically present in the plaintiffs' house was not Hutchinson. Reassured by the telephone directory, and so believing that they were dealing with P. G. M. Hutchinson, the plaintiffs concluded[127] the sale and allowed the car to be taken away. In due course the car came into the hands of the defendant. The cheque given to the plaintiffs by 'Hutchinson' was not met, and the plaintiffs sued the defendant for the return of the car or for damages in the tort of conversion.

Sellers and Pearce LJJ held that the contract between the plaintiffs and 'Hutchinson' was void: although, if 'Hutchinson' had paid cash for the car, the contract would have been valid, the fact that he wished to take the car in exchange for a cheque brought his identity into play. And the checking of the telephone directory helped to show that the identity of 'Hutchinson' was crucial to the plaintiffs.[128] The general approach taken by the judges is, however, instructive. All three judges—including Devlin LJ, who dissented—took as their starting-point that, in a contract concluded face to face, there is a presumption that the parties physically present are intended to be the parties to the contract.[129] And Sellers LJ[130] said that the question to be asked was the objective test: 'How ought the promisee to have interpreted the promise?' Sellers and Pearce LJJ therefore took the view[131] that, on the facts, 'Hutchinson' was not entitled reasonably to conclude that the plaintiffs were prepared to contract with a person other than the real Hutchinson.

[127] There was an argument (which was not accepted) that the contract had already been concluded before 'Hutchinson' produced his cheque-book—and so before his identity (which reflected upon his creditworthiness) became relevant: [1961] 1 QB 31, 49, 58.

[128] [1961] 1 QB 31, 48, 58. See, however, *Dennant* v. *Skinner and Collom* [1948] 2 KB 164, 168 (quoted above, p. 29).

[129] [1961] 1 QB 31, 50, 57, 66.

[130] Ibid., at p. 53, following Slade J at first instance, who had himself followed the approach of Goodhart, (1941) 57 LQR 228.

[131] Following the finding of Slade J at first instance. The case was, however, a borderline one, and Pearce LJ was less enthusiastic than Sellers LJ in so deciding: [1961] 1 QB 31, 59. However, Devlin LJ at p. 67 thought that the presumption that the man physically present was the intended contracting party was *not* rebutted.

The final case to consider is *Lewis* v. *Averay*,[132] which again involved the sale of a car to a man passing himself off as an identifiable third person. Lewis sold his car to a man calling himself 'Green', whom Lewis thought was a well-known actor.[133] The Court of Appeal unanimously held that the contract was not void for mistake of identity. Phillimore LJ[134] accepted that the approach taken in *Ingram* v. *Little*—that there is a presumption, in contracts concluded face to face, that the persons physically present are intended to be the contracting parties—was correct; but he held that there was no rebuttal of the presumption on the facts. Megaw LJ applied[135] the objective test of *Ingram* v. *Little*: How should the promisee interpret the promise?

However, Lord Denning MR took a bolder view: that a mistake of identity does not as such render a contract void.[136] He said that this was in full accord with the presumption derived from *Ingram* v. *Little* relating to contracts concluded face to face, but clearly there is a fundamental difference. The majority in *Ingram* v. *Little* regarded the presumption as *rebuttable*: indeed, they held that, on the facts, it had been rebutted. However, Lord Denning MR's presumption appears to be *irrebuttable*. The contract is still voidable for fraud; but it is not void.[137] Moreover, Lord Denning's approach is wholly objective: it is the fact that the two parties outwardly appear to have agreed that makes the contract not void;[138] there is no question of what one party actually did conclude and reasonably ought to have concluded about

---

[132] [1972] 1 QB 198.

[133] 'Richard Greene, who played Robin Hood in the "Robin Hood" series': [1972] 1 QB 198, 203 (Lord Denning MR). No point was taken about the different spelling of the surname; and the case was considered on the assumption that the man had held himself out clearly as being Richard Greene, although both counsel in argument accepted that there was no clear representation of identity: ibid., at pp. 201, 202.

[134] Ibid., at p. 208.

[135] Although with some reservation: ibid., at pp. 208–9.

[136] Ibid., at p. 207.

[137] Notice that this is another instance of Lord Denning MR's preference for contracts to be voidable, rather than void, for mistake: see also in relation to mistakes as to terms: p. 23, above; and common mistakes: p. 238, below. The reason is clear: the third party purchaser of the car in *Lewis* v. *Averay* deserves to be protected in preference to the original seller, who provided the opportunity for the fraud to be practised: [1972] 1 QB 198, 207. Cf. the recommendation of the Law Reform Committee to abrogate the distinction between void and voidable contracts, in case of identity mistakes, in favour of innocent third parties: 12th Report (Transfer of Title to Chattels) (1966) Cmnd. 2958, para. 15. See also the same problem in relation to rescission for misrepresentation: p. 102, below.

[138] [1972] 1 QB 198, 207.

the other's intentions. We have seen that this is a view taken by Lord Denning in other areas of formation of contracts.[139]

(d) Conclusions

It is clear that the general view in the cases is that an identity mistake, if operative, renders a contract void, on the basis that there is a failure in the formation of the contract. This could be expressed in the terms of the objective test: A will be held to have contracted with B, in spite of his (subjective) intention to contract with C, if he so conducted himself that B was entitled reasonably to think, and did in fact think, that he was a person with whom A was prepared to contract.[140] However, the cases do not generally use the objective test explicitly in this area, for two reasons. First, because it is usually clear that B knows that he is not the person with whom A intends to contract: in most of the cases B has himself induced A to make the mistake of identity by a misrepresentation that he is C.

Second, and more important, the efforts of the judges are concentrated on the difficult question of whether it was really B's *identity* about which A was mistaken; or whether it was some other attribute of his character—for example, his creditworthiness—which he mistook.[141] This can be an elusive and difficult enquiry[142]—rather similar to the distinction between the 'substance' and the 'quality' of the subject-matter of a contract, which is relevant in the case of common mistakes.[143]

An alternative approach is that of Lord Denning MR, suggesting that identity mistakes ought not to render contracts void, but only voidable.[144] This is not, however, the law. Although it has been a consistently stated view of Lord Denning,[145] it has not been followed by other judges in England and is in conflict with those cases which have held contracts void for mistakes of identity: in particular, the

---

[139] p. 22, above.

[140] 'How ought the promisee to have interpreted the promise?': *Ingram* v. *Little* [1961] 1 QB 31, 53; *Lewis* v. *Averay* [1972] 1 QB 198, 208; *Chitty*, §356.

[141] *Dennant* v. *Skinner and Collom* [1948] 2 KB 164, 168; p. 29, above.

[142] The distinction between identity and attributes was criticized by Lord Denning MR in *Lewis* v. *Averay* [1972] 1 QB 198, 206.

[143] See pp. 233 ff., below.

[144] *Lewis* v. *Averay* [1972] 1 QB 198, 207; p. 34, above.

[145] See also *Solle* v. *Butcher* [1950] 1 KB 671, 691–3; p. 22, above; pp. 238–9, below.

decision of the House of Lords in *Cundy* v. *Lindsay*.[146] It is also, on the views advanced in this chapter, contrary to principle: the question of the identity of the parties—just as the question of the terms of the contract itself—is an issue relating to the formation of the contract, and should be considered in accordance with the usual objective test of formation.

[146] (1878) 3 App. Cas. 459. See also, for example, *Hardman* v. *Booth* (1863) 1 H. & C. 803; *Ingram* v. *Little* [1961] 1 QB 31. *Cundy* v. *Lindsay* was cited in *Lewis* v. *Averay* [1972] 1 QB 198, but was not referred to by Lord Denning MR in his judgment; and in *Solle* v. *Butcher* [1950] 1 KB 671, 693 Denning LJ sought to distinguish *Cundy* v. *Lindsay*, in a way which was described by Gresson P in *Fawcett* v. *Star Car Sales Ltd.* [1960] NZLR 406, 412 as 'a somewhat cavalier method of disposing of a House of Lords judgment'.

2

Written Terms and Contracts Reduced to Writing

The ascertainment of the obligations contained in a contract is, no doubt, often relatively straightforward: the objective test is applied to the words spoken by the parties, in the case of oral contracts; and if the contract is in written form, the written document will set out the terms.[1] However, there can be problems in cases where the contract is not wholly reduced to writing, and one party seeks to introduce into the contract a written term about which the other did not actually know but to which he had access; or where the contract is reduced to writing but one party (who has perhaps even signed the document) seeks to escape from the contract by claiming that the written document does not reflect his understanding of the agreement. This chapter will consider whether there are any principles which underlie the courts' decisions on these issues—looking particularly to the relevance of the parties' respective positions and conduct at the time the contract was entered into.

It is clear that the general approach remains that of the objective test for the formation of the contract.[2] In *Hardwick Game Farm* v. *Suffolk Agricultural Poultry Producers Association*[3] Diplock LJ said,

The task of ascertaining what the parties to a contract of any kind have agreed shall be their legal rights and liabilities to one another as a result of the contract . . . is accomplished not by determining what each party actually thought those rights and liabilities would be, but by what each party by his words and conduct reasonably led the other party to believe were the acts which he was undertaking a legal obligation to perform. There are some rights and liabilities which arise by implication of law from the nature of the contract itself such as a contract of sale of goods or land, a contract of

---

[1] The express terms, that is. There may also of course be implied terms, but these will not be dealt with in detail in this book.

[2] *Smith* v. *Hughes* (1871) LR 6 QB 597; p. 8, above.

[3] [1966] 1 WLR 287, 339.

carriage or bailment, a contract of service or a contract of insurance. In offering to enter into a contract of a particular kind a party leads the other party reasonably to believe that he undertakes a legal obligation to perform all those acts which a person entering into a contract of that kind usually performs, unless his words or conduct are such as would make it reasonably clear to the other party that this is not so . . . In English law this general rule has become subject to a special rule that where parties have agreed to embody their contract in a written document they are presumed to have agreed to be bound by all the terms included in the written document and by no other terms except those which arise by implication of law from the nature of the contract itself; and this is so whether they have both read and understood the written document or not. Whatever the historical origin of this rule . . . its justification today is that it is so well established that any party to a contract by agreeing that its terms shall be embodied in a written document so conducts himself as to lead the other to believe that he intended the written document to set out all the rights and liabilities of each party towards the other which do not arise by implication of law from the nature of the contract itself.

1. INCORPORATION OF WRITTEN TERMS

The first situation to consider is where there is no formal written contract, but one party claims that the contract includes a term or terms which were on a written notice to which the other party had access. For example, this has arisen in cases where tickets have been issued under a contract, and the ticket has contained a term, or has referred to some other document containing a term, which the party supplying the ticket alleges has been incorporated into the contract.

The basic rule which can be deduced from the cases[4] is that the party seeking to introduce the term will be successful in so doing if he takes reasonable steps to bring the term to the other party's attention; thus it will be a question of fact.[5] What, though, is the underlying principle here? It can be seen that the early cases developed the rule by reference to the objective test.

In *Harris* v. *Great Western Railway Co.*[6] the plaintiff (acting through an agent) deposited luggage with the defendants, and received a

---

[4] The most heavily relied upon is perhaps *Parker* v. *South Eastern Railway Co.* (1877) 2 CPD 416.

[5] Ibid., at p. 422.

[6] (1876) 1 QBD 515.

ticket which contained on the back a clause limiting the defendants' liability. The plaintiff's agent knew that the ticket contained conditions, but did not choose to read them. It is not surprising that the plaintiff was held bound by the clause: it would be remarkable if a person who knows of the existence of terms proposed by the other party could escape being bound by them simply by choosing not to read them. The reasoning behind this was put by Blackburn J:[7]

by assenting to the contract thus reduced to writing, he represents to the other side that he has made himself acquainted with the contents of that writing and assents to them, and so induces the other side to act upon that representation by entering into the contract with him, and is consequently precluded from denying that he did make himself acquainted with those terms. But then the preclusion only exists when the case is brought within the rule so carefully and accurately laid down by Parke B in delivering the judgment of the Exchequer in *Freeman* v. *Cooke*,[8] that is, if he 'means his representation to be acted upon, and it is acted upon accordingly: or if, whatever a man's real intentions may be, he so conduct himself that a reasonable man would take the representation to be true, and believe that it was meant that he should act upon it, and did act upon it as true.'

This makes it quite clear that the underlying principle is that, as long as one party has given the other party the *chance* of seeing the written term, the fact that the second party then agrees to the contract means that the first party is entitled to hold the second to the written term, provided that he actually (and on reasonable grounds) believes that the second party agrees. In short, it is an application of the principle which we have already seen stated by Blackburn J in *Smith* v. *Hughes*[9]—the objective test for the formation of a contract.[10]

We can see, then, that a party may be bound, under the objective

---

[7] Ibid., at p. 530.

[8] (1848) 2 Ex. 654, 663; see pp. 8–9, above.

[9] (1871) LR 6 QB 597, 607; see p. 8, above.

[10] The statement of Blackburn J in *Harris* v. *Great Western Railway Co.* was doubted by Lord Devlin in *McCutcheon* v. *David Macbrayne, Ltd.* [1964] 1 WLR 125, 134: 'when a party assents to a document forming the whole or a part of his contract, he is bound by the terms of the document, read or unread, signed or unsigned, simply because they are in the contract; and it is unnecessary and possibly misleading to say that he is bound by them because he represents to the other party that he has made himself acquainted with them'. However, we have seen that Blackburn J's approach is consonant with the general test for the formation of a contract: and see *Hardwick Game Farm* v. *Suffolk Agricultural Poultry Producers Association* [1966] 1 WLR 287, 339 (Diplock LJ), quoted above, pp. 37 f. See also pp. 43 ff., below.

test, by terms—whether he has read them or not—in documents of which he is aware;[11] or of which he reasonably ought to have been aware;[12] but not by terms in documents of which he is not aware and it is not reasonable for the other party to think that he is aware.[13] So one must examine what each party actually knew of the proposed terms, and what each was entitled to assume from the other's words and conduct, to ascertain whether the objective test is satisfied, and thus whether the written terms are incorporated into the contract.

The content of the term in question will be relevant to its incorporation. An unreasonable term is not automatically excluded from the contract.[14] If the term is such as one would normally expect in such a contract, it may be easier to establish that the party seeking to incorporate the term was entitled to assume that the other party knew about it; but the more onerous the term, the less reasonable it will be to assert that the other party can be taken to have assented to it, without better steps being taken to attempt to draw it to his attention.

This can be illustrated by the decision in *Interfoto Picture Library Ltd.* v. *Stiletto Visual Programmes Ltd.*,[15] where the plaintiffs sent to the defendants (at their request) 47 transparencies of photographs. A clause[16] in the delivery note provided for the return of the transparencies on a particular date, after which a holding fee of £5 a day a

---

[11] *Harris* v. *Great Western Railway Co.* (1876) 1 QBD 515; provided that he knows that the document contains terms which are intended to be contractually binding, and does not think that it is just a receipt, e.g. *Chapelton* v. *Barry UDC* [1940] 1 KB 532.

[12] *Parker* v. *South Eastern Railway Co.* (1877) 2 CPD 416; *Hood* v. *Anchor Line (Henderson Brothers), Ltd.* [1918] AC 837; *Thompson* v. *London, Midland and Scottish Railway Co.* [1930] 1 KB 41 (an extreme case, in which the plaintiff was bound by a condition printed on p. 552 of a timetable for which she would have had to pay 6*d*. It might not be decided the same way today: cf. *Hollingworth* v. *Southern Ferries Ltd., The Eagle* [1977] 2 Lloyd's Rep. 70, 78).

[13] *Henderson* v. *Stevenson* (1875) LR 2 HL (Sc.) 470; *Richardson, Spence & Co.* v. *Rowntree* [1894] AC 217.

[14] *Gibaud* v. *Great Eastern Railway Co.* (1921) 125 LT 76. There are *statutory* controls on terms in certain contracts on the ground of unreasonableness: see esp. the Unfair Contract Terms Act 1977.

[15] [1989] QB 433. See also *J. Spurling* v. *Bradshaw* [1956] 1 WLR 461, 466 (Denning LJ: 'the more unreasonable a clause is, the greater the notice which must be given of it'); *Thornton* v. *Shoe Lane Parking Ltd.* [1971] 2 QB 163, 170, 172.

[16] Notice that this was not an *exclusion* clause. Dillon LJ ([1989] QB 433, 438) made it clear that, although the cases which have developed the rules have generally been concerned with exclusion clauses—which have therefore been construed narrowly against the person seeking to rely on the clause—the rules are not limited to exclusion clauses, and apply to any contractual provision which is particularly onerous for one party.

transparency would be charged. This holding fee was 'extremely high, and . . . exorbitant.'[17] It was unlikely that the defendants had read the clause. The Court of Appeal held that the clause referring to the holding fee was not incorporated in the contract,[18] because it was unusually onerous: the plaintiffs therefore had a commensurately greater responsibility to attempt to bring it to the defendants' attention, before they were entitled to rely upon it.

Bingham LJ,[19] whilst noting that there is in English law no over-riding principle of good faith, pointed out that the cases which have concerned incorporation of terms by sufficiency of notice are to be seen as part of a general approach, whereby fairness and reason-ableness of the parties are relevant to determining their obligations under the contract:[20]

The tendency of the English authorities has, I think, been to look at the nature of the transaction in question and the character of the parties to it; to consider what notice the party alleged to be bound was given of the particular condition said to bind him; and to resolve whether in all the circumstances it is fair to hold him bound by the condition in question.

The relative positions of the parties will clearly be relevant in determining what one is entitled reasonably to assume about the other's intentions concerning the terms of the contract. For example, if one party knows that the other is incapable of understanding the written terms, he ought not to be entitled to rely on them without explaining them.[21] But the fact that the two parties are of *equal* bargaining strength can in some circumstances be highly relevant. For example, if two parties, of equal bargaining power, are in the same trade, it may be possible to imply terms which are standard in the trade. In *British Crane Hire Corporation Ltd.* v. *Ipswich Plant Hire Ltd.*[22] the plaintiffs and defendants were both plant hire companies. The plaintiffs hired a crane to the defendants at short notice, in an emergency. The defendants were held bound by a term in the plaintiffs' conditions of hire, which were of a kind standard in the

---

[17] [1989] QB 433, 436 (Dillon LJ). It was not argued that the provision might have been void as a penalty: ibid. For penalty clauses, see pp. 211 ff., below.

[18] The contract therefore did not provide for what sum should be paid for late return of the transparencies; so the plaintiffs were awarded a *quantum meruit* of only £3.50 a transparency a week.

[19] [1989] QB 433, 439 ff.

[20] Ibid., at p. 445.

[21] Cf. *Hitchman* v. *Avery* (1892) 8 TLR 698; p. 45, below.

[22] [1975] QB 303.

trade, although they were not sent to the defendants until *after* the contract was formed. Because of the relationship between the parties, when the defendants requested the crane urgently, the plaintiffs were entitled to conclude that the defendants were accepting it on the terms of the plaintiffs' own printed conditions.[23]

There is also a rule whereby a term can be incorporated into a contract by a 'course of dealing'; this is separate from the *British Crane* situation. In the case of a 'course of dealing', there must have been a regular, consistent course of dealing by the parties on the same terms over a long period. However, 'course of dealing' may also be analysed as an application of the objective test of formation of the contract.[24] Lord Pearce in *Hardwick Game Farm* v. *Suffolk Agricultural Poultry Producers Association* said,[25]

The court's task is to decide what each party to an alleged contract would reasonably conclude from the utterances, writings or conduct of the other. The question, therefore, is not what [S] themselves thought or knew about the matter but what they should be taken as representing to [G, the other contracting party] about it or leading [G] to believe. The only reasonable inference from the regular course of dealing over so long a period is that [S] were evincing an acceptance of, and a readiness to be bound by, the printed conditions of whose existence they were well aware although they had not troubled to read them. Thus the general conditions became part of the oral contract.

We have seen that these cases involve, at root, an application of the objective test of *Smith* v. *Hughes*.[26] The circumstances of the contract and the relative positions and conduct of the parties are considered to ascertain whether the party seeking to impose a term can be allowed to say that it was reasonable for him to think that the other party was agreeing to it. For the objective test to be satisfied, of course, the party imposing the term must also *in fact* think that the other is agreeing. If he knows that there is no actual agreement, that is fatal. However, it must be noticed that simply because he knows that the other party has not actually read the written term which he is seeking to incorporate does not mean that he cannot rely on it. The

---

[23] Ibid., at p. 311 (Lord Denning MR). Sir Eric Sachs at p. 313 made it clear that it will be quite different if the parties 'are in wholly different walks of life . . . where one, for instance, is an expert in a line of business, and the other is not'.

[24] *Smith* v. *Hughes* (1871) LR 6 QB 597; p. 8, above.

[25] [1969] 2 AC 31, 113.

[26] (1871) LR 6 QB 597.

failure to read may simply show that the other party is *taking the risk* of there being conditions to which he would not agree. The principle therefore can be reduced to this: that as long as sufficient steps have been taken to attempt to draw the other's attention to the existence of the term, the party imposing it may be able to say that he honestly and reasonably thought that the other party was either agreeing to the term or taking the risk of its existence.[27]

2. SIGNATURE ON WRITTEN DOCUMENTS

A particular problem can arise in relation to documents which have been signed by a party who wishes none the less to assert that he did not agree to the terms contained in the document. One might expect that this would present only the same questions as those discussed in the preceding section: after all, a signed document can be seen as simply a particular example of a contract reduced to writing. However, the fact that a person has written his signature on the written contract will naturally make it more difficult for him to assert that he did not intend to be bound by its terms. But it is clear from the cases that a signature is not conclusive proof of agreement. What we need to consider is what rules the judges have developed in relation to signatures on contracts; and what is the underlying rationale of those rules.

(a) The Signature Rule

The courts have taken a clear line in relation to signed documents. Scrutton LJ said in *L'Estrange* v. *F. Graucob, Ltd.*,[28]

In cases in which the contract is contained in a railway ticket or other unsigned document, it is necessary to prove that an alleged party was aware, or ought to have been aware, of its terms and conditions. These cases have no application when the document has been signed. When a document containing contractual terms is signed, then, in the absence of fraud, or, I will add, misrepresentation, the party signing it is bound, and it is wholly immaterial whether he has read the document or not.

Under this test, as soon as it is shown that a party has signed the document, he is bound by its terms unless he can show fraud or

---

[27] *Hood* v. *Anchor Line (Henderson Brothers), Ltd.* [1918] AC 837, 845.
[28] [1934] 2 KB 394, 403.

misrepresentation by the other party. In addition to these exceptions, however, we must also consider certain other situations not set out in Scrutton LJ's statement: cases where the person signing cannot read, or speaks a different language from that of the document; and the doctrine of *non est factum*.

(i) Fraud and Misrepresentation

It has long been said[29] that fraud is an exception to the strict rule that a party is bound by the entire contents of a document which he has signed. In *L'Estrange* v. *F. Graucob, Ltd.*,[30] Scrutton LJ added misrepresentation as an exception. The operation of fraud and misrepresentation here must be distinguished from when they operate generally so as to vitiate contracts.[31] The fraud or misrepresentation is not here being used to avoid the whole contract. It is being used by one party who wishes to assert that there is a contract, but that, because of the fraud or misrepresentation of the other party, certain terms upon which that other party wishes to rely were not incorporated into the contract.

For example, in *Curtis* v. *Chemical Cleaning and Dyeing Co.*,[32] the plaintiff sought to recover damages from the defendant cleaners in respect of stains caused to a white satin wedding dress during cleaning. The defendants attempted to rely on an exclusion clause on a ticket which the plaintiff had signed when she took the dress into the shop. It was held that the defendants could not rely on the clause, because their agent had misrepresented the scope of the clause to the plaintiff when she had questioned it. The defendants would therefore have been able to rely on the clause only in its form as (mis)represented by their agent:[33] that is, the clause was only incorporated in the form in which it had been misrepresented to be.

(ii) Illiteracy

Cases have occasionally occurred of parties who are able to sign their

---

[29] See e.g. *Parker* v. *South Eastern Railway Co.* (1877) 2 CPD 416, 421 (Mellish LJ).

[30] [1934] 2 KB 394, 403, set out above. See also Maugham LJ at p. 406.

[31] For details on which, see Part II below.

[32] [1951] 1 KB 805. See also *Jacques* v. *Lloyd D. George & Partners Ltd.* [1968] 1 WLR 625.

[33] [1951] 1 KB 805, 809. For a similar principle in relation to unsigned contracts, see *Mendelssohn* v. *Normand, Ltd.* [1970] 1 QB 177.

names, without being able to understand the contents of the document because they are illiterate. Such a case was *Hitchman* v. *Avery*,[34] where the defendant was held not bound by the contract which he had signed: it was clear that his mind had not assented to any such contract as was contained in the agreement. However, it was crucial to the facts that the defendant, on being presented with the contract and being asked to read it, had told the plaintiff's representative that he could not read. If the plaintiff (and the plaintiff's agent) had not known of the defendant's illiteracy, the defendant might have been bound by the contract.[35]

(iii) Foreign Languages

A contracting party who cannot understand the language of the written document is in a similar position to one who cannot read at all: but it is clear that the courts have taken a firm line in such cases. In *The Luna*,[36] the master of a Dutch shipping vessel understood and spoke very little English, and could not read English at all; none the less he signed a contract. He was bound by its contents. However, it might not seem a harsh decision: the master knew he was signing a contract, but he did not attempt to read it and did not ask any questions about it.[37] He might therefore be said to have taken the risk of what the document contained—he could have prevented the problem by simply asking questions about the contents of the document.

The Luna may be contrasted with *George Harvey* v. *Ventilatorenfabrik Oelde GmbH*,[38] where the plaintiff, an Englishman, signed a contract in duplicate, in English, which did not profess on its face to incorporate any other contractual terms. However, there were terms in German (of which the plaintiff was unaware) on the back of only

---

[34] (1892) 8 TLR 698. Cf. *Lloyds Bank plc* v. *Waterhouse, The Independent*, 27 February 1990.

[35] Ibid. Wright J said that then he 'might have been *estopped* by the fact of his signature to the agreement from resisting its effect'. See also *Lloyds Bank plc* v. *Waterhouse, The Independent*, 27 February 1990; pp. 50–1, below.

[36] [1920] P. 22. Cf. *Thompson* v. *London, Midland and Scottish Railway Co.* [1930] 1 KB 41 (a case which did not involve a signature, and so was decided on the principles relating to notice) where Sankey LJ said at p. 56 that if 'the conditions in the time table were printed in Chinese, so that you could not understand them . . . it probably could not be said you would be bound by the condition'.

[37] [1920] P. 22, 24.

[38] (1988) 6-CLD-06-29.

one of the copies of the contract. The Court of Appeal held that the plaintiff was not bound by the German terms, because he was misled by the form of the different documents.

(iv) *Non est factum*

Non est factum has also been acknowledged to be an exception to the signature rule;[39] however, we shall see that it is a narrow exception.

The plea of *non est factum*, literally, involves an assertion by a party that a document 'is not his deed'. Originally[40] it applied to situations where the person sought to be held liable did not in fact sign the document; but then (by the sixteenth century) it was held to cover situations where a person had executed a deed under a mistake; and, later, it was held to apply to other written contracts.[41]

If the plea of *non est factum* is successful, the whole document which contained the signature is *void*. This is clearly a drastic consequence, since not only can neither party rely on it but nor can any third party;[42] the courts have therefore adopted a very restrictive test.

The modern approach is set out in the judgments of the House of Lords in *Saunders* v. *Anglia Building Society*.[43] Broadly, there are three requirements which must be satisfied by the person seeking to avoid the document:

(1) that he was under a disability, which made him permanently or temporarily unable through no fault of his own to have any real understanding of the purport of the document—whether this disability is as a result of defective education, illness or innate incapacity;[44]

---

[39] *L'Estrange* v. *F. Graucob, Ltd.* [1934] 2 KB 394, 406 (Maugham LJ); *Blay* v. *Pollard and Morris* [1930] 1 KB 628.

[40] *Saunders* v. *Anglia Building Society* [1971] AC 1004, 1015 (Lord Reid), 1024 (Lord Wilberforce).

[41] *Foster* v. *Mackinnon* (1869) LR 4 CP 704, 712.

[42] The plea of *non est factum* has often arisen where an innocent third party has relied on a signed document: *Saunders* v. *Anglia Building Society* [1971] AC 1004, 1016 (Lord Reid).

[43] [1971] AC 1004.

[44] Ibid., at p. 1016 (Lord Reid). Lord Reid included the requirement that the person must be unable to understand the document *without explanation*. This must, however, be viewed cautiously, since it might be said that a normal person of full capacity, but without legal training, would be unable to understand many standard legal documents without explanation. Lord Reid made it clear that a person of full capacity might be able to avoid a contract on the ground of *non est factum* only in exceptional cases: ibid.

(2) that there was a radical[45] difference between the document which he actually signed and the document which he thought he was signing;

(3) that he was not careless.[46]

Non est factum is designed only for exceptional cases. Its purpose is to protect a vulnerable person—the mere fact of a disability is enough, it need not be known by the other party.[47] However, such a person is protected only if the consequences of the signed document are very serious for him (it must be *very* different from what he thought)[48] and he must prove that he was not at fault—that he was not negligent. The party against whom the contract is avoided does not lose the benefit because of any fault on his part; he may honestly and reasonably have thought that the disabled party was agreeing to the contract. *Non est factum* is therefore an exception to the objective test—but a very narrow exception, based on a policy of protecting persons who are incapable of understanding a written contract.

(b) The Rationale of the Signature Rule

The cases involving signatures on written contracts are clearly applying a policy in favour of limiting the circumstances in which the binding effect of a signature can be avoided. This is most clearly shown by the cases on *non est factum*, where the consequences of holding that the plea is successful are the most severe in that it makes the whole written contract void, with sometimes harsh consequences for innocent third parties. But even in the cases where the contract is not sought to be avoided, but merely a particular term is claimed not to have been incorporated, the courts are reluctant not to give the signature its full effect:

---

[45] Ibid., at p. 1017. Various other words are used to describe this: 'fundamental'; 'serious'; 'very substantial' (Lord Reid at p. 1017); 'essentially different in substance'; 'basically' (Lord Wilberforce at p. 1026). It is clear that a very narrow test is intended; compare the restrictive test for avoiding a contract at common law on the basis of a common mistake: *Kennedy* v. *The Panama, New Zealand and Australian Royal Mail Co. Ltd.* (1867) LR 2 QB 580, 587; *Bell* v. *Lever Brothers Ltd.* [1932] AC 161, 218, pp. 233–7, below.

[46] The burden is on the party seeking to avoid the contract to show that he took care: [1971] AC 1004, 1019 (Lord Hodson).

[47] *Lloyds Bank plc* v. *Waterhouse, The Independent,* 27 February 1990.

[48] See n. 45, above.

It would be very dangerous to allow a man over the age of legal infancy to escape from the legal effect of a document he has, after reading it, signed, in the absence of an express misrepresentation by the other party of that legal effect.[49]

However, we have seen that there are certain exceptions to the binding nature of a signature; and if we look again a little more closely at these, we can see the underlying rationale of the signature rule.

Several cases have expressed the basic view that the signature constitutes evidence of the party's agreement to the contract.[50] Thus, as between the parties, it seems that the one party is entitled to rely upon the other's signature as showing his agreement. Viewed in this light, the exceptions to the signature rule based on fraud and misrepresentation make sense: a party is entitled to rely upon his belief that the other has agreed to the written document by signing it; but he is not entitled so to rely if that signature was procured by the first party's fraud or misrepresentation—that is, his deliberate or innocent misrepresentation about the contents or meaning of the document which has been signed. We can see therefore that one party's actions in obtaining the signature—even by an *innocent* misrepresentation[51]—preclude him from relying on the signature.

This view of the underlying principle has been taken in certain Canadian cases—and it has there been taken further than has been generally accepted in England. Consider, for example, the situation where one party presents the other with a written offer to contract, which contains very many terms, and the other has insufficient time in which to read all the small print. He signs the contract. If there is a clause in the middle of the document about which he did not know, and to which he would not have agreed, is he bound by it? The English authorities[52] have generally only allowed a person to avoid the consequences of his signature if he has been *actively* misled by the other party about the terms of the contract. Here, there is no active misleading, merely the fact that the party signing does not have sufficient time to read the document.

---

[49] *Blay* v. *Pollard and Morris* [1930] 1 KB 628, 633 (Scrutton LJ).

[50] *Curtis* v. *Chemical Cleaning and Dyeing Co.* [1951] 1 KB 805, 808; *Parker* v. *South Eastern Railway Co.* (1877) 2 CPD 416, 421; *L'Estrange* v. *F. Graucob, Ltd.* [1934] 2 KB 394.

[51] As was the case in *Curtis* v. *Chemical Cleaning and Dyeing Co.* [1951] 1 KB 805.

[52] In particular, *L'Estrange* v. *F. Graucob, Ltd.* [1934] 2 KB 394.

The most obvious answer is that such a situation must be so common in the pressurized world of commerce that to allow parties to escape contracts simply on the ground that they have not read them would be disastrous. After all, a person can ask questions about the contents of a document he is being asked to sign;[53] and if he fails to ask, then he can be taken by his signature as having accepted the risk of what may be in the contract. However, it might not be so simple. Situations can arise where the party offering the written document knows that the other party is not willing to accept a particular term, and there are good reasons why the party who signs has not asked about the terms. This is what happened in the Canadian case of *Tilden Rent-a-Car Co.* v. *Clendenning*.[54]

In that case, the defendant hired a car from the plaintiffs at an airport; the plaintiffs' clerk knew that the defendant was in a hurry and that he did not read the document before signing it. The contract contained an unusual exclusion clause, which was held not to be binding. The Ontario Court of Appeal applied the objective test for the formation of a contract. The plaintiffs would only have been allowed to hold the defendant to the contract including the term if, at the time of the contract, they had actually believed that he was agreeing to the term, and they had reasonable grounds for that belief. But here, the plaintiffs knew that the defendant had not read the document, and had no reason to believe that he was agreeing to it. Dubin JA said,[55]

Consensus ad idem is as much a part of the law of written contracts as it is of oral contracts. The signature to a contract is only one way of manifesting assent to contractual terms. . . .

The justification for the rule in *L'Estrange* v. *F. Graucob, Ltd.*[56] appears to have been founded upon the objective theory of contracts, by which means

---

[53] And so, provided that he asks the right questions, he will discover the truth about the contents of the document (if the other party is honest), or (if the other party is not honest about the contents of the document) he will procure a misrepresentation upon which he will be able to rely under *Curtis* v. *Chemical Cleaning and Dyeing Co.* [1951] 1 KB 805.

[54] (1978) 83 DLR (3d) 400. See also *Colonial Investment Co. of Winnipeg, Man.* v. *Borland* (1911) 1 WWR 171 (affd. on different grounds, (1912) 2 WWR 960); *Gray-Campbell Ltd.* v. *Flynn* [1923] 1 DLR 51 (esp. the dissenting judgment of Beck JA). In all of these cases, the fact that the term was unusual or unexpected by the particular signatory was important to show that the other party was not entitled to rely upon the signature as showing assent to it.

[55] (1978) 83 DLR (3d) 400, 404.

[56] [1934] 2 KB 394.

parties are bound to a contract in writing by measuring their conduct by outward appearance rather than what the parties inwardly meant to decide. This, in turn, stems from the classic statement of Blackburn J in *Smith* v. *Hughes*.[57]

This approach must clearly be followed cautiously, to ensure that mere failure to read a document cannot entitle a party who has signed the document to escape the consequences of his signature. In *Tilden Rent-a-Car Co.* v. *Clendenning* it was crucial that the plaintiffs' clerk knew that the defendant did not read the terms because he was in a hurry; and, indeed, the plaintiffs held out their service as involving speedy completion of the contract. The transaction was therefore of a kind—and known to the plaintiffs as being of a kind—invariably carried out in a hurried, informal manner.[58] The circumstances of a signature will need to be considered very carefully before holding that it is not binding where there has been no active misleading of the party signing. It will not be enough for the signatory simply to show that the other party knew that he was in a hurry and did not read the document. It is necessary to distinguish simple failure to read, where the signing party is taking the risk of what the document contains, from situations where it is not reasonable from the failure to read to think that the signature denotes assent. However, provided that such cases can, on their facts, be dealt with, the approach of *Tilden Rent-a-Car Co.* v. *Clendenning* is a straightforward application of the objective test of formation of a contract, following *Smith* v. *Hughes*.[59]

Indeed, this approach[60] has been used in the English courts. In *Lloyds Bank plc* v. *Waterhouse*,[61] a father (who was unable to read) signed a guarantee of his son's debts in favour of a bank. The guarantee was, however, more extensive than the father realized: it

---

[57] (1871) LR 6 QB 597, 607; quoted at p. 8, above.

[58] (1978) 83 DLR (3d) 400, 405.

[59] (1871) LR 6 QB 597, 607; p. 8, above.

[60] Which was discussed in Spencer, *Signature, Consent, and the Rule in L'Estrange v. Graucob* [1973] CLJ 104.

[61] *The Independent*, 27 February 1990; Cartwright, [1990] LMCLQ 338. A signed contract was also overridden and set aside by reason of one party's knowledge of the other's mistake in *Watkin* v. *Watson-Smith, The Times*, 3 July 1986. Notice also that in *Walters* v. *Morgan* (1861) 3 De G. F. & J. 718, 724 Lord Campbell LC said that a Court of Equity would refuse specific performance of a signed contract if there was 'a contrivance on the part of the purchaser, better informed than the vendor of the real value of the subject to be sold, to hurry the vendor into an agreement without giving him the opportunity of being fully informed of its real value, or time to deliberate and take advice respecting the conditions of the bargain'.

was an all-monies guarantee, but the father claimed that he thought he was signing a guarantee limited to a particular loan taken out by the son. The father sought to escape the guarantee when the bank called upon him. Sir Edward Eveleigh[62] said that, because the father made no pretence at reading the document, and expressed to the bank concern to limit the extent of his risk, he was not bound since his signature did not of itself entitle the bank reasonably to assume that he was agreeing to its terms.

It therefore seems clear that the cases involving signature can be set in the context of the objective test. The words and conduct of the parties at the time of contracting are crucial to the ascertainment of the obligations under the contract. The reason that a signature is prima facie binding is because it induces the other party to rely upon it; but if the other party is at fault in having by fraud or innocent misrepresentation caused the other to put his signature to the document, he can no longer rely upon the signature as showing assent. The language of estoppel creeps into the cases again here: for example, Wright J in *Hitchman* v. *Avery*[63] spoke of a party having been 'estopped by the fact of his signature to the agreement from resisting its effect'. However, it may be better not to consider it to be an estoppel as such. For example, in *Gallie* v. *Lee*[64] Salmon LJ, in the context of a plea of *non est factum*, said,

If, however, a person signs a document because he negligently failed to read it, I think he is precluded from relying on his own negligent act for the purpose of escaping from the ordinary consequences of his signature. In such circumstances he cannot succeed on a plea of *non est factum*. This is not in my view a true estoppel, but an illustration of the principle that no man may take advantage of his own wrong.

However one describes the basis of the signature rule, it seems clear that the principles of the objective test of *Smith* v. *Hughes*, and the close analysis of the parties' respective words and conduct which that imports, lie at the heart of the cases on the binding effect of a signature on a written contract.

[62] *Obiter*, although Woolf LJ 'recognised the attractions' of this analysis; the main grounds on which the father escaped the guarantee were *non est factum* and misrepresentation.

[63] (1892) 8 TLR 698; p. 45, above. See also *Colonial Investment Co. of Winnipeg, Man.* v. *Borland* (1911) 1 WWR 171, 187; *Gray-Campbell Ltd.* v. *Flynn* [1923] 1 DLR 51, 59.

[64] [1969] 2 Ch. 17, 48, approved by Lords Hodson and Pearson on appeal in *Saunders* v. *Anglia Building Society* [1971] AC 1004, 1019, 1038. See also pp. 13 ff., above.

3. RECTIFICATION OF WRITTEN CONTRACTS

We have seen[65] that if the parties have agreed to embody their contract in a written document, it will be presumed that the document contains the terms agreed between them. However, there are situations where one party may claim that the written contract does not properly reflect the agreement; and he may request that the written document be rectified,[66] so that he can enforce the true agreement. A claim for rectification can arise in two separate circumstances; where the parties can be shown to have come to an agreement, but the document by some mistake does not accurately reflect it ('common mistake');[67] or where one party has obtained the written document in terms to which the other party did not intend to agree ('unilateral mistake').[68]

(a) Rectification for Common Mistake

In the case of 'common' mistake, the parties have agreed the terms of the contract, and rectification is simply directed to remedying the defective *expression* of the agreement. Thus, one must separate the agreement between the parties from the words used to implement that agreement. Rectification for common mistake can deal only with the words, not with the underlying agreement. For example, in *Frederick E. Rose (London) Ltd.* v. *William H. Pim Jnr. & Co. Ltd.*,[69] the parties contracted in writing for the sale of 'horsebeans'. That was the word upon which they had actually agreed. However, they had both been under a misunderstanding: what the plaintiff buyer needed was a particular kind of horsebean, 'feveroles'.[70] The Court

---

[65] See pp. 37–8, 43, 46–7, 48, above.

[66] Rectification is an equitable remedy. This may well have influenced the language and general approach taken by the courts in relation to rectification: see n. 89, below.

[67] This mistake is 'common', since both parties are in agreement about the terms, but they share the mistake in their expression of the terms in the document: see p. 4, n. 4, above.

[68] This is known as 'unilateral' mistake, since only one party does not agree to (i.e. is mistaken about) the written terms; the parties are therefore at cross-purposes: see p. 4, n. 3, above.

[69] [1953] 2 QB 450.

[70] They used the word 'horsebean', although they both meant 'feverole'; yet a wholly objective meaning was attributed to the words by the court: Spencer, [1973] CLJ 104, 113.

of Appeal refused rectification, since the mistake was in the underlying agreement; the document itself was an accurate expression of
what the parties had in fact agreed. 'Rectification is concerned with
contracts and documents, not with intentions. In order to get rectification it is necessary to show that the parties were in complete
agreement on the terms of their contract, but by an error wrote them
down wrongly.'[71]

For a written contract to be rectified on the ground of common
mistake, the following conditions must be satisfied:[72]

(1) the parties must have had a common intention[73] in regard to
the particular provisions of the contract, together with some
outward expression of that common intention;

(2) the common intention must continue up to the time of the
execution of the contract;

(3) there must be clear evidence that the instrument as executed[74]
does not accurately represent the true agreement of the parties
at the time of its execution;

(4) it must be shown that the instrument, if rectified as claimed,
would accurately represent the true agreement of the parties at
the time of its execution.

(b) Rectification for Unilateral Mistake

In the case of a unilateral mistake, the parties are not in fact in agreement at the time of the execution of the written contract; one party
wishes to contract on the terms of the written document, whereas

[71] [1953] 2 QB 450, 461 (Denning LJ). Note, however, that Denning LJ generally took
a wholly objective approach to the formation of a contract; the outward expression of
the parties' intentions determined the existence and terms of the contract: p. 22, above.
One would therefore expect him to look to the outward meaning of the words used,
rather than what both parties intended the words to convey, to establish the terms.

[72] *Agip S.p.A.* v. *Navigazione Alta Italia S.p.A.* [1984] 1 Lloyd's Rep. 353, 359 (Slade
LJ); *Snell's Equity*, 29th edn., 1990, pp. 628–30. The burden of proof is on the party
seeking to assert that he should not be bound by his signature; and this burden, whilst
still the civil standard of the balance of probability, will require convincing proof to
counteract the cogent evidence of the parties' intention displayed by the written
document: *Thomas Bates & Son Ltd.* v. *Wyndham's (Lingerie) Ltd.* [1981] 1 WLR 505, 514
(Buckley LJ), 521 (Brightman LJ); *Agip S.p.A.* v. *Navigazione Alta Italia S.p.A.*, above, at
p. 359.

[73] Although it is not necessary to show an actual (oral) enforceable contract before
the document is executed: *Joscelyne* v. *Nissen* [1970] 2 QB 86.

[74] It is immaterial which of the parties committed the agreement to paper; the
author of the mistake is not precluded from claiming rectification: *Ball* v. *Storie* (1832) 1
Sim. & St. 210, 219.

the other intends different terms. However, the written document is prima facie the contract, and the question is, on what principle can a party to that document be heard to say that he should not be bound by it? A number of different expressions have been used in the cases to describe the principle; but the key is that the party against whom rectification is ordered must actually have *known* of the other party's disagreement with the terms in the written contract at the time when it was executed. We shall see, therefore, that the courts are, in essence, saying that one party is entitled to rely on the fact that the other party has assented to the written contract, unless his entitlement to rely is displaced by his own contrary knowledge.

And, if there is such knowledge, it seems entirely proper to allow rectification. In some situations the difference between unilateral and common mistakes may be simply one of timing. Assume the following facts. A and B agree on a set of terms for their contract. They execute a formal written document which, by its omission of a term, is more favourable to A. B will seek to avoid the strict consequences of the written contract, by claiming rectification. If, at the time the document was executed, both parties still thought that the document reflected the agreed terms—that is, they were both innocent of the error in the written contract—the mistake is common. If, however, by the time he signed the contract A realized that the document had been drawn in his favour, the mistake is unilateral. If B could have obtained rectification for the common mistake in the situation where A was ignorant of the mistake in the document, B should be in no worse position where A in fact knew of B's mistake. If, however, there was no such prior agreement between A and B, and if A did not in fact know that B was not assenting to the written terms, it is not so clear that B should be able to strike down the written contract.

There are a few older cases which appear to have allowed rectification against a person who did not have knowledge of the other party's disagreement with the terms of the written contract. In *Paget* v. *Marshall*,[75] for example, a landlord was granted, at his own election, either rescission or rectification of a lease in which he claimed he had included some property by mistake. The mistake was clearly not common, since the lessee thought he was taking the whole property. In granting the remedy, Bacon V-C said[76] that there

---

[75] (1884) 28 Ch. D. 255. See also *Harris* v. *Pepperell* (1867) LR 5 Eq. 1.
[76] (1884) 28 Ch. D. 255, 266.

was no fraud: 'I cannot impute to him the intention of taking advantage of any incorrect expression in [the letter offering the lease].'

However, these older cases were later explained[77] or doubted,[78] and it has been made clear that there must be knowledge by the party against whom rectification is ordered.[79] In *A. Roberts & Co. Ltd.* v. *Leicestershire County Council*,[80] for example, Pennycuick J stated a general principle:

a party is entitled to rectification of a contract upon proof that he believed a particular term to be included in the contract, and that the other party concluded the contract with the omission or a variation of that term in the knowledge that the first party believed the term to be included.

The cases have used various expressions to describe the circumstances in which rectification can be awarded for unilateral mistake. It has been said to rest on the *fraud* of the party seeking to resist rectification;[81] or on an *estoppel* by which the party who obtained the contract in its written form is by his conduct in procuring the agreement of the other party to the document estopped from denying that the contract included the term intended by the other party;[82] or the *sharp practice* of the party who obtains the document in his favour;[83] or the *'equity of the position'*, in that the conscience of

[77] *May* v. *Platt* [1900] 1 Ch. 616, 623.

[78] *Riverlate Properties Ltd.* v. *Paul* [1975] Ch. 133, 142–4.

[79] This applies only to bargains between the parties; if there is no bargain, but merely a gratuitous transaction (such as a voluntary settlement), there is no reason in principle to require knowledge on the part of the recipient of the gift before the document embodying the gift is rectified to give better effect to the intentions of the donor: *Re Butlin's Settlement Trusts* [1976] Ch. 251; *Gibbon* v. *Mitchell* [1990] 3 All ER 338.

[80] [1961] Ch. 555, 570. See also *Garrard* v. *Frankel* (1862) 30 Beav. 445, 451, explained in *Riverlate Properties Ltd.* v. *Paul* [1975] Ch. 133, 142.

[81] *Blay* v. *Pollard and Morris* [1930] 1 KB 628, 633; *May* v. *Platt* [1900] 1 Ch. 616, 623; *A. Roberts & Co. Ltd.* v. *Leicestershire County Council* [1961] Ch. 555, 570.

[82] *Agip S.p.A.* v. *Navigazione Alta Italia S.p.A.* [1983] 2 Lloyd's Rep. 333, 342 (Leggatt J), [1984] 1 Lloyd's Rep. 353, 365 (Slade LJ); *Thomas Bates & Son Ltd.* v. *Wyndham's (Lingerie) Ltd.* [1981] 1 WLR 505, 520–1 (Eveleigh LJ); *A. Roberts & Co. Ltd.* v. *Leicestershire County Council* [1961] Ch. 555, 570; *Snell's Equity*, pp. 630–1.

[83] *Riverlate Properties Ltd.* v. *Paul* [1975] Ch. 133, 140, doubted in *Thomas Bates & Son Ltd.* v. *Wyndham's (Lingerie) Ltd.* [1981] 1 WLR 505, 515 (Buckley LJ) and 520–1 (Eveleigh LJ). However, it seems that the words 'sharp practice' were chosen by the Court of Appeal in *Riverlate Properties Ltd.* v. *Paul* simply as a shorthand expression, which was intended to emphasize the knowledge of the party obtaining the document that the other party would not agree to the written terms. As such, this is consistent with Buckley and Eveleigh LJJ's own views in *Thomas Bates & Son Ltd.* v. *Wyndham's (Lingerie) Ltd.*

the party obtaining the document in his favour is affected by his
having known at the time of contracting that the other party would
not have agreed to the document as written, taken with his failure to
draw that other party's attention to his mistake.[84]

All these formulations depend upon the fact that the party against
whom rectification is ordered knew, at the time that the document
was executed, that the other party did not realize its terms and
would not have agreed to it. This has been clearly stated in *Agip
S.p.A.* v. *Navigazione Alta Italia S.p.A.*[85] In that case, the defendants
let two ships to the plaintiffs under two charterparties, each of which
contained a price escalation clause. The original discussions in
relation to the clause had assumed that it would be expressed in
Italian lire. However, the defendants had, during the drafting,
changed the figure to the equivalent sum in US dollars. The
defendants' agent had then retyped the document, with the effect
that the change was not so obvious; however, the judge found that
this had been done simply for the sake of the tidiness of the
document: it was not from any ulterior motive of concealing the
change.[86] The defendants invoked the price escalation clause, and
the plaintiffs claimed that it should be rectified to substitute the
original figure in lire, which would have resulted in the escalation
being considerably lower. Rectification was refused, on the basis that
the defendants did not realize that the plaintiffs were mistaken when
they executed the charterparties; and it was entirely the fault of the
plaintiffs that they had not noticed the change. Slade LJ reviewed
various cases[87] which had stated the principles by which rectification
is granted. His conclusion was that, apart from cases such as fraud,
undue influence, and fiduciary relationships, to which special
considerations apply, a contract would not be rectified for unilateral
mistake unless the party resisting rectification had knowledge of the
other party's mistaken belief about the terms of the contract; and the
knowledge must be *actual* knowledge—constructive knowledge is
not sufficient.[88]

[84] *Thomas Bates & Son Ltd.* v. *Wyndham's (Lingerie) Ltd.* [1981] 1 WLR 505, 515
(Buckley LJ).

[85] [1983] 2 Lloyd's Rep. 333 (Leggatt J), [1984] 1 Lloyd's Rep. 353 (Court of Appeal).

[86] [1983] 2 Lloyd's Rep. 333, 337.

[87] In particular, *A. Roberts & Co. Ltd.* v. *Leicestershire County Council* [1961] Ch. 555,
Riverlate Properties Ltd. v. *Paul* [1975] Ch. 133, and *Thomas Bates & Son Ltd.* v.
Wyndham's (Lingerie) Ltd. [1981] 1 WLR 505.

[88] *Agip S.p.A.* v. *Navigazione Alta Italia S.p.A.* [1984] 1 Lloyd's Rep. 353, 365; see also

(c) Conclusion

Rectification for common mistake does not involve any interference with the actual agreement concluded by the parties—it simply involves the rewriting of the formal document to bring it into line with that agreement. However, rectification for unilateral mistake involves a closer consideration of the agreement. One party (A) thinks that the terms of the contract are X; the other (B) thinks that they are Y. There is a formal written document which embodies terms X. The basic approach of the cases has been to say that, in order to displace the presumption that the terms of the agreement were X, B must show that A actually knew, at the time of the execution of the document, that B was mistaken in his understanding about what the document said.

Although these rules relating to rectification have been developed quite separately,[89] we can set the remedy in the context of the other rules relating to formation of contracts, which have already been discussed. The fact that the contract has been set out in writing means that each party is entitled to assume that the writing properly reflects the assent of the other. However, the writing is not conclusive; one party may be able to displace the other's reliance on the written contract by showing that that other's knowledge at the time of the contract disentitles him from so relying. The relative knowledge[90] of each party at the time of the contract about the intentions of the other as regards the terms of the contract is crucial in determining the terms which will be enforceable.

Leggatt J at [1983] 2 Lloyd's Rep. 333, 343: 'Knowledge means knowledge. If it be negatived subjectively it cannot be reinstated by some objective test. There is no room for any doctrine of constructive knowledge.'

[89] Primarily because rectification is an equitable remedy; the Courts of Equity therefore originally developed the rules independently of the common law rules for the formation of a contract. Moreover, the fact that rectification is an equitable remedy may explain the fierce insistence of the judges that there must be *actual* knowledge of the party against whom rectification is ordered: if there is no such actual knowledge, his conscience will be clear and he ought to be able to rely on the written contract; see *Riverlate Properties Ltd.* v. *Paul* [1975] Ch. 133, 141.

[90] Although in the case of rectification this must be *actual* knowledge. Equity operates on conscience, and only if there is actual knowledge will conscience be affected: n. 89, above. This is not wholly consistent with the common law approach, where the fact that a person ought not *reasonably* to have thought that the other party was agreeing will prevent him holding that other party to his terms: *Smith* v. *Hughes* (1871) LR 6 QB 597; p. 8, above.

II
MISREPRESENTATION

3

Remedies for Misrepresentation: Introduction

1. THE ESSENCE OF MISREPRESENTATION

Put simply, a misrepresentation is a false statement; a person represents something wrongly. For an action by a plaintiff to be based on a misrepresentation by a defendant it will generally be necessary for the false statement to have caused some loss, or to have caused an undesirable state of affairs (for example, the plaintiff having agreed to become a party to a transaction to which he would not have agreed had he known the truth) which the plaintiff requires to be remedied. In the context of misrepresentation as a vitiating factor in the formation of contract, we are concerned with the false statement in circumstances where a contract is entered into, and so with such questions as the impact of the statement on the validity of the contract, and the remedies which may be available as between the parties to the contract.

It has become customary in the books which deal with this topic to begin by defining a misrepresentation, and the requirements for an action based on misrepresentation, and only then to consider the various remedies which are available. 'Misrepresentation' is usually defined as a false statement of fact; and it is said that for an action to lie the statement must be material and have been relied upon by the person to whom it was made, or have induced him to enter the contract.[1]

This is not, however, the most satisfactory method of dealing with misrepresentation. One of the main difficulties with the subject is that there is a wide range of remedies, founded in tort, contract, and

[1] See e.g. Spencer Bower and Turner, *The Law of Actionable Misrepresentation*, 3rd edn., 1974, pp. 36 ff., 130 ff.; Treitel, pp. 254–64; Anson, pp. 209–15; CFF, pp. 257–65; Allen, *Misrepresentation*, 1988, ch. 2.

equity, and under statute. These various remedies have been built up over the years without any serious attempt by either the judges or Parliament to create a unified theory of misrepresentation. Each of the remedies has its own rules—including its own rules about what sort of statements will give rise to a remedy.[2]

For example, it would be misleading to begin by saying that all remedies require the statement to be one of fact; a fraudulent misrepresentation of law attracts the same remedies as a fraudulent misrepresentation of fact.[3] And the remedies for breach of contract which are available in cases of misrepresentation require the representation to have been incorporated as a term of the contract— which involves very different questions from the other remedies.[4] Many of the books treat incorporation of representations as a separate area altogether, and limit misrepresentation to 'mere' representations: those misrepresentations made leading up to the contract which are not incorporated as terms of the contract. However, this is artificial, since it is not possible to examine fully the underlying policy in imposing liability (and in particular different heads of liability) for pre-contractual statements without considering also whether (and why) the statement is to have contractual force.

This book will deal separately with the rules for each remedy. As has been said above, each will require a false statement to have been made, which causes loss or some other undesirable state of affairs for which the plaintiff seeks a remedy. It will be seen in due course that, although the tests which are to be applied may differ from one remedy to another, there is on some points a common underlying principle. However, it will be clearer, in order to follow the cases and to analyse a given set of facts, if the remedies are treated separately.

First, however, it will be helpful to look briefly at two questions: why any remedy should be given for a misrepresentation; and what sort of remedy will generally be appropriate.

2. WHY REMEDY A MISREPRESENTATION?

False statements may of course be made in a wide range of circumstances. We are here concerned with such statements made in the

---

[2] See *Derry* v. *Peek* (1889) 14 App. Cas. 337, 359–60, where Lord Herschell criticized the use of rescission cases to determine the requirements of the tort of deceit.
[3] See pp. 71 ff., below.   [4] See pp. 133 ff., below.

context of contractual negotiations, and the justification for granting remedies—and the choice of the appropriate remedy—may be very different in that context from a non-contractual context. However, there are particular problems which are generally associated with attaching liability to statements, which were discussed by Lord Reid in connection with liability in tort for negligent statements:[5]

The most obvious difference between negligent words and negligent acts is this. Quite careful people often express definite opinions on social or informal occasions even when they see that others are likely to be influenced by them; and they often do that without taking that care which they would take if asked for their opinion professionally or in a business connection. . . .

Another obvious difference is that a negligently made article will only cause one accident, and so it is not very difficult to find the necessary degree of proximity or neighbourhood between the negligent manufacturer and the person injured. But words can be broadcast with or without the consent or the foresight of the speaker or writer.

There are two separate points here: that statements can easily be made 'off the cuff'; and that words can travel further than expected. The second point should not give trouble in the context of mis-representations during pre-contractual negotiations. As long as remedies are limited to statements made by (or on behalf of) one contracting party to the other, there should be no danger from unauthorized or unforeseen repetition. However, there is some substance in the first point. Words are too easily spoken—and some-times too easily written. Of course, the fact that they are spoken (or written) by one negotiating party to the other—and so they are used with a view to a particular advantage for the speaker (or writer)—might suggest that some degree of responsibility should attach; and so Lord Reid's concern should not be so great in a *pre-contractual* misrepresentation.[6]

However, there is a refinement which can be introduced here: the state of mind of the representor. Whilst one might expect the law to exhibit some caution in attributing liability to statements made

---

[5] *Hedley Byrne & Co. Ltd.* v. *Heller & Partners Ltd.* [1964] AC 465, 482–3. See also at p. 534 (Lord Pearce); and see pp. 115–16, below.

[6] *Hedley Byrne & Co. Ltd.* v. *Heller & Partners Ltd.* was concerned specifically with statements *not* made in the context of a contract; liability in contract for statements made by one contracting party to the other had long been accepted as being capable of giving rise to a remedy in contract: cf. *Le Lievre* v. *Gould* [1893] 1 QB 491, 498; *Nocton* v. *Lord Ashburton* [1914] AC 932, 955. But the general point about caution in attaching liability to statements still holds.

during contractual negotiations, one would also expect a greater readiness to hold liable a representor who could be said to be more culpable. It is convenient to consider here various states of mind which may exist in a misrepresentor; they can be regarded as forming a scale, beginning with the most culpable:

(1) D (the misrepresentor) *knows* or *believes* that his statement is not true.
(2) D *suspects* that it might not be true.
(3) D makes the statement *not caring* whether or not is is true.
(4) D *honestly* believes that his statement is true; but he has *no reasonable grounds* for that belief: that is, he ought to realize that it is untrue.
(5) D *honestly* believes that his statement is true; and he has *reasonable grounds* for that belief: that is, he has no reason to think that it is untrue.

It should be noted from the outset that many of the remedies which are available for misrepresentation hinge on the state of mind of the representor. There is an added complication, however; that the terminology of the cases in discussing this state of mind varies, depending on the period in which the case in question was decided. The modern cases use a threefold classification: the misrepresentation is made fraudulently; or negligently; or innocently. We shall see later[7] that a representor is fraudulent if he has any of the states of mind listed in categories (1) to (3) above. He will be negligent, generally,[8] if he has the state of mind referred to in (4); and he will be innocent only if he falls within category (5).

It must be borne in mind in considering the cases that this threefold classification was developed only in the 1960s. Although the modern definition of fraud was laid down in 1889,[9] it was not established until 1963[10] that there could be any separate general remedy for negligent misrepresentation. Before the 1960s there was therefore no significance in a misrepresentation having been made

---

[7] p. 109, below.
[8] See pp. 124–5, below.
[9] In *Derry* v. *Peek* (1889) 14 App. Cas. 337: see p. 109, below.
[10] *Hedley Byrne & Co. Ltd.* v. *Heller & Partners Ltd.* [1964] AC 465; p. 120, below. But this was not immediately held to extend to pre-contractual misrepresentations: see p. 123 below. In addition, a remedy in damages for (effectively) negligent misrepresentation was introduced by s. 2(1) Misrepresentation Act 1967: see p. 132, below. Before 1963 there might be a remedy for negligent misrepresentations in

negligently, and all misrepresentations which were not fraudulent were termed 'innocent': it is only since the 1960s that the term 'innocent' has been regarded as restricted to representations which are neither fraudulent nor negligent. In this book the modern, threefold classification will be used.

Given that the state of mind of the misrepresentor may be classified as fraudulent, negligent, or innocent, one would expect that most, or the most severe, remedies would be available against a fraudulent misrepresentor. However, it may be expected that even an innocent representor—who is by definition both honest and reasonable in his belief in the truth of his statements—may be open to some remedies being awarded against him. Because he is the least culpable, it may be that the more severe financial remedies will be inappropriate to award against him. However, in the context of a misrepresentation which led up to the representee agreeing to enter into a contract with the representor, the representor's innocent state of mind does not wholly exonerate him. As between the two parties it is not true to say that there is nothing to choose between them— that they are both innocent. One might look at the actions of the parties, as well as at their states of mind, to determine their responsibility: the representor made the false statement, and so introduced into the negotiations the element which disturbed the balance of the negotiations. This may in itself merit some remedies against him.

3. WHAT KIND OF REMEDY?

It will be useful to bear in mind the kinds of remedy which may be appropriate for misrepresentations; it is important to consider the purpose which may be served by each remedy. Broadly speaking, there are three types of remedy which may be available.

First, given the context in which we are considering the misrepresentation to have been made—the misrepresentation will have led up to a contract—it may be desirable to allow the representee to escape from that contract, on the basis that he would not have

particular, narrow situations, such as a fiduciary relationship between the parties or an implied term of care under a contract: *Nocton* v. *Lord Ashburton* [1914] AC 932, 952–6, pp. 117 ff., below. But this did not involve negligence being recognized as a separate category of misrepresentations.

entered into it had he known the truth. This points towards the
remedy of rescission.[11]

Second, the misrepresentation may have caused loss to the
representee, in the sense that he has less than he once had. A
remedy may therefore be required to put back into the pocket of the
representee what he has lost because of the misrepresentation. We
shall see[12] that this points to the remedy of damages, assessed on the
tort measure.

Third, since the misrepresentation has led up to a contract, it may
have engendered false expectations which were to be fulfilled by
virtue of the contract. It may therefore be appropriate to give effect
to those expectations as if the representation had been true rather
than false. This points towards the remedy of damages, assessed on
the contract measure.[13]

As between the two damages remedies, it may be expected that
the courts will award the tort measure more readily than the contract
measure. The effect of awarding damages on a contractual basis is
generally to impose a guarantee of the truth of the statement, and so
to attach a higher responsibility for the statement than an award of
damages on the tort measure, which ensures only that the representee is no worse off than he was before the false statement was
made.[14]

Furthermore, it is sometimes suggested that a justification for
awarding damages based on the contract measure is that, since it
effectively requires the defendant to pay an amount equivalent to his
failure to perform his contract, it can act as an incentive to a potential
contract-breaker to perform, rather than break, his contract.[15]
However, this cannot operate as a justification for awarding contract
measure damages for misrepresentation. The representor cannot
'perform' in the sense of turning a false statement into a true statement.[16]

[11] See Ch. 4, below.
[12] See p. 106, below.
[13] See pp. 105–6, below.
[14] See Burrows, *Remedies for Torts and Breach of Contract*, 1987, p. 150. It should not,
however, be assumed that, in any given situation, the measure of damages calculated
on the contract measure will be larger than that calculated on the tort measure. See
p. 106 n. 5, below.
[15] See Beale, *Remedies for Breach of Contract*, 1980, pp. 157 ff.; Fuller & Perdue, (1936)
46 Yale LJ 52, 61; Atiyah, (1978) 94 LQR 193, 197–8.
[16] Beale, *Remedies for Breach of Contract*, pp. 166–7; *Pulsford* v. *Richards* (1853) 17
Beav. 87, 95–6.

However, even an award of damages on the tort measure imposes on a representor a financial responsibility for his statements, and we shall see that the courts have been cautious in ascribing such a responsibility to a representor who is only negligent. However, as discussed above, there is reason for holding even a wholly innocent misrepresentor to account for his statements; and the remedy of rescission is in many ways the most suitable, since it allows the representee to extricate himself from the contract.[17] It is a response to the fact that a pre-contractual misrepresentation, even an innocent one, has disturbed the balance of the negotiations, and therefore operates to vitiate the contract from the very beginning. It is therefore proposed to begin by discussing the remedy of rescission for misrepresentation in some detail.

[17] If rescission is not available, a misrepresentation may in an appropriate case still be available as a defence to an action for specific performance: *Lamare* v. *Dixon* (1873) LR 6 HL 414. Thus, although the misrepresentee cannot escape the contract entirely, he may be able to avoid having to *perform* the contract, and instead submit to paying damages for breach.

4

Rescission for Misrepresentation

1. TERMINOLOGY

It is necessary to begin by explaining the meaning of the word 'rescission', since there has been some confusion in the cases and in the textbooks. If a contract is rescinded for misrepresentation, it is avoided *ab initio*: it is treated as if there had never been a contract at all, and performance which has taken place under the contract must be reversed. In this respect, this remedy for misrepresentation is similar to the avoidance of a contract for duress or undue influence.[1]

If, say, there is a contract under which A has agreed to deliver 50 bags of coal to B, for £10 a bag, and at the time that the contract is rescinded A has delivered 20 bags (and B has paid £200 to A); then the effect of the contract being rescinded is that B must return the 20 bags to A, and A must return the £200 to B.[2]

With rescission must be contrasted another remedy, which will be referred to in this book as 'termination'. Termination is a remedy which is sometimes available for breach of contract,[3] but it operates differently from rescission. In the case of both rescission and termination, the future, unperformed obligations of the contract are released. However, in the case of termination, the obligations which have already been performed, or have already accrued, are left undisturbed. In the example given above, termination of the contract for the bags of coal would discharge both A's obligation to deliver the remaining 30 bags and B's obligation to pay the remaining £300.

---

[1] See Part III, below.

[2] Of course, there will be problems in rescinding a contract if, for example, it is not possible to reverse performance; this is discussed below, pp. 93 ff., but does not detract from this general explanation of how rescission operates if it is available.

[3] See p. 133 n. 122, below.

The 20 bags already delivered, and the £200 already paid, would not, however, be required to be returned.

Rescission and termination are clearly very different remedies. There has sometimes been confusion because the cases have used the word 'rescission' to mean termination—the distinction between the two being made by calling termination 'rescission for breach', as opposed to 'rescission *ab initio*' for misrepresentation. It is, however, too easy to drop the additional words 'for breach' and '*ab initio*'; sometimes it is therefore not clear to which remedy reference is being made. There is judicial authority that the different concepts should, for clarity, have clearly distinct nomenclature[4] and it is proposed throughout this book to refer to rescission to mean only rescission *ab initio*.

2. COMMON LAW AND EQUITY

The rules concerning the availability of rescission as a remedy for pre-contractual misrepresentations were developed during the nineteenth century. By 1867[5] it was established that rescission was available both at common law and in equity; however, the rule at common law was that rescission was limited to misrepresentations which were fraudulent.[6] In *Kennedy* v. *The Panama, New Zealand and Australian Royal Mail Co. Ltd.*[7] Blackburn J, giving the judgment of the Court refusing rescission to a shareholder who had subscribed for shares in response to a prospectus which contained an innocent[8] misrepresentation, said[9]

There is . . . a very important difference between cases where a contract may be rescinded on account of fraud, and those in which it may be rescinded on the ground that there is a difference in substance between the thing

[4] *Johnson* v. *Agnew* [1980] AC 367, 392–3 and *Photo Production Ltd.* v. *Securicor Transport Ltd.* [1980] AC 827, 844 (Lord Wilberforce).

[5] *Kennedy* v. *The Panama, New Zealand and Australian Royal Mail Co. Ltd.* (1867) LR 2 QB 580.

[6] The earlier position appears to have been that the remedy granted by the common law was damages for deceit; rescission was granted (originally only in the case of fraudulent misrepresentations: see n. 11, below) by equity. See *Attwood* v. *Small* (1838) 6 Cl. & Fin. 232, 395 (Lord Lyndhurst); 444, 466 (Lord Brougham); 502 (Lord Wynford).

[7] (1867) LR 2 QB 580: a pre-Judicature Act case, decided in a common law court, which necessarily deals only with the common law rule.

[8] That is, not fraudulent: since the case was decided before 1963, the Court did not consider whether the representation might have been negligent. See pp. 64–5, above.

[9] (1867) LR 2 QB 580, 587.

bargained for and that obtained. It is enough to shew that there was a fraudulent representation as to *any part* of that which induced the party to enter into the contract which he seeks to rescind; but where there has been an innocent misrepresentation or misapprehension,[10] it does not authorize a rescission unless it is such as to shew that there is a complete difference in substance between what was supposed to be and what was taken, so as to constitute a failure of consideration.

It became recognized, however, that the circumstances in which equity would grant rescission of a contract on the ground of mis-representation were wider; it is therefore in practice the equitable jurisdiction which has generally been exercised, and which will be discussed in the following pages. It was established by 1881[11] that rescission is not restricted to fraudulent misrepresentations; even innocent misrepresentations may give rise to this remedy.

It is not altogether clear whether at first a *wholly* innocent mis-representation sufficed, or whether some degree of negligence on the part of the representor was required.[12] In *Derry* v. *Peek*,[13] however, Lord Herschell made it quite clear that a wholly innocent (that is, non-negligent) misrepresentation would give rise to rescission:

Where rescission [on the ground of misrepresentation of a material fact] is claimed it is only necessary to prove that there was a misrepresentation; then, however honestly it may have been made, however free from blame the person who made it, the contract, having been obtained by misrepresentation, cannot stand.

In essence, equity will allow rescission of a contract[14] if there was a

---

[10] That is, a non-fraudulent misrepresentation, or a mistake. This statement of the jurisdiction of the common law in relation to common mistakes has been adopted in subsequent cases: see p. 236, below.

[11] *Redgrave* v. *Hurd* (1881) 20 Ch. D. 1, 12–13 (Jessel MR); Pollock, *Principles of Contract*, 1876, p. 467; *Fane* v. *Fane* (1875) LR 20 Eq. 698; *Adam* v. *Newbigging* (1888) 13 App. Cas. 308, 320. It appears that in the 1850s the House of Lords still assumed that fraud was necessary for rescission in equity: *Reynell* v. *Sprye* (1852) 1 De G. M. & G. 660, 708; *Smith* v. *Kay* (1859) 7 HLC 750.

[12] Cases which used language suggesting a requirement of negligence include *Pulsford* v. *Richards* (1853) 17 Beav. 87, 94; *Reese River Silver Mining Co.* v. *Smith* (1869) LR 4 HL 64, 79; *Mathias* v. *Yetts* (1882) 46 LT 497, 503. However, these are not unequivocal, and were decided before the modern definition of fraud was laid down in *Derry* v. *Peek* (1889) 14 App. Cas. 337.

[13] (1889) 14 App. Cas. 337, 359.

[14] If a second contract is also so closely connected with the first that they can be regarded as interdependent, the second contract may also in some cases be rescinded: *Holliday* v. *Lockwood* [1917] 2 Ch. 47.

misrepresentation which was material and was relied upon by the representee in entering into the contract. These criteria require explanation, however; and it must be added that, even if the test is satisfied, rescission may be denied if the defendant can establish any one of a number of 'bars' to rescission.

3. REQUIREMENTS OF THE REMEDY OF RESCISSION

(a) The Statement

In order to give rise to the remedy of rescission for misrepresentation, there must first be a representation—that is, a statement[15] made by one party to a contract[16] (or his agent) to the other party[17] (or his agent). It is generally said[18] that the misrepresentation, to give rise to the remedy of rescission in equity, must be a statement of fact: it is not sufficient if the misrepresentation is a statement of law, of opinion, or of intention. This, however, must be qualified. It appears from the cases that any fraudulent statement suffices; only if it is not fraudulent is there a requirement that the statement be of fact.[19]

(i) Fraudulent Statements

The definition of fraud is discussed below;[20] suffice it to say for present purposes that it includes both knowledge of the falsehood of the statement and recklessness regarding its truth.

Fraudulent misrepresentations of intention and opinion can be dealt with quickly. Both intention and opinion describe the representor's mind. A person who makes a statement about what he presently intends to do, or what his present opinion is on a subject, must know whether or not he is telling the truth. In this context, then, fraud can only mean misrepresentation with knowledge of the falsehood: there is no place for recklessness. On the other hand, if a

---

[15] For the problems of 'misrepresentation' by silence, see pp. 88 ff., below.
[16] The 'representor', or 'misrepresentor'.
[17] The 'representee', or 'misrepresentee'.
[18] See the books cited at p. 61 n. 1, above.
[19] This points to one circumstance in which a plaintiff may wish to allege fraud, in spite of the difficulty of proof: see p. 111, below.
[20] p. 109. The modern definition was developed in the context of the tort of deceit, rather than rescission.

person misrepresents what is his actual intention, or his actual opinion, he can be regarded as misrepresenting a fact: the fact of what is going on in his head at the time.

This is the way in which the courts have approached the point: although they have developed the rules that misrepresentations of intention and opinion do not vitiate a contract,[21] they regard a fraudulent statement as a statement of fact. For example, in *Brown* v. *Raphael*[22] Lord Evershed MR said,

a statement of opinion is always to this extent a statement of fact, that it is an assertion that the vendor does in fact hold the opinion which he states.

And, in *Edgington* v. *Fitzmaurice*,[23] in the context of statements of intention, Bowen LJ said,

There must be a misstatement of an existing fact: but the state of a man's mind is as much a fact as the state of his digestion.

Misrepresentations of law are, however, different. Such a misrepresentation may be phrased in terms simply of an opinion about the law on a particular subject: in such a case the rules relating to misrepresentation of opinion would apply. However, if the misrepresentation is simply one of law[24] the cases show that liability in respect of the statement depends upon whether it was made fraudulently or not.

Some commentators[25] suggest that *all* misrepresentations of law should be treated as misrepresentations of opinion, on the ground that any representation of law can be only an expression of the belief of the representor that the law is as stated; he cannot ever be categoric. This is not, however, convincing. The cases do not deal with the matter in this way; and we shall see that even a non-fraudulent misrepresentation which appears to be a misrepresentation of opinion may give rise to rescission if it can be said that it really is, or includes, a statement of fact because the representor is in

[21] See pp. 74 ff., below.

[22] [1958] Ch. 636, 641. See also *Anderson* v. *Pacific Fire and Marine Insurance Co.* (1872) LR 7 CP 65, 69 (Willes J).

[23] (1885) 29 Ch. D. 459, 483. The case concerned the requirement of a statement of fact in the tort of deceit, rather than for rescission.

[24] This issue is not as easy to determine as at first appears: the distinction between a statement of fact and a statement of law is often difficult to establish. This is discussed below.

[25] See e.g. Spencer Bower and Turner, *The Law of Actionable Misrepresentation*, 3rd edn., 1974, pp. 61–2; *Clerk & Lindsell on Torts*, 16th edn., 1989, para. 18-09.

a superior position of knowledge *vis-à-vis* the representee.[26] There is, however, no such rule in the case of misrepresentations of law, where liability hinges simply on the question of whether the misrepresentation was made fraudulently.

The context in which this has most commonly arisen is that of claims for recovery of premiums paid under a contract of insurance, where the party claiming such recovery was induced to enter the contract by a misrepresentation about the validity of the contract. Generally, there has been a misrepresentation that the party has an insurable interest in the life of the person insured under the contract, which will thereby enable him to recover under the contract upon the death of the insured. Such cases raise other issues,[27] but they discuss the general rule that misrepresentations of law do not allow a remedy, and they show that the rule extends only to non-fraudulent statements. In *Harse* v. *Pearl Life Assurance Company*,[28] for example, the Court of Appeal refused relief where the statement was made innocently. Collins MR said,[29]

The statement . . . was not a statement of fact, but one of the law, and was made innocently, as the jury have found. Unless there can be introduced the element of fraud, duress, or oppression, or difference in the position of the parties which created a fiduciary relationship to the plaintiff so as to make it inequitable for the defendants to insist on the bargain that they had made with the plaintiff, he is in the position of a person who has made an illegal contract and has sustained a loss in consequence of a misstatement of law, and must submit to that loss.

On the other hand, in similar cases where it was established that the statement was made fraudulently,[30] relief was granted, specifically on the ground that fraud was involved.[31] Furthermore, a similar distinction has been made in cases which concern representations

[26] *Smith* v. *Land and House Property Corporation* (1884) 28 Ch. D. 7; p. 80, below.

[27] In particular, the recovery of money paid pursuant to an illegal contract. Fraud can, however, also override the illegality of a contract: see Goff and Jones, ch. 21 (especially at p. 411).

[28] [1904] 1 KB 558.

[29] Ibid., at p. 563.

[30] There is no discussion in these cases on the definition of fraud which is to be applied, although it must be assumed that the definition is the same as that in the tort of deceit.

[31] *The British Workman's and General Assurance Company Ltd.* v. *Cunliffe* (1902) 18 TLR 502 (in spite of the headnote, which is misleading); *Tofts* v. *Pearl Life Assurance Company Ltd.* [1915] 1 KB 189; *Hughes* v. *Liverpool Victoria Legal Friendly Society* [1916] 2 KB 482.

made by a third party concerning the ability of a company to contract: in a case where the misrepresentation was construed as a statement of law, relief was on that ground refused;[32] but in another case[33] the representation was construed as a statement of fact, and relief was granted. Bowen LJ said,[34]

I am not prepared to say—and I doubt whether, if a man who wilfully misrepresented the law—would be allowed in equity to retain any benefit he got by such misrepresentation.

It therefore seems that a clear rule can be deduced,[35] that a fraudulent misrepresentation of law will found a remedy, although a non-fraudulent misrepresentation of law will not of itself[36] do so.

(ii) Non-Fraudulent Statements

The general rule is that a non-fraudulent misrepresentation, to give rise to the remedy of rescission, must be a representation of *fact*. It is not sufficient if the representation is one of law, intention, or opinion. However, it is necessary to consider how the distinctions between these different types of representation are made, and what the justification is for not allowing misrepresentations of law, intention, and opinion to give rise to the remedy.

(A) Non-fraudulent Misrepresentations of Law

It has already been illustrated that the courts have taken the view that misrepresentations of law should not of themselves give rise to the remedy of rescission unless they were made fraudulently. Two further questions need to be answered: what is a misrepresentation of law, as distinct from a misrepresentation of fact? And why is such a distinction made?

(I) Law and Fact Distinguished
The distinction between a misrepresentation of law and one of fact is not clear-cut. Many representations can be said to contain elements of both fact and law. There

---

[32] *Rashdall* v. *Ford* (1866) LR 2 Eq. 750.
[33] *West London Commercial Bank Ltd.* v. *Kitson* (1884) 13 QBD 360.
[34] *Ibid.*, at pp. 362–3; *obiter*.
[35] Such a rule was deduced in *Oudaille* v. *Lawson* [1922] NZLR 259.
[36] i.e. without there being present any other vitiating factor, such as duress.

are, however, certain indications in the cases[37] of how to draw the distinction.[38] If the issue is one of the existence of a public general statute, that will clearly be regarded as an issue of law. In *Sharp Brothers & Knight* v. *Chant*,[39] for example, rent was paid in excess of that payable under the Increase of Rent and Mortgage Interest (War Restrictions) Act 1915, and in ignorance of the existence of the statute; the overpayment was held to be irrecoverable because the mistake was of law.

However, an issue of the construction of a statute, or its applicability to a given set of facts, can raise difficulties. In *William Whiteley Ltd.* v. *The King*,[40] duties paid by the suppliant[41] to the Inland Revenue on the mistaken basis that its employees were 'male servants' for the purpose of the Revenue Act 1869 were held not to be recoverable on the ground of mistake, since the mistake was one of law. By contrast, in *Solle* v. *Butcher*[42] rent was paid in respect of a flat which had been repaired and improved after having suffered war damage, on a mistaken assumption that the rent was not subject to any statutory limitation. Since the flat as altered was still the *same* flat as the unaltered flat for the purposes of the Rent Restriction Acts, the rent was in fact limited. A majority of the Court of Appeal[43] held that this was a mistake of fact, and allowed a remedy for the mistake.[44] Bucknill LJ said[45] that 'it was a question of fact whether the flat had been so restored, altered and reconstructed as to destroy its identity'. Jenkins LJ, however, dissenting,[46] thought that it was 'simply a mistake as to the effect of certain public statutes on the contract made': that is, a mistake of law. It is easy to sympathize

---

[37] The relevant cases are drawn from various areas of the law where the law/fact distinction is applied, such as contracts entered into, and payments made, under mistake, and not simply (in fact, rarely) from misrepresentation. The same rules, however, apply also to misrepresentation.

[38] One area in which the law/fact distinction is not fully worked out is in the question of the interpretation of documents. Sometimes the issue is regarded as a question of law (*Ord* v. *Ord* [1923] 2 KB 432) although in general the courts have interpreted statements about the legal effect of a document as being questions of fact: *Lewis* v. *Jones* (1825) 4 B. & C. 506, 512; *Hirschfeld* v. *The London, Brighton and South Coast Railway Co.* (1876) 2 QB 1 (*quaere* whether this was, however, a fraudulent misrepresentation of law, which attracted a remedy on the principles set out at pp. 72–4, above); *Wauton* v. *Coppard* [1899] 1 Ch. 92; *Horry* v. *Tate & Lyle Refineries Ltd.* [1982] 2 Lloyd's Rep. 416 (in which the law/fact issue was not, however, discussed). Cf. *Curtis* v. *Chemical Cleaning and Dyeing Co.* [1951] 1 KB 805.

[39] [1917] 1 KB 771.   [40] (1909) 101 LT 741.

[41] The claim was a petition of right.   [42] [1950] 1 KB 671.

[43] Bucknill and Denning LJJ.   [44] See p. 238, below.

[45] [1950] 1 KB 671, 685.   [46] Ibid., at p. 705.

with Jenkins LJ. The factual question of whether the flat was still the same flat after the alteration was not a factual issue *in vacuo*. The only purpose in asking the question whether the flat was the same flat or not was to ask whether it was a flat—a 'dwelling-house'—to which the statutes[47] applied. It therefore seems rather closer in principle to *William Whiteley Ltd.* v. *The King*.

This last case may show a willingness on the part of some judges to find a mistake, or misrepresentation, of fact, rather than law, in order to allow remedies to be granted accordingly. The courts may also be seen to lean towards a finding of the mistake, or misrepresentation, being one of fact, rather than law, in their application of a test laid down in *Cooper* v. *Phibbs*.[48] It was there held that the question of the ownership of property of which the plaintiff took a lease (but which was found to belong to him already) was one of fact, since it related not to the general law, but to the private rights of the plaintiff.[49] Lord Westbury said,[50]

It is said, '*Ignorantia juris haud excusat;*' but in that maxim the word '*jus*' is used in the sense of denoting general law, the ordinary law of the country. But when the word '*jus*' is used in the sense of denoting a private right, that maxim has no application. Private right of ownership is a matter of fact; it may be the result also of matter of law; but if parties contract under a mutual mistake and misapprehension as to their relative and respective rights, the result is, that that agreement is liable to be set aside as having proceeded upon a common mistake.

Moreover, if an English court has to consider a question of foreign law, it regards it as a question of fact,[51] and this extends to the law of misrepresentation.[52]

---

[47] In particular s. 1 of the Increase of Rent and Mortgage Interest (Restrictions) Act 1920.

[48] (1867) LR 2 HL 149.

[49] It is interesting to notice that the mistake about ownership derived from an ambiguous statement in a private Act of Parliament: see (1867) LR 2 HL 149, 162–4 (Lord Cranworth).

[50] (1867) LR 2 HL 149, 170. The principle also applies to the law of misrepresentation: *André & Cie. SA* v. *Ets. Michel Blanc & Fils* [1979] 2 Lloyd's Rep. 427, 431 (Lord Denning MR).

[51] There are practical reasons for this: see Dicey and Morris, *The Conflict of Laws*, 11th edn., 1987, ch. 9. See, however, *Furness Withy (Australia) Pty. Ltd.* v. *Metal Distributors (UK) Ltd., The Amazonia*, [1989] 1 Lloyd's Rep. 403, 408, where Gatehouse J declined to apply this in relation to a common mistake of Australian law.

[52] *André & Cie. SA* v. *Ets. Michel Blanc & Fils* [1979] 2 Lloyd's Rep. 427, 430–1 (Lord Denning MR). Indeed, Lord Denning there went so far as to say that the 'distinction between law and fact is very illusory. It is so difficult to define that I hope the time will soon come when it will be discarded.'

(II) Rationale of Exclusion of Remedies for Misrepresentations of Law The reason for denying remedies for mistakes (and misrepresentations) of law is not coherently stated in the cases. The maxim 'ignorance of the law is no excuse' has often been backed by the argument that everyone is presumed to know the law;[53] but this is clearly unconvincing as a justification.[54] There are, however, two more particular justifications which may be advanced for the rule.

First, there is an argument based on general access to the law. Since the law is public, it is equally possible for each party to a transaction to discover the law, and so each must take responsibility for his own assumptions about what the law is. This argument is not in itself adequate to justify the rule. It is not true that the law is easy and general of access;[55] and even if such an argument goes some way towards justifying the rule that a *mistake* of law generally gives rise to no remedy, it ought not necessarily to preclude a remedy for a *misrepresentation* of law, where one party has taken it upon himself to state the law on a topic.

The second argument is based on the security of contracts.[56] If mistake (or misrepresentation) of law were to be allowed as a ground of rescission, it would tend to undermine contracts to an unacceptable degree—precisely because it is too easy to make such mistakes. This idea is present in some of the cases concerned with mistake of law,[57] and is essentially a method of eliminating a potentially large class of persons who might wish to escape from their contractual

---

[53] *Brett* v. *Rigden* (1568) 1 Plowden 340, 342 (concerning the law relating to wills); Hale, *History of the Pleas of the Crown*, pt. I, ch. 6 (criminal law); *Bilbie* v. *Lumley* (1802) 2 East 469, 472 (mistaken payments: action for money had and received).

[54] Indeed, it can be argued that the rule is to some extent a historical accident: Lord Wright of Durley, *Legal Essays and Addresses*, 1939, p. xix; Goff and Jones, pp. 117–19; *Hydro Electric Commission of Township of Nepean* v. *Ontario Hydro* (1982) 132 DLR (3d) 193, 201–11. The law relating to recovery of money paid under a mistake of law is currently under review by the Law Commission.

[55] See Furmston, (1981) 1 LS 37. Lord Hailsham of St Marylebone in *Hamlyn Revisited: The British Legal System Today*, 1983, p. 28, points out how vast is the output of primary and secondary legislation under modern governments: and this is not taking into account the difficulties of ascertaining the common law on any particular point.

[56] See Birks, *An Introduction to the Law of Restitution*, 1985, rev. 1989, pp. 164–7; *Table-Talk of John Selden*, 2nd edn., 1696, p. 89: 'Ignorance of the Law excuses no man; not that all Men know the Law, but because 'tis an excuse every Man will plead, and no man can tell how to confute him.'

[57] *Bilbie* v. *Lumley* (1802) 2 East 469, 472 (Lord Ellenborough CJ: 'Every man must be taken to be cognizant of the law; otherwise there is no saying to what extent the excuse of ignorance might be carried. It would be urged in almost every case'); *Rogers* v. *Ingham* (1876) 3 Ch. D. 351, 356–7 (James LJ).

obligations. Again, this idea might be more particularly apposite to the question of mistake of law, but the courts have none the less applied the rule to eliminate the remedy of rescission for simple, innocent misrepresentations of law.

However, sometimes a misrepresentation of law *does* give rise to a remedy. We have already seen that this will be the case if the misrepresentation was made fraudulently; the fraud of the representor overrides the policy which favours limiting the effect of misrepresentations of law.[58] And there are other circumstances which have been recognized as making a mistake (or misrepresentation) of law actionable. In *Kiriri Cotton Co. Ltd.* v. *Dewani*[59] Lord Denning said,

It is not correct to say that everyone is presumed to know the law. The true proposition is that no man can excuse himself from doing his duty by saying that he did not know the law on the matter. *Ignorantia juris neminem excusat.* Nor is it correct to say that money paid under a mistake of law can never be recovered back. The true proposition is that money paid under a mistake of law by itself and without more, cannot be recovered back. . . . If there is something more in addition to a mistake of law—if there is something in the defendant's conduct which shows that, of the two of them, he is the one primarily responsible for the mistake—then it may be recovered back. . . . Likewise, if the responsibility for the mistake lies more on the one than the other—because he has misled the other when he ought to know better— then again they are not *in pari delicto* and the money can be recovered back.

This shows that there is nothing intrinsic in the nature of a mistake, or misrepresentation, of law which requires it to go unremedied; but before a remedy will be granted there must be something more in the facts than a simple mistake, or misrepresentation, of law: something to tip the scales against the party resisting the remedy. In the case of mistake, it may be expected that the courts would take a strong line in favour of upholding the contract, and so deny rescission simply on the ground of mistake of law. However, it is not so obvious that the courts should lean against granting remedies in the case of a misrepresentation of law. It might be thought to be more consistent with the generosity with which rescission is granted for wholly innocent misrepresentations if the courts were to treat the fact that a defendant has misrepresented the law as sufficient to show that the

---

[58] pp. 72 ff., above.

[59] [1960] AC 192, 204. The case concerned the recovery of money paid pursuant to an illegal contract. See also *Rogers* v. *Ingham* (1876) 3 Ch. D. 351.

responsibility lies with him (and therefore rescission is available against him). However, the courts have not gone so far, and have limited recovery to fraudulent misrepresentations of law.

(B) *Non-fraudulent Misrepresentations of Intention*

A representation of intention is a statement of the representor's *present* plan for his *future* conduct. If the statement of intention is not fraudulent, it must be an honest statement of his present plan. Therefore, the statement can only be a 'misrepresentation' in the sense that it is a statement of what will happen in the future, which is subsequently not carried out. As soon as it is put in this way, it should be clear why the courts are reluctant to allow rescission for such a 'misrepresentation': to allow the representee to escape from the contract on the basis of such a representation would be to attribute a force to the statement of intention which is not appropriate to a statement not incorporated into a contract. If a person with whom I am contracting makes a statement about what he intends to do in the future, I can hold him to it—and have remedies against him in the event of his failure to perform it—if I get him to promise as a term of the contract that he will do as he says. If I do not obtain a contractual promise to that effect, I should not be able to hold him to it.[60]

(C) *Non-fraudulent Misrepresentations of Opinion*

As in the case of statements of intention, a statement of opinion, if it is not fraudulent, must be honestly made: it is therefore only a 'misrepresentation' in the sense that the representor offers an honest view on a particular topic, which is in fact incorrect. The basic rule here is that such a misrepresentation of opinion cannot give rise to the remedy of rescission, although sometimes what appears on its face to be a statement of opinion is found to be, or to include, a statement of fact which can give rise to the remedy.

[60] Cf. *Jorden* v. *Money* (1854) 5 HLC 185. Such a misrepresentation may, however, afford a defence to an action by the 'misrepresentor' for specific performance of the contract: *Lamare* v. *Dixon* (1873) LR 6 HL 414. There is also an entirely separate question: whether there should be any remedy available for a statement of intention which was honest when made, but where the representor has changed his mind before the contract is entered into (i.e. it would be false if then restated). This is discussed below, pp. 87–8.

In *Smith* v. *Land and House Property Corporation*,[61] for example, the written particulars of a hotel at an auction sale described it as let to 'a very desirable tenant, Mr Frederick Fleck'. It appeared, however, that Mr Fleck was not a desirable tenant: he had failed to pay rent to the plaintiff vendor as it fell due, and he had paid part of that which was due only when the plaintiff had threatened to distrain.[62] The defendant purchaser, who bought the property after the auction since the reserve price was not reached at the auction, refused to complete the purchase, and obtained rescission of the contract in the action brought by the vendor. The Court refused to accept the plaintiff's argument that the representation was merely one of opinion. Bowen LJ said,[63]

In a case where the facts are equally well known to both parties, what one of them says to the other is frequently nothing but an expression of opinion. The statement of such opinion is in a sense a statement of a fact, about the condition of the man's own mind, but only of an irrelevant fact, for it is of no consequence what the opinion is.[64] But if the facts are not equally known to both sides, then a statement of opinion by the one who knows the facts best involves very often a statement of a material fact, for he impliedly states that he knows facts which justify his opinion.

It is therefore clear that the words used by the representor are not conclusive about the legal nature of his representation. Whether or not he phrases his statement in terms of opinion, it is necessary to look further, to the circumstances in which the statement was made, and in particular to the relative and respective positions of the parties, to determine whether it is to be regarded as a statement simply of opinion, or whether the circumstances imply a statement of fact. The crucial point, in the test proposed by Bowen LJ, is the parties' respective knowledge (or, rather, access to[65] knowledge) of

---

[61] (1884) 28 Ch. D. 7.

[62] The reference to the tenant being very desirable had in fact been inserted by the auctioneers, not on instructions from the plaintiff.

[63] (1884) 28 Ch. D. 7, 15. Followed by the Privy Council in *Bisset* v. *Wilkinson* [1927] AC 177, where, however, the statement in question was held to be only one of opinion since the representor had no superior knowledge.

[64] Unless, of course, the opinion is not in fact held, in which case the remedies for fraud apply: see pp. 71–2, above.

[65] Lord Evershed MR in *Brown* v. *Raphael* [1958] Ch. 636, 642, commenting on Bowen LJ's test, said, 'Observe that he is not saying that one party must know all the facts; it suffices for the application of the principle if it appears that between the two parties one is better equipped with information or the means of information than the other.'

the facts. A superior position in this respect can therefore carry with it a higher obligation not to misrepresent the facts.[66]

(b) Materiality and Reliance

The requirements that the statement be material, and that the statement be relied upon by the representee in entering into the contract,[67] are inevitably interlinked. Materiality describes a factual aspect of the statement, and involves the idea that the statement is of its nature capable of having influenced the representee—of having (to some degree) induced him to contract; reliance (or inducement) describes the particular relationship which the statement had—or is deemed to have had—to the contract.

Materiality is in some senses an obvious requirement:[68] the misrepresentation must be relevant to the contract. If a vendor of a car tells his prospective purchaser that he went to Scarborough for his holiday this year, whereas in fact he went to Egypt, there is a false statement of fact, but it is quite irrelevant to the contract. However, if he says that the car has never been abroad, whereas he in fact took it on his holiday to Egypt, it is certainly material, since it is relevant to the history of the car, and therefore to its condition. The basic position is that materiality is determined objectively; the

[66] It appears to be necessary that the representor should hold himself out as having superior knowledge, before the representee is entitled to rely on the representation as being one of fact, rather than opinion: *Bisset* v. *Wilkinson* [1927] AC 177, 183-4. The cases do not consider how clear a representation of superior knowledge is required; but in principle one would expect that if a reasonable man would think that, in the circumstances, one party had relevant superior knowledge, and the other party in fact believes that he does have the knowledge, then the second party should be entitled to regard the statement as one of fact, rather than opinion: cf. the general 'objective' test adopted by the courts in construing statements: *Smith* v. *Hughes* (1871) LR 6 QB 597; *The Hannah Blumenthal* [1983] 1 AC 854; Ch. 1, above.

[67] *Attwood* v. *Small* (1838) 6 Cl. & Fin. 232, 448 (Lord Brougham); *Pulsford* v. *Richards* (1853) 17 Beav. 87, 96 (Romilly MR).

[68] An alternative view is that materiality is not a separate requirement, but is simply relevant to the burden of proof of reliance: any misrepresentation which induces a person to enter into a contract should be a ground for rescission, *whether or not* it would have so induced a reasonable person; materiality just raises a presumption that a particular representee relied upon the statement. See Goff and Jones, p. 168; *Museprime Properties Ltd.* v. *Adhill Properties Ltd.* [1990] 2 EGLR 196, 201–2; Chitty, §427. It has also been said that a *fraudulent* misrepresentor will not be allowed to say that his representation was not material: *Smith* v. *Kay* (1859) 7 HLC 750; however, the courts have still enquired into materiality in cases of fraud: see e.g. *Smith* v. *Chadwick* (1884) 9 App. Cas. 187.

question is whether 'the Court sees on the face of [the statement] that it is of such a nature as would induce a person to enter into the contract, or would tend to induce him to do so, or that it would be a part of the inducement, to enter into the contract';[69] and if the mis-statement is trivial in the context of the contract, it will not be material.[70]

The close relationship between the requirements of materiality and reliance is shown by the cases which discuss how reliance is proved. If it is shown that the misrepresentation was material, then it may be inferred that the representee relied upon it in entering into the contract. In *Mathias* v. *Yetts*[71] Jessel MR said,

if a man has a material misstatement made to him which may, from its nature, induce him to enter into the contract, it is an inference that he is induced to enter into the contract by it. You need not prove it affirmatively. The man who makes the material misstatement to induce the other to enter into the contract cannot be heard to say that he did not enter into it, to some extent, at all events, on the faith of that statement, unless he can prove one of two things: either in fact that the man did not rely upon it, and made inquiries and got information which showed that the misstatement was untrue, and still went on with the contract, that is one thing; or else that he said, expressly or impliedly, 'I do not care what your representations are; I shall not inquire about them. I shall enter into the contract taking the risk.'

This makes it clear that the materiality of the statement gives rise to an inference of fact—that the statement induced the representee to enter into the contract: that he relied upon the statement in entering into the contract. This is a rebuttable inference, as Jessel MR points out;[72] but the effect is to put on to the representor the burden of

[69] *Smith* v. *Chadwick* (1882) 20 Ch. D. 27, 44 (Jessel MR), a case concerning the tort of deceit; for similar statements by the same judge in relation to rescission, see *Redgrave* v. *Hurd* (1881) 20 Ch. D. 1, 21; *Mathias* v. *Yetts* (1882) 46 LT 497, 502.

[70] *Smith* v. *Chadwick* (1882) 20 Ch. D. 27, 55, 70 (a misrepresentation about £3,000 out of £301,000: the case concerned the tort of deceit).

[71] (1882) 46 LT 497, 502. See also Sir James Hannen at p. 505 and Lindley LJ at p. 507.

[72] An earlier statement of Jessel MR on the same point, in *Redgrave* v. *Hurd* (1881) 20 Ch. D. 1, 21, referred to the inference being one of law, rather than of fact. This was criticized in the Court of Appeal (*Smith* v. *Land and House Property Corporation* (1884) 28 Ch. D. 7, 16 (Bowen LJ)) and in the House of Lords (*Smith* v. *Chadwick* (1884) 9 App. Cas. 187, 196 (Lord Blackburn)), and it is clear that the presumption is only a rebuttable presumption of fact. Jessel MR also stated the presumption in similar terms to his statement in *Mathias* v. *Yetts* (1882) 46 LT 497, 502, in the context of the tort of deceit in *Smith* v. *Chadwick* (1882) 20 Ch. D. 27 (reported immediately after *Redgrave* v.

showing that the representee did not in fact rely on the representation.[73]

The idea of reversing the burden of proof of reliance in this manner is a consequence of one difficulty in the law of misrepresentation. It is of its nature difficult to establish why one entered into a contract.[74] There are many forces which influence a person's mind, and if a representee were required to prove that it was because of the representation that he in fact decided to enter into the contract, it might often be almost impossible to prove.[75] Moreover, it is clear from the cases that the misrepresentation need not be the only inducing factor, in order to found rescission: as long as it was an inducing factor, that is sufficient.[76]

If the representee can be shown to have known of the falsehood of the statement, he can clearly not rely on it. There is, however, a grey area: what if he had the *means* of finding out the truth? The rule is[77] that

The mere fact that a party has the opportunity of investigating and ascertaining whether a representation is true or false is not sufficient to deprive him of his right to rely on a misrepresentation. . . . The person who has made the misrepresentation cannot be heard to say to the party to whom he has made that representation, 'You chose to believe me when you might have doubted me, and gone further'. The representation once made relieves the party from an investigation, even if the opportunity is afforded.

Hurd, above, in the same volume of the Law Reports). As counsel in *Smith* v. *Kay* (1859) 7 HLC 750 Jessel had (without success) resisted such an analysis.

[73] If, however, the statement is ambiguous, the representee must prove that he relied on the false meaning: *Smith* v. *Chadwick* (1884) 9 App. Cas. 187 (deceit).

[74] *Reynell* v. *Sprye* (1852) 1 De G. M. & G. 660, 708 (Lord Cranworth). A similar idea, of reversing the burden of proof of reliance, and for similar reasons, has also been used in the context of promissory estoppel: *Brikom Investments Ltd.* v. *Carr* [1979] QB 467, 482–3; and proprietary estoppel: *Greasley* v. *Cooke* [1980] 1 WLR 1306, 1311.

[75] Inevitably it will be at least as difficult to disprove reliance, since the representor is required to show what did *not* influence the *other* party's mind: so the representor is often given an almost impossible task, thus favouring the representee over the representor.

[76] *Mathias* v. *Yetts* (1882) 46 LT 497, 502 (Jessel MR). The same point was also made by Lord Cranworth in *Reynell* v. *Sprye* (1852) 1 De G. M. & G. 660, 708 and Lord Wynford in *Attwood* v. *Small* (1838) 6 Cl. & Fin. 232, 502. These last two statements both refer to this as the rule in the case of *fraudulent* misrepresentations; however, at the time that the cases were decided, fraud was a requirement for rescission in equity: see n. 11, above; the rule cannot therefore be so limited, but should apply to all cases where rescission is now available for misrepresentation.

[77] *Redgrave* v. *Hurd* (1881) 20 Ch. D. 1, 22–3 (Baggallay LJ).

However, this may not apply, and the representee may be prevented from relying on the statement, if there are suspicious circumstances which put him on notice of the falsehood,[78] or if he does in fact enquire into the truth of the statement, but does so negligently.[79]

It is not, however, sufficient that the representee *in fact* relied on the statement; in addition the representor must have *intended* the statement to act as an inducement. This requirement is seen most clearly in cases involving fraud, where it is said that 'general fraudulent conduct signifies nothing . . . It must be shown that the attempt [to overreach] was made, and made with success.'[80] However, it appears that this is a requirement also of non-fraudulent misrepresentations. Although there is (*ex hypothesi*) no requirement in such cases of an intention to mislead, none the less the representor must make the statement with a view to the representee entering into the contract.[81]

(c) Changes of Circumstances

It has so far been assumed that there is simply a misrepresentation of fact, which is then relied upon by the representee in entering into the contract. But there may be a delay between the time of the representation and the contract being concluded. A question therefore arises about the consequences of such a delay.

Reliance upon the representation is tested at the time of the contract. If the statement, when made, was false but (by virtue of a change in the facts) has become true by the time the contract is entered into, there can be no question of rescission; at the time that

---

[78] Ibid.

[79] *Attwood* v. *Small* (1838) 6 Cl. & Fin. 232. He is then relying on his own enquiry rather than on the statement of the representor. The line may, however, be very fine.

[80] Ibid., at pp. 447–8 (Lord Brougham). See also *Way* v. *Hearn* (1862) 13 CB (NS) 292, 303, 305; and, for the tort of deceit, *Andrews* v. *Mockford* [1896] 1 QB 372, 378.

[81] *Redgrave* v. *Hurd* (1881) 20 Ch. D. 1, 21 (Jessel MR, who also says that the inference of reliance is drawn from a material misrepresentation 'calculated' to induce the representee to enter into the contract. He appeared, however, to be using the word in its sense of 'capable of' inducing or 'likely to' induce, rather than 'intended to' induce: see *The Oxford English Dictionary*, 2nd edn., 1989, 'Calculated', meanings 2 and 1 respectively; and cf. Jessel MR's formulation in *Mathias* v. *Yetts* (1882) 46 LT 497, 502, quoted at p. 82, above: 'a material misstatement . . . which *may, from its nature, induce*'); *Smith* v. *Chadwick* (1884) 9 App. Cas. 187, 196 (Lord Blackburn: this was a case of fraud, but the statement is made generally).

the statement is relied on, it is not a misrepresentation.[82] If, however, the statement was true when made, but has become false by the time it is relied upon—that is, by the time the contract is entered into— the question is whether the representor can shelter behind the fact that his statement was true when he made it; or whether the representee can require to be informed of the change in circumstances. In essence, on whom is the risk of a change in facts between the representation and the contract?

In general, the risk is placed on the representor. This rule is expressed in two different ways: either it is said that there is a duty on the representor to communicate a change in the circumstances[83] or that the representation is to be treated as a continuing representation, which is therefore a *mis*representation at the time at which it is relied upon.[84]

In *With* v. *O'Flanagan*,[85] for example, With agreed by a contract dated 1 May 1934 to buy from O'Flanagan a medical practice for £4,000. He had been told by O'Flanagan in January 1934 that the practice was 'doing at the rate of £2,000 a year'; after that representation had been made, however, O'Flanagan became seriously ill, and his practice (which was looked after by various locum tenentes) declined until in the three weeks before the contract it produced only £15 (of which £10 was from a single patient).[86] After With took possession of the practice, no patient came for three days; he therefore sought to rescind the contract.

The Court of Appeal allowed rescission. Lord Wright MR[87] gave the alternative reasons already mentioned; that either O'Flanagan had failed in his duty to communicate the change, or his representation had been a continuing one. Romer LJ, however, put the point narrowly. He said,[88]

---

[82] Spencer Bower and Turner, *The Law of Actionable Misrepresentation*, p. 84; *Briess* v. *Woolley* [1954] AC 333, 353–4 (concerning, however, the tort of deceit).

[83] *With* v. *O'Flanagan* [1936] Ch. 575, 583 (Lord Wright MR); *Traill* v. *Baring* (1864) 4 De G. J. & S. 318, 326 (Knight Bruce LJ), 329 (Turner LJ).

[84] *With* v. *O'Flanagan* [1936] Ch. 575, 584 (Lord Wright MR); *Re an Arbitration between Marshall and Scottish Employers' Liability and General Insurance Co. Ltd.* (1901) 85 LT 757; *Smith* v. *Kay* (1859) 7 HLC 750, 769 (Lord Cranworth).

[85] Above, n. 84.

[86] During April 1934 With discovered that the practice was being looked after by a locum tenens; O'Flanagan's agent assured him that 'the present locum is quite efficient and is looking after the practice satisfactorily': [1936] Ch. 575, 577.

[87] [1936] Ch. 575, 583–4.

[88] Ibid., at p. 586 (italics added).

if at a later date and before the contract is actually entered into, owing to a change of circumstances, *the representation then made would to the knowledge of [the representor] be untrue* . . . [the representor] cannot hold [the representee] to the bargain.

If this is exhaustive as a statement of principle, it limits the remedy to changes of facts of which the representor *knows*: in effect, only those statements which, if they were repeated at the time of the contract, would be fraudulent.[89] Although the concept of a duty to communicate the changed facts would be harsh if it were not limited to cases where the representee knew (or at least had the means of knowing) the change, it is not obvious that such a limitation should be imposed. We have already seen that a wholly innocent mis-representation can give rise to rescission; there is a corresponding argument that the mere fact that a representation (though true when made) has become false before the contract is entered into ought to entitle the representee to avoid the contract. The granting of rescission for a wholly innocent misrepresentation appears to be based, as discussed above,[90] on the idea that the representee deserves to be protected against even an innocent misrepresentor, who has taken upon himself a level of responsibility simply by having made the statement; as between them, the scales are tipped in favour of the representee. It is of course arguable that where the statement is true when made, there is nothing to tip the scales against the representor unless the mere fact of having put a state-ment into the negotiations carries with it a continuing responsibility for its truth. But, given the clear policy of the law of rescission in favour of the representee, it seems that the better view is indeed to impose upon the representor a continuing responsibility for the truth of his statement—even if he does not know of the changed circumstances which render the statement false.

---

[89] It is not altogether clear whether Lord Wright MR intended the rule to be so limited. The third judge in *With* v. *O'Flanagan*, Clauson J, simply agreed with the other two. An explanation for Romer LJ's language may, however, be found in it source, which seems quite clearly to be the judgment of Turner LJ in *Traill* v. *Baring* (1864) 4 De G. J. & S. 318, 329, which was quoted in Lord Wright MR's judgment at p. 583. That case, however, dealt with a change of *intention*: see below. In case of a misrepresen-tation of intention, the only circumstance in which rescission will be available is where the misrepresentation was fraudulent: see pp. 71–2 and 79, above. It is in that context therefore quite natural to require the change of circumstances to be known by the representor. Moreover, *Traill* v. *Baring* was decided in 1864, when it was not yet clear that rescission was available for an innocent misrepresentation.

[90] p. 67.

Another difficult, related area is the question whether a change of law, intention, or opinion between the (true) statement and the time of the contract can give rise to rescission. The only authorities appear to be in the area of representations of intention;[91] and here there is a conflict. In *Traill* v. *Baring*[92] P, a Life Assurance Society, had a risk of £3,000 which it wished to reinsure. It proposed to R, another society, that R should take £1,000 of this risk by way of reinsurance, whilst a further £1,000 would be reinsured with V, a third society, and the balance of the risk would be retained by P. In the event, and before R contracted to reinsure its share, P changed its mind and reinsured[93] the whole £2,000 balance with V. It was held that R was entitled to rescind its contract, on the basis that P had been under a duty to communicate its change of intention.

In *Wales* v. *Wadham*,[94] however, Tudor Evans J took the clear view that the rule in *With* v. *O'Flanagan*[95] could only apply to statements of fact, and not of intention. The defendant 'made an honest statement of her intention which was not a representation of fact, and I can find no basis for holding that she was under a duty in the law of contract to tell [the plaintiff] of her change of mind'.[96] The case involved general statements by a wife to her husband during her marriage that she objected in principle to remarriage after divorce; and specific statements during the period the marriage was breaking up that she had no intention to remarry. After she separated from her husband, but before they agreed on terms for her financial provision, the wife changed her views, to the extent of having agreed to marry another man in due course once her pending divorce was made absolute. Tudor Evans J's judgment on the question of rescission for misrepresentation[97] seems to have been influenced by the facts that the husband did contemplate the possibility that the wife might change her mind; and that the statement by the wife that she did not intend to remarry was, in the

[91] Presumably, though, arguments could be applied to representations of law and opinion similar to those in relation to the cases concerning representations of intention.

[92] (1864) 4 De G. J. & S. 318.

[93] At first instance, Stuart V-C (sub. nom. *Trail* v. *Baring* (1864) 4 Giff. 485, 490) thought it was not merely a change of intention, because the reinsurance had actually taken place.

[94] [1977] 1 WLR 199, 211. *Traill* v. *Baring* was not cited.

[95] [1936] Ch. 575.

[96] [1977] 1 WLR 199, 211.

[97] The case was also decided on three other grounds.

circumstances, limited to a statement of present intention and could not carry any implication that she would not change her mind: it was made in an attempt to save the marriage. Given, also, that the decision was made without reference to *Traill* v. *Baring*,[98] it is not on its face conclusive authority that a change of intention can never found rescission. However, it has received a brief note of approval on this issue by the House of Lords.[99]

It may be that the resistance to allowing rescission for changes of intention between the making of the statement and the time of the contract is founded on a concern to avoid undermining the distinction between statements of fact and of intention. As discussed earlier,[100] the justification for refusing legal consequences for statements of intention is that it would be to attribute too great a force to a statement about the future: if a representee wishes to hold a representor to such a statement, he should get him to make a contractual promise to that effect. That rule certainly applies to statements of intention which are still honestly held at the time of the contract; but it should not necessarily prevent the remedy where the change occurs before the contract is entered into (and therefore the statement, if repeated at that time, would clearly be fraudulent and so actionable).

(d) Silence as Misrepresentation

The remedy of rescission has so far been discussed on the basis that a false *statement* of fact is required. That is of course the easiest case. It is, however, possible for the remedy to be granted even in the absence of such a statement: a statement may be made which, strictly, is true, but in the circumstances in which it is made is so misleading that it communicates in addition a falsehood; or no words may be used but *conduct* of the defendant may communicate a falsehood; or (even though no words and no conduct can be relied upon by the plaintiff to found his claim for rescission) the relationship between the parties may be such as to place an obligation on one party (or, sometimes, both parties) to make disclosure of material facts, and the defendant may have failed to fulfil this obligation. The first two of these catagories are only variations of the

[98] (1864) 4 De G. J. & S. 318.
[99] *Livesey* v. *Jenkins* [1985] AC 424, 439.
[100] p. 79, above.

basic rules of misrepresentation; there is still a misleading of the plaintiff by an identifiable, positive (albeit sometimes innocent) action on the part of the defendant. The third category is rather different. It is not a case of one party having actively disturbed the balance of negotiation between the parties, but the imposition of a duty attaching by virtue simply of the relative positions of the parties.

(i) True, but Misleading, Statements

A positive statement of fact, whilst being literally true, may still be only a half truth; it may carry an implication of additional facts—those additional facts being untrue. For example, in *Dimmock* v. *Hallett*[101] land was described at an auction sale as 'lately in the occupation of Mr. R. Hickson, at an annual rent of £290 15s.' This was true; and the natural implication was that the land was capable of being let for that value. However, it was not stated by the vendor that Mr Hickson had vacated the property, and the vendor had been able to find other prospective tenants only at a lower rent. It was therefore characterized as a misrepresentation. And in *Nottingham Patent Brick and Tile Co.* v. *Butler*,[102] a vendor's solicitor was asked to confirm the vendor's statement that land was subject to covenants; he failed to do so—and said that he did not know of the covenants. This was held to constitute a misrepresentation which bound the vendor, since the solicitor failed to add that he had not read the documents of title.

(ii) Misrepresentation by Conduct

In many areas of the law, deeds can carry the same consequences as words.[103] It would be quite absurd if, for example, a nod of the head could not carry the same responsibility as the word 'yes'. In the law of misrepresentation this is also true;

a single word, or (I may add) a nod or a wink, or a shake of the head, or a smile from the purchaser intended to induce the vendor to believe the existence of a non-existing fact, which might influence the price of the

---

[101] (1866) 2 Ch. App. 21.
[102] (1886) 16 QBD 778.
[103] e.g., in the context of formation of a contract, *Brogden* v. *Metropolitan Railway Co.* (1877) 2 App. Cas. 666.

subject to be sold, would be a sufficient ground for a Court of Equity to refuse a decree for a specific performance of the agreement.[104]

What matters, then, is whether the false fact has been communicated, not whether words have been used to make the communication. For example, the action of an agent of a lessor of property in covering up active patches of dry rot has been held to constitute a fraudulent misrepresentation which was intended to deceive prospective tenants.[105]

Most cases involve words, rather than conduct; perhaps because it is words which will generally constitute the clearest misrepresentations. There is no detailed consideration in the cases of the test to be applied in analysing conduct: in principle one would expect that the conduct must in fact have led the plaintiff to believe the false fact, and that it was reasonable for him so to believe.[106]

(iii) Obligations of Disclosure

There is no general duty to speak in negotiations leading up to a contract; nor is there even a duty on one party to the negotiations to disabuse the other party of a mistake of fact which the first party is aware that the other is making.[107] The problem is the familiar one of imposing a liability for omissions. However, there are certain circumstances in which it has been thought acceptable to impose such a liability: either because of the relationship between the parties, or because of the nature of the contract itself. The two main categories of cases[108] are where there is a fiduciary relationship between the parties, and where the contract is within the class known as contracts *uberrimae fidei*.

---

[104] *Walters* v. *Morgan* (1861) 3 De G. F. & J. 718, 724 (Lord Campbell LC).

[105] *Gordon* v. *Selico Co. Ltd.* [1985] 2 EGLR 79 (Goulding J; this issue was not challenged on appeal, [1986] 1 EGLR 71): the remedy there sought was for the tort of deceit. For a representation inherent in the wearing of an Oxford cap and gown, see *R.* v. *Barnard* (1837) 7 Car. & P. 784 (in relation to a criminal charge of false pretences).

[106] Cf. *Smith* v. *Hughes* (1871) LR 6 QB 597; *The Hannah Blumenthal* [1983] 1 AC 854; Ch. 1, above.

[107] If one party knows that the other is mistaken about the *terms* of the contract, however, he cannot hold the mistaken party to his (the first party's) terms. *Smith* v. *Hughes* (1871) LR 6 QB 597; pp. 7–8, above.

[108] For a comprehensive account of the law in this area, see Spencer Bower, Turner, and Sutton, *The Law Relating to Actionable Non-Disclosure*, 2nd edn., 1990. Statute has sometimes intervened to impose duties of disclosure: see e.g. Financial Services Act 1986, ss. 47, 133 (criminal offences related to making statements or *dishonestly*

(A) Fiduciary Relationship[109]

If the relationship between the parties is fiduciary, obligations automatically attach to the fiduciary. This area is closely related to undue influence and the rules developed by the Courts of Equity to regulate transactions entered into between trustees and their beneficiaries (the 'self-dealing' and 'fair-dealing' rules), where the fiduciary nature of the relationship between the parties is crucial to the ascertainment of the obligations attaching.[110] If the party is a trustee, then the highest duties of frankness and disclosure attach;[111] but if there is no trust as such—and even if there is no established category of fiduciary relationship between the parties—then an analysis of the relationship is necessary to determine whether one has placed himself in a position which rendered it incumbent upon him to give the best advice to the other.

For example, in *Tate* v. *Williamson*[112] a purchaser contracted to purchase property from his cousin, who had 'contracted habits of extravagance at the university. . . . with scarcely a friend to counsel him, and towards the close of his life he became addicted to drinking, and died prematurely at the age of twenty-four'. Lord Chelmsford LC said[113] that 'openness and fair dealing were the more necessary when he was negotiating with an extravagant and necessitous young man, deprived at the time of all other advice, eager to raise money, and apparently careless in what manner it was obtained'.

(B) Contracts Uberrimae Fidei[114]

Certain categories of contract have come to be regarded as carrying

---

concealing material facts for the purpose of inducing another to enter or refrain from entering into certain investment agreements or insurance contracts: notice that the additional requirement of dishonesty is imposed in relation to concealment of facts, thus narrowing the duty in relation to omissions to speak), 146–7 and 150, 163–4 and 166 (compensation for misleading statements or *omissions* in listing particulars and prospectuses).

[109] Spencer Bower *et al.*, *The Law Relating to Actionable Non-Disclosure*, pts. IV and V.

[110] See Ch. 8 and Ch. 9 s. 2(*d*), below.

[111] *Tito* v. *Waddell (No. 2)* [1977] Ch. 106, 241; Ch. 9 s. 2(*d*), below. The duties are owed only to the beneficiary: *Low* v. *Bouverie* [1891] 3 Ch. 82 (where the issue was not rescission but the tort of deceit. Cf., however, s. 137(8) Law of Property Act 1925).

[112] (1866) LR 2 Ch. App. 55, 61.

[113] Ibid., at pp. 66–7.

[114] Spencer Bower *et al.*, *The Law Relating to Actionable Non-Disclosure*, pt. II.

obligations of full and frank disclosure. The most common of these is the contract of insurance,[115] where

> The special facts, upon which the contingent chance is to be computed, lie most commonly in the knowledge of the insured only: the under-writer trusts to his representation, and proceeds upon confidence that he does not keep back any circumstance in his knowledge, to mislead the under-writer into a belief that the circumstance does not exist, and to induce him to estimate the risque, as if it did not exist.
>
> The keeping back such circumstance is a fraud, and therefore the policy is void.[116] Although the suppression should happen through mistake, without any fraudulent intention; yet still the under-writer is deceived, and the policy is void; because the risque run is really different from the risque understood and intended to be run, at the time of the agreement.[117]

This duty of disclosure of all material facts extends to all contracts of insurance, whatever the nature of the risk,[118] and the test of materiality is whether the fact 'would influence the judgment of a prudent insurer in fixing the premium, or determining whether he will take the risk'.[119] This can impose a heavy obligation on an insured, and there have been calls to limit the obligation of disclosure to those facts which a reasonable man in the position of the applicant would disclose;[120] there has, however, been no

---

[115] See Clarke, *The Law of Insurance Contracts*, 1989, esp. ch. 23; Ivamy, *General Principles of Insurance Law*, 1986, chs. 12–14. Another contract *uberrimae fidei* is the contract entered into between members of a family, known as a family arrangement: for example, where a dispute over the division of property within a family is settled by contract: *Gordon* v. *Gordon* 3 Swans. 400; *Greenwood* v. *Greenwood* (1863) 2 De G. J. & S. 28.

[116] It is now clearly established that a breach of the duty of disclosure, like a positive misrepresentation, makes a contract voidable, not void: *Banque Keyser Ullmann SA* v. *Skandia (UK) Insurance Co. Ltd.* [1990] QB 665, 770–1; *Mackender* v. *Feldia AG* [1967] 2 QB 590.

[117] *Carter* v. *Boehm* (1766) 3 Burr. 1905, 1909 (Lord Mansfield).

[118] *London Assurance* v. *Mansel* (1879) 11 Ch. D. 363, 367 (Jessel MR).

[119] Marine Insurance Act 1906, s. 18(2). The definition is treated as generally applicable: *Locker and Woolf Ltd.* v. *Western Australian Insurance Co. Ltd.* [1936] 1 KB 408, 415 (Scott LJ); *Lambert* v. *Co-operative Insurance Society Ltd.* [1975] 2 Lloyd's Rep. 485.

[120] Law Reform Committee 5th Report (1957) Cmnd. 62; *Lambert* v. *Co-operative Insurance Society Ltd.* [1975] 2 Lloyd's Rep. 485, 491; Law Com. No. 104: *Insurance Law: Non-Disclosure and Breach of Warranty* (1980), para 4.47. In practice, because the insurer is in a better position than the insured to have in mind the sorts of fact which could affect the risk, the existing test of materiality in insurance contracts is more onerous than that in relation to the general rules of rescission for misrepresentation. However, the Association of British Insurers' Statement of Long Term Insurance Practice states that a member will not reject on the ground of non-disclosure unless the fact was one which the proposer could *reasonably* be expected to disclose.

such change in the law.[120a] The duty of disclosure in insurance contracts is reciprocal—the insurer must also disclose to the insured all facts known to him which are material either to the nature of the risk sought to be covered or to the recoverability of a claim under the policy which a prudent insured would take into account in deciding whether or not to place the risk for which he seeks cover with that insurer.[121]

4. BARS TO RESCISSION

Once the requirements of rescission have been satisfied, the misrepresentee has the right to rescind the contract unless one or more of the following bars to rescission is established.[122]

(a) Impossibility of Restitution

The basic concept of rescission[123] is that the contract is treated as if it had never been entered into. This involves the reversal of performance which has taken place under the contract. There will naturally be a problem, therefore, if such a reversal is impossible:

> If you are fraudulently induced to buy a cake you may return it and get back the price; but you cannot both eat your cake and return your cake.[124]

[120a] Although the Government did announce in 1983 its intention of legislating for consumer insurance contracts: Hansard, Apr. 28 1983, Written Answers, House of Commons, col. 376.

[121] *Banque Keyser Ullmann SA* v. *Skandia (UK) Insurance Co. Ltd.* [1990] QB 665, 772, approved in the House of Lords sub nom. *Banque Financière de la Cité SA* v. *Westgate Insurance Co. Ltd.* [1990] 2 All ER 947, 950, 960. At first instance, [1990] QB 665, 699 ff., Steyn J also held that damages were available as a remedy for a breach of the duty to disclose. This latter point (but not the issue of the duty of the insurer to disclose) was reversed by the Court of Appeal, [1990] QB 665, 773–81, and this view was reinforced by the Court of Appeal in *Bank of Nova Scotia* v. *Hellenic Mutual War Risks Association (Bermuda) Ltd., The Good Luck* [1990] QB 818, 885 ff., in relation to the obligation to disclose *during* the currency of the contract. The approach of the Court of Appeal in *Banque Keyser Ullmann SA* v. *Skandia (UK) Insurance Co. Ltd.* was approved by the House of Lords: [1990] 2 All ER 947, 959, 960 (although Lord Bridge reserved his opinion: at p. 951). See also *Carter* v. *Boehm* (1766) 3 Burr. 1905, 1909 (Lord Mansfield).

[122] The Misrepresentation Act 1967, s. 1, abolished two other bars to rescission: that the misrepresentation had become a term of the contract; and that the contract had been performed. A representee may also be prevented from claiming rescission—as any other remedy for misrepresentation—if he is so bound by an exclusion clause in the contract (subject to s. 3 Misrepresentation Act 1967, as substituted by s. 8 Unfair Contract Terms Act 1977.)

[123] See p. 68, above.

[124] *Clarke* v. *Dickson* (1858) El. Bl. & El. 148, 152 (Crompton J).

On this issue, there was a difference between the rules of common law and equity. Because the common law had little machinery available to adjust the rights of the parties—such as ordering an account of any benefit obtained by the rescinding party—it took a very narrow view of the requirement of restitution, and would not recognize a rescission unless the contract could be unwound, and any property transferred under it could be returned *in specie.*

However, equity could take account of profits, or make an allowance for deterioration of property, and

the practice has always been for a Court of Equity to give this relief whenever, by the exercise of its powers, it can do what is practically just, though it cannot restore the parties precisely to the state they were in before the contract.[125]

So, for example, although the fact that the plaintiff has had the use of property for a period before rescission might have prevented his obtaining rescission at common law,[126] it is not a bar to rescission in equity, since money can be ordered to be paid by way of compensation for lost rent; and compensation can be ordered for the value of stock taken over upon the purchase of a business, but since then used up, when the contract for the purchase is being rescinded.[127] A mere decrease in value of property does not prevent rescission,[128] although a change in the nature of property may: for example, where the contract was for shares in an unincorporated association which, before rescission was claimed, had been incorporated.[129]

Moreover, there is in the cases an indication of another distinction which is relevant to the question of the ability to make restitution. In *Spence* v. *Crawford,*[130] the House of Lords emphasized that the standard to be applied differed according to whether the misrepresentations were made fraudulently or not. Lord Wright said,[131]

[125] *Erlanger* v. *New Sombrero Phosphate Co.* (1878) 3 App. Cas. 1218, 1279 (Lord Blackburn).

[126] *Hunt* v. *Silk* (1804) 5 East 449 (concerning breach, rather than misrepresentation).

[127] *Alati* v. *Kruger* (1955) 94 CLR 216.

[128] *Armstrong* v. *Jackson* [1917] 2 KB 822. *A fortiori* where the decrease in value is directly related to the misrepresented worth of the property: *Adam* v. *Newbigging* (1888) 13 App. Cas. 308.

[129] *Western Bank of Scotland* v. *Addie* (1867) LR 1 Sc. & Div. 145, 165–6; *Clarke* v. *Dickson* (1858) El. Bl. & El. 148.

[130] [1939] 3 All ER 271; cf. *Lagunas Nitrate Company* v. *Lagunas Syndicate* [1899] 2 Ch. 392, 423, 433–4.

[131] [1939] 3 All ER 271, 288.

The court will be less ready to pull a transaction to pieces where the defendant is innocent, whereas in the case of fraud the court will exercise its jurisdiction to the full in order, if possible, to prevent the defendant from enjoying the benefit of his fraud at the expense of the innocent plaintiff.

And Lord Thankerton[132] put the point more narrowly:

[a fraudulent misrepresentor] is not entitled in bar of restitution to found on dealings with the subject purchased, which he has been enabled by his fraud to carry out.

He put a hypothetical example: that if the contract was for shares which enabled the purchaser to take control of a company, and the purchaser had since disposed of other shares so that the subject shares were necessary to retain control, the purchaser might be able to resist rescission if he had been innocent in his misrepresentation; not if he had been fraudulent.

(b) Affirmation

Misrepresentation makes a contract only voidable at the instance of the misled party; it does not make it void. If, therefore, a person who has a right to rescind chooses *not* to rescind, but to require the contract to continue, he will *affirm* the contract. His election to affirm is final; he can no longer change his mind and rescind the contract on the basis of the misrepresentation in question.[133]

The question, though, is what constitutes affirmation. If a contracting party were to say clearly, 'I know that I can rescind on the basis of your misrepresentation, but I elect not to do so', that would obviously amount to affirmation. Contracting parties are, however, rarely so clear, and it is necessary to look to their actions, as well as their words, to deduce their intention.[134]

The first question is what degree of knowledge on the part of the rescinding party is required before any words or actions can amount to affirmation. The basic point is that it is not sufficient that he knows of the facts which give rise to the right to rescind: in addition it is necessary for the rescinding party to know that he has the right

---

[132] Ibid., at p. 281.

[133] Com. Dig. Election, C.2: 'If a man once determines his Election, it shall be determined for ever.'

[134] Com. Dig. Election, C.1: 'A Determination of a Man's Election shall be made by express Words, or by Act.'

to rescind, yet he chooses with that knowledge not to exercise the right.[135]

The second question is what, short of a statement of election, is sufficient to constitute affirmation. As in the formation of contract[136] one would expect that the conduct of the representee would be viewed objectively from the perspective of the representor: the question should be whether the representor reasonably could, and in fact did, believe that the representee's words and actions indicated that he had decided not to rescind the contract.

This position was taken in *Peyman* v. *Lanjani*,[137] where Stephenson LJ put it in the language of estoppel:[138]

In fact and in law men's intentions must be judged by their actions, and a man's acts may convey to any reasonable person standing in the shoes of the other party to a contract, as clearly as any words, an intention to repudiate or to affirm the contract. If the other party, relying on acts having the latter effect, suffers detriment or prejudice, there is unequivocal, and irrevocable, affirmation.

(c) Lapse of Time

Essentially, lapse of time involves the passage of such a time that the representee ought no longer to be allowed to rescind the contract. What will constitute such a time will, of course, vary from contract to contract: whilst it might still be reasonable to rescind a contract for the purchase of an antique vase which turns out to be a fake three months after the contract was concluded, it would hardly be reasonable to wait three months to reject a bottle of milk which turned out to be semi-skimmed rather than full cream.

Lapse of time is a separate bar from affirmation. A representee may affirm the contract immediately after the contract has been concluded, if he discovers the misrepresentation and decides not to rescind. Alternatively, rescission may be barred by lapse of time

---

[135] *Peyman* v. *Lanjani* [1985] Ch. 457, 486–7. This case did not deal with affirmation in the context of rescission for misrepresentation, but discussed affirmation generally; see Stephenson LJ at p. 489. Cf. the rules for waiver by a landlord of the right to forfeit a lease: *Matthews* v. *Smallwood* [1910] 1 Ch. 777, 786.

[136] *Smith* v. *Hughes* (1871) LR 6 QB 597; *The Hannah Blumenthal* [1983] 1 AC 854; see Ch. 1, above.

[137] [1985] Ch. 457, 488.

[138] On the question of whether a formal estoppel—with detrimental reliance—should be necessary in applying an objective test of interpreting a party's intentions, see p. 15, above.

without affirmation ever taking place, if the representee either does not discover his right to rescind, or does not decide whether to affirm. However, in practice affirmation and lapse of time are closely linked, since the passage of time without rescission can provide evidence of affirmation.[139]

Lapse of time does not operate to bar rescission in the case of a fraudulent misrepresentation, until the fraud is discovered.[140] In the case of a non-fraudulent misrepresentation,[141] however, time is measured from the time of the contract, whether or not the representee knows the statement to be untrue. One would expect that the length of time which bars rescission would be linked to the time it ought reasonably to take the misled party to discover the truth.[142]

In *Leaf* v. *International Galleries*,[143] for example, the defendants sold to the plaintiff in 1944 a painting which they (without fraud) described as a Constable. It was not until 1949, when he wished to sell the painting, that the plaintiff discovered that it was not by Constable. Counsel for the plaintiff argued that time did not begin to run until the discovery of the misrepresentation; however, the Court of Appeal held that the lapse of five years had barred rescission.[144]

It seems that Denning LJ viewed 'discoverability' as the key to the measure of 'reasonable time':[145]

[139] *Clough* v. *The London and North Western Railway Co.* (1871) LR 7 Ex. 26, 35.

[140] *Rolfe* v. *Gregory* (1865) 4 De G. J. & S. 576, 579; *Armstrong* v. *Jackson* [1917] 2 KB 822, 830.

[141] The cases discussing the point were decided before 1963, and so did not distinguish in their terminology between negligent and innocent misrepresentations; see pp. 64–5, above.

[142] Cf. *Torrance* v. *Bolton* (1872) LR 8 Ch. App. 118, 124, where James LJ, speaking of the case where the representee has 'some notice of what he has done' referred to 'a reasonable time to ascertain his position, and to take advice from persons capable of advising him as to what he ought to do'.

[143] [1950] 2 KB 86. See also *Attwood* v. *Small* (1838) 6 Cl. & Fin. 232.

[144] Denning LJ used the analogy of the right to reject goods for breach of a condition. Such a right to reject is limited by the rule that, once the buyer has 'accepted' the goods, he can only claim damages for breach: s. 11(1)(c) Sale of Goods Act 1893 (now s. 11(4) Sale of Goods Act 1979). And s. 35 Sale of Goods Act 1893 (now s. 35(1) Sale of Goods Act 1979) provides that there is a deemed acceptance when 'after the lapse of a reasonable time, he retains the goods without intimating to the seller that he has rejected them'. Since Leaf's right to reject the picture for breach of the condition of the contract that the artist was Constable was barred by this provision, Denning LJ ([1950] 2 KB 86, 90–1) took the view that the claim to rescind the contract for misrepresentation was also barred: 'an innocent [i.e. non-fraudulent] misrepresentation is much less potent than a breach of condition; and a claim to rescission for innocent misrepresentation must at any rate be barred when a right to reject for breach of condition is barred'.

[145] Ibid., at p. 91.

The buyer has accepted the picture. He had ample opportunity for examination in the first few days after he had bought it. Then was the time to see if
the condition or representation was fulfilled. Yet he has kept it all this time.

It was made clear by Jenkins LJ that the rule is one of policy, to
promote finality of transactions:[146]

it may be said that the plaintiff had no occasion to obtain any further
evidence as to the authorship of the picture until he wanted to sell; but in my
judgment contracts such as this cannot be kept open and subject to the
possibility of rescission indefinitely. . . . it behoves the purchaser either to
verify or, as the case may be, to disprove the representation within a
reasonable time, or else stand or fall by it. If he is allowed to wait five, ten, or
twenty years and then reopen the bargain, there can be no finality at all.

(*d*) Third Party Rights

Since misrepresentation makes a contract only voidable, the ability
of the representee to avoid the contract—that is, to rescind it—is
limited by the general rule in relation to voidable contracts that if a
third party has bona fide and for value obtained rights in the subject-
matter of the contract, the contract ceases to be capable of avoidance.[147] This is a rule of policy, whereby the rights of innocent third
parties are held to prevail over the rights of the party who could
have avoided the contract, but did not do so in time.[148]

It is only *innocent* third parties who have the protection of this
rule. If the third party has notice of the defect in the original contract,
the rights which he obtains in the subject-matter of the contract are
subject to the right of the misled party to rescind. The cases have not
examined in detail what constitutes 'notice' in this context; but in

---

[146] Ibid., at p. 92. See also Evershed MR at pp. 94–5.

[147] *Cundy* v. *Lindsay* (1878) 3 App. Cas. 459, 463–4.

[148] This rule is not limited to equitable remedies, but applies also to contracts
voidable at common law: *White* v. *Garden* (1851) 10 CB 919. In the case of a mistake
sufficiently fundamental to make a contract *void* (rather than simply *voidable*), there is
no restriction by reference to third parties, since the contract is so vitiated from the
beginning that it never creates even temporary rights in the mistaken party: *Cundy* v.
Lindsay (1878) 3 App. Cas. 459; *Bell* v. *Lever Brothers Ltd.* [1932] AC 161; see pp. 26–8,
above; pp. 233–5, below. The rights of third parties can therefore hinge on fine
distinctions: whether the contract was void or voidable; and whether the misled party
managed to rescind the contract before the third party acquired his rights in the
subject-matter: see e.g. *Car and Universal Finance Co. Ltd.* v. *Caldwell* [1965] 1 QB 525,
n. 162, below.

one case[149] Lord Denning MR appears to have thought that a person will have notice if he actually knows of the defect in title, or if he has a suspicion and refrains from asking questions; but not if he is just blundering or negligent.

(e) Section 2(2) Misrepresentation Act 1967

Section 2(2) reads:

Where a person has entered into a contract after a misrepresentation has been made to him otherwise than fraudulently, and he would be entitled, by reason of the misrepresentation, to rescind the contract, then, if it is claimed, in any proceedings arising out of the contract, that the contract ought to be or has been rescinded, the court or arbitrator may declare the contract subsisting and award damages in lieu of rescission, if of opinion that it would be equitable to do so, having regard to the nature of the misrepresentation and the loss that would be caused by it if the contract were upheld, as well as to the loss that rescission would cause to the other party.

This subsection places a restriction on the ability of a misrepresentee to rescind the contract, by giving the court a discretion to award damages in lieu of rescission. The following points may be noted.

First, the subsection operates only where the misrepresentation is made 'otherwise than fraudulently'—that is, it is negligent or innocent.[150]

Second, the subsection applies 'Where a person has entered into a contract after a misrepresentation has been made to him . . .' This will exclude cases of non-dislosure in, for example, contracts *uberrimae fidei*.[151]

Third, the subsection operates not only where the representee asks for rescission in court proceedings, but also where the representee has already rescinded,[152] but the contract comes to be raised

---

[149] *Car and Universal Finance Co. Ltd.* v. *Caldwell* [1965] 1 QB 525, 533, relying on *Jones* v. *Gordon* (1877) 2 App. Cas. 616, 629 (Lord Blackburn). Lord Denning MR was sitting as the trial judge.

[150] If the misrepresentee is concerned to avoid the court exercising its discretion— for example, if there was a relatively trivial misrepresentation which the misrepresentee now wishes to use as a means of extricating himself from a contract which has (for other reasons) turned out to be a bad bargain—he will have an incentive to attempt to prove fraud on the part of the representor.

[151] Cf. *Banque Keyser Ullmann SA* v. *Skandia (UK) Insurance Co. Ltd.* [1990] QB 665, 790, discussing similar wording in s. 2(1) Misrepresentation Act 1967; applied to s. 2(2) by the Court of Appeal in *Ramphul* v. *Toole* (unreported) 17 March 1989.

[152] Rescission is an extrajudicial remedy: see p. 101, below.

in subsequent litigation. In effect, the court's power extends to resurrecting the already rescinded contract.[153] In this, section 2(2) differs from the other bars to rescission. It means that the representee who has rescinded cannot be sure that his rescission will not be reversed.

Fourth, the circumstances in which the court is likely to exercise its discretion are indicated by the closing words of the subsection. It is a balancing exercise: the court must consider

(1) the nature of the misrepresentation;
(2) the loss that would be caused (presumably, to the representee) by the misrepresentation if the contract were upheld;
(3) the loss that rescission would cause to the representor.

The court is therefore likely to exercise its discretion where the representation is relatively trivial, and where rescission would be unduly harsh to the representor.[154]

Fifth, the subsection applies only where the representee could, apart from the subsection, rescind the contract. That appears to mean that the court obtains the discretion to award damages in lieu of rescission only if there is no other bar to rescission—such as impossibility of restitution.[155]

Sixth, the subsection does not specify the measure of damages. In relation to the statutory discretion under section 50 Supreme Court Act 1981 to award damages in addition to, or in substitution for, the equitable remedies of injunction or specific performance, it has been held that damages are to be assessed on the same basis as damages at common law. Therefore, in relation to specific performance, for example, the damages are to be assessed on the same basis as

[153] *Atlantic Lines & Navigation Co. Inc.* v. *Hallam Ltd., The Lucy* [1983] 1 Lloyd's Rep. 188, 202.

[154] Ibid. See Law Reform Committee 10th Report (Innocent Misrepresentation) 1962, Cmnd. 1782, paras. 11–13, which proposed the provision embodied in the subsection. The court will not normally exercise its discretion to refuse rescission in cases of commercial insurance contracts, where the rules governing material misrepresentation fulfil an important 'policing' function in ensuring that brokers make fair representations to underwriters: *Highlands Insurance Co.* v. *Continental Insurance Co.* [1987] 1 Lloyd's Rep. 109, 118.

[155] Mustill J in *Atlantic Lines & Navigation Co. Inc.* v. *Hallam Ltd., The Lucy* [1983] 1 Lloyd's Rep. 188, 201–2 appears to have assumed that this would be so. Cantley J in *Alton House Garages (Bromley) Ltd.* v. *Monk* (unreported) 31 July 1981, held that 'the court is given a judicial discretion to choose, on equitable grounds, between rescission and damages in lieu of rescission. If the party claiming rescission is not entitled to rescission, there is no such choice.'

damages for breach of contract.[156] It is likely that damages under section 2(2) Misrepresentation Act 1967 will also follow common law principles of assessment; but the more appropriate common law measure to follow is the tort measure, since rescission, like tort damages, is designed to return to the status quo.[157]

5. THE NATURE OF RESCISSION

Rescission for misrepresentation is not a court-given remedy. A party misled by a misrepresentation into entering into a contract need not obtain a court order to rescind the contract; rescission is effectedd[158]

by an unequivocal act of election [by the misrepresentee] which demonstrates clearly that he elects to rescind [the contract] and to be no longer bound by it.

If a dispute arises concerning the right of the misrepresentee to rescind, a court may of course be involved in adjudicating upon that question. But if it decides that the rescission was justified, the court order merely confirms the validity of the original rescission: it does not of itself rescind the contract.[159]

The question remains, however: what is a sufficient 'unequivocal act of election' by the misrepresentee? It is clear from the cases that a direct communication by the misrepresentee to the misrepresentor that he elects to rescind will suffice. The problem is what, if anything, short of that will have a similar effect.

[156] *Johnson* v. *Agnew* [1980] AC 367, 400.

[157] See also Treitel, p. 279; Cartwright, *Damages for Misrepresentation* [1987] Conv. 423, 428–9.

[158] *Car and Universal Finance Co. Ltd.* v. *Caldwell* [1965] 1 QB 525, 531 (Lord Denning MR). See also *Reese River Silver Mining Co. Ltd.* v. *Smith* (1869) LR 4 HL 64, 73 (Lord Hatherley LC); *Abram Steamship Co. Ltd.* v. *Westville Shipping Co. Ltd.* [1923] AC 773, 781 (Lord Atkinson); *Alati* v. *Kruger* (1955) 94 CLR 216, 224. In the case of a contract to take shares in a company, different principles apply: in addition to indicating a desire to rescind, the shareholder must take steps to have his name removed from the register of members of the company. Rescission of the allotment of shares will take place when an action for removal is begun: *Re Scottish Petroleum Co.* (1883) 23 Ch. D. 413.

[159] Subject to the operation of s. 2(2) Misrepresentation Act 1967: see p. 99, above. If a claim to rescind is first raised in court proceedings, rather than directly between the parties, the rescission (if ultimately found to be valid) dates not from the court order, but from the moment that the claim was first raised: *Reese River Silver Mining Co. Ltd.* v. *Smith* (1869) LR 4 HL 64, 73.

In *Car and Universal Finance Co. Ltd.* v. *Caldwell*,[160] Caldwell sold a car to a man calling himself Norris, and was induced to allow Norris to take the car away in return for a cheque; the cheque was not met, and Caldwell reported the fraud to the police. He also telephoned the AA to ask them to look for the car. It was held that, although the car was not in fact recovered for some time, the contract between Caldwell and 'Norris' was rescinded by Caldwell's action in attempting to recover it. As Lord Denning MR said,[161]

It is not sufficient for him, of course, to keep it in his own mind or write down a note in his own private sitting room. However, conduct such as we have here, namely, telling the bank, the police and the A.A. 'Find this car if you possibly can. Get it back. It is mine,' seems to me an unequivocal act of rescission.

One should not press this case too far, however.[162] It is important to note that it involved fraud. The Court of Appeal emphasized that the general rule is that rescission is effected by the rescinding party communicating his election to the party who made the misrepresentation. Where, however, there is fraud, and the misrepresentor deliberately ensures that actual communication is impossible, the misrepresentee need not so communicate.[163]

The rationale behind this exception to the general rule seems similar to estoppel. It is the deliberate action of the misrepresentor in evading communication which prevents him insisting on the right to be told of the election to rescind.[164]

---

[160] [1965] 1 QB 525.

[161] Ibid., at p. 532; sitting as the trial judge.

[162] The Law Reform Committee 12th Report (Transfer of Title to Chattels) (1966) Cmnd. 2958, para. 16, thought that *Car and Universal Finance Co. Ltd.* v. *Caldwell* went 'far to destroy the value of s. 23 of the Sale of Goods Act [1979], which provides that where the seller of goods has a voidable title which has not been avoided at the time of the sale, the buyer acquires a good title to the goods provided he buys them in good faith and without notice of the seller's defect of title'. They therefore recommended that the *Caldwell* rule should be reversed, and that 'unless and until notice of the rescission of the contract is communicated to the other contracting party an innocent purchaser from the latter should be able to acquire a good title'.

[163] The Court declined to comment on the case of a non-fraudulent misrepresentation, where the misrepresentor cannot be found.

[164] Sellers and Upjohn LJJ both emphasized that, although the rights of third parties will be affected, the position as regards rescission must be viewed between only the two contracting parties; hence, the evasion of communication in crucial: [1965] 1 QB 525, 551, 555.

6. RATIONALE OF THE REMEDY OF RESCISSION

Rescission is a quite drastic remedy: it involves the unwinding of the whole contract. We have seen that it is limited by certain 'bars', which mitigate its drastic nature to some degree. But, given that it is available even for wholly innocent misrepresentations, it is clear that the courts have taken the view that a party deserves in principle to be able to extricate himself from a contract when he has been misled by a factual statement relevant to the contract, without showing any particular state of mind of the other party; without showing that the misrepresentation was the crucial factor which induced him to contract; and without showing any loss flowing from the misrepresentation beyond having entered into the contract.

The justification for such a one-sided position is precisely the one-sidedness of the bargaining position of the parties. It is the fact that the representor has taken it upon himself—even wholly innocently—to make a statement relevant to the other party's entering into the contract which justifies favouring that other party. The balance of the negotiations has been disturbed. This idea lay behind the words of Lord Brougham in *Attwood* v. *Small*:[165]

It must be a falsehood which is not common to both parties to inquire into and ascertain, a falsehood which is not open to the eyes of either the one or the other party, but which is within the knowledge of one party, not within the knowledge of the other, and consequently to one party telling the other, who has no other means of satisfying himself excepting listening to what is told him by the party alone knowing it, he *adhibens fidem* entered upon the contract, in which case equity will relieve him against it, because he had no other means of knowing, and he trusted to that representation alone, not to his own inquiry.

The justification for granting rescission for an innocent misrepresentation put forward by Jessel MR in *Redgrave* v. *Hurd*[166] was *either* that 'A man is not to be allowed to get a benefit from a statement which he how admits to be false'; *or* it is 'moral fraud . . .

---

[165] (1838) 6 Cl. & Fin. 232, 447, drawing upon the judgment of Lord Eldon in *Edwards* v. *McLeay* (1818) 2 Swans. 287, 289. The judges were here talking of rescission for fraudulent misrepresentation, since that was then the established ground of rescission: see nn. 6, 11 above. Cf. *Whittaker* v. *Campbell* [1984] QB 318, 327, where Robert Goff LJ saw rescission as a means of preventing unjust enrichment by the representor.

[166] (1881) 20 Ch. D. 1, 12–13.

where a man, having obtained a beneficial contract by a statement which he now knows to be false, insists upon keeping that contract'. Neither of these is satisfactory, since they look to the later knowledge of the falsehood as only retrospectively vitiating the contract. The better view is that it is the simple unbalancing of the bargain, by one party having made a material false statement during the negotiations, which justifies a remedy for misrepresentation.

5

Damages for Misrepresentation

There are various separate remedies in damages which may be available for a misrepresentation made by one party to the other during the course of negotiations leading up to a contract. These remedies—at common law and under statute—have been developed over the years without any attempt to integrate them into a unified theory of damages for misrepresentation. It may therefore happen that more than one remedy in damages is available on a single set of facts—either as alternative remedies, or sometimes cumulatively. This chapter will consider separately each remedy in damages: in the torts of deceit and negligence; under section 2(1) of the Misrepresentation Act 1967; and for breach of contract; as well as certain other money remedies for misrepresentation. The question of cumulation of these separate remedies—as well as their relationship to the remedy of rescission—will be considered in Chapter 6. But at the outset it must be noted that the remedies in damages will generally fall into two categories: those in which the damages are assessed on the tort measure and those assessed on the contract measure.

1. THE TORT MEASURE v. THE CONTRACT MEASURE

There is a basic distinction between damages assessed on the tort measure and damages assessed on the contract measure. The purpose of awarding damages on the contract measure is to put the plaintiff, so far as money can do it, in the same position as if the contract had been performed.[1] In the context of misrepresentation this means that damages on the contract measure will generally[2] be

---

[1] *Robinson* v. *Harman* (1848) 1 Ex. 850, 855.

[2] Sometimes, however, damages for breach of contract may be calculated on a different basis: see *Esso Petroleum Co. Ltd.* v. *Mardon* [1976] QB 801; p. 138, below.

calculated to put the plaintiff in the financial position in which he would have been if the misrepresentation had been true.

Tort measure damages have a different purpose. They are not designed to fulfil the expectation created by the representation, but to compensate the plaintiff for loss suffered: they put back into the pocket of the plaintiff what he once had, but no longer has, as a result of the tort.[3] In the context of misrepresentation, therefore, the aim is generally to put the plaintiff in the financial position in which he would have been if he had not entered into the contract.[4]

An illustration may assist in seeing the difference. Assume that A, in selling his car to B, makes a misrepresentation about the age of the car: the car is really 10 years old; A says that it is only 7 years old. B pays £1,000 for the car. The value of a 10-year-old car is £700; the value of a 7-year-old car is £1,200.

If damages are assessed on the contract measure, the question will be, how much worse off is B immediately after the transaction than he *should have been*, had the representation been true? The answer is £500: he should have had a car worth £1,200; he has a car worth only £700.

If the tort measure is applied, however, the question is, how much worse off is B immediately after the transaction than he *was before*? To this question the answer is £300: he started with £1,000 in his pocket; he has obtained a car worth only £700.[5]

---

[3] *McConnel* v. *Wright* [1903] 1 Ch. 546, 554–5 (dealing with an action under the Directors Liability Act 1890). It will be seen that the detailed rules relating to the recoverable losses (e.g. consequential losses) differ from one cause of action to another; but the same 'out-of-pocket' measure is used as the basis of calculation in all the remedies which employ the tort measure.

[4] *Holmes* v. *Jones* (1907) 4 CLR 1692, 1709; *Smith Kline & French Laboratories Ltd.* v. *Long* [1989] 1 WLR 1, 6. It may happen that, looking at the effect of the misrepresentation on the contract as a whole, the contract is still so profitable that there is no loss: *Holmes* v. *Jones*, above. See also *Doyle* v. *Olby (Ironmongers) Ltd.* [1969] 2 QB 158, 171; Burrows, *Remedies for Torts and Breach of Contract*, 1987, pp. 150–4.

[5] On these facts, therefore, the better measure for a plaintiff to seek is the contract measure. It will not, however, always be so: the reason that the contract measure was here greater than the tort measure is that the bargain was a good one: if the misrepresented fact had been true, B was getting a good bargain by getting the car for £200 less than its market value. If the bargain is a bad one for the plaintiff, it will generally be better for him to try to obtain tort measure damages, rather than contract measure damages, to extricate himself from the financial effects of his contract. There will also be other considerations in the choice of the particular damages remedy to be sought—for example, if there are consequential losses which may be recoverable under some, but not other, remedies. The illustration in the text is intended to show only the simplest distinction between the tort and the contract measures.

2. THE TORT OF DECEIT

In order to establish the tort of deceit, it must be shown that the defendant

(1) made a material misrepresentation;
(2) was fraudulent; and
(3) intended the plaintiff to act upon the representation;

and that the plaintiff

(1) acted on the misrepresentation; and
(2) suffered loss by so doing.[6]

These requirements will be discussed in turn.

(a) Misrepresentation

The paradigm case of deceit involves a false statement of fact by the defendant. However, there are variations on this which can still give rise to the action.

(i) Statements of Law, Intention, and Opinion

In some cases it has been said that the representation must be of fact;[7] however, a fraudulent statement of intention or opinion is in effect a statement of fact, and so is actionable.[8] Moreover, we saw in the context of the remedy of rescission that a misrepresentation of law is actionable if it is made fraudulently. The fraud overrides the policy of the law in limiting relief in respect of statements of law. It must be arguable that the same rule ought to apply in the tort of deceit, and a fraudulent misrepresentation of law ought to be actionable.

---

[6] *Bradford Third Equitable Benefit Building Society* v. *Borders* [1941] 2 All ER 205, 211 (Viscount Maugham).
[7] See e.g. *Bradford Third Equitable Benefit Building Society* v. *Borders* [1941] 2 All ER 205, 211.
[8] See p. 71, above.

(ii) Misrepresentation by Conduct or Silence

As with the other remedies, there is nothing to limit misrepresentations to words; conduct which communicates a statement can equally give rise to the tort of deceit.[9]

However, the courts have taken a more restrictive approach to *silence* as a ground of deceit, than in relation to rescission. For deceit, there must be a positive statement, or a partial statement which is itself misleading:[10]

mere omission, even though such as would give reason for setting aside a contract,[11] is not, in my opinion, if it does not make the substantive statements false, a sufficient ground for maintaining an action of deceit.

(iii) Construction of the Statement

There can, of course, be ambiguity in a statement; one question, therefore, is whose interpretation is to be applied to ascertain whether it is a *mis*representation? We have seen elsewhere[12] that in general an objective view is taken of the meaning of words used by parties to a contract. However, in the context of the tort of deceit, the question of the meaning of the statement is inextricably bound up with the requirement of fraud. Since the defendant cannot be liable unless he is fraudulent—which is essentially a subjective requirement[13]—the courts have tended to take a subjective approach to the interpretation of the statement.

The question is not whether the defendant in any given case honestly believed the representation to be true in the sense assigned to it by the court on an objective consideration of its truth or falsity, but whether he honestly believed the representation to be true in the sense in which he understood it albeit erroneously when it was made.[14]

---

[9] *Gordon* v. *Selico Co. Ltd.* [1985] 2 EGLR 79; p. 90 n. 105, above.

[10] *Arkwright* v. *Newbold* (1881) 17 Ch. D. 301, 320 (Cotton LJ); see also James LJ at pp. 317–18; *Peek* v. *Gurney* (1873) LR 6 HL 377, 403; *Bradford Third Equitable Benefit Building Society* v. *Borders* [1941] 2 All ER 205, 211. Cf., however, *Brownlie* v. *Campbell* (1880) 5 App. Cas. 925, 950; *Smith* v. *Hughes* (1871) LR 6 QB 597, 605.

[11] e.g. in the context of a fiduciary relationship, or a contract *uberrimae fidei*: see pp. 90 ff., above.

[12] See Ch. 1, above.

[13] See p. 109, below.

[14] *Akerhielm* v. *De Mare* [1959] AC 789, 805. See also *Angus* v. *Clifford* [1891] 2 Ch. 449, 472.

(b) Fraud

(i) The Meaning of Fraud

The essence of the tort of deceit is fraud. The meaning of fraud was clearly established by the House of Lords in *Derry* v. *Peek*.[15]

In that case, the defendants were directors who issued a prospectus inviting the public to subscribe for shares in their company. The prospectus contained a misrepresentation; the plaintiff, who alleged that he bought shares relying upon the misrepresentation, claimed damages for deceit. The Court of Appeal found the defendants liable, because the directors, although they believed their statement to be true, had no reasonable grounds for that belief. The House of Lords rejected that test. Unreasonableness of belief does not itself constitute fraud; it can only be evidence of dishonesty.[16] Lord Herschell summed up the requirements:[17]

First, in order to sustain an action of deceit, there must be proof of fraud, and nothing short of that will suffice. Secondly, fraud is proved when it is shewn that a false representation has been made (1) knowingly, or (2) without belief in its truth, or (3) recklessly, careless whether it be true or false. . . . To prevent a false statement being fraudulent, there must, I think, always be an honest belief in its truth. . . . Thirdly, if fraud be proved, the motive of the person guilty of it is immaterial.

The key division is therefore between fraud—which is deceit—and an honest belief in truth—which is not. It is the state of the defendant's mind which matters. Did he actually believe what he said, or not? What he *ought* to have realized about the meaning of his words is relevant only to the question of whether a court will believe him. Negligence, or unreasonable grounds for belief, do not constitute fraud.[18]

---

[15] (1889) 14 App. Cas. 337. The effect of this decision was reversed by the Directors Liability Act 1890: see n. 114, below. This Act was, however, limited to the factual context of *Derry* v. *Peek*, and did not change the basis of the tort of deceit.

[16] Ibid., at p. 352.

[17] Ibid., at p. 374.

[18] Lord Herschell's language could in one respect be misinterpreted. He says that it is fraud if the defendant is 'careless whether it be true or false'. In context, this clearly does not mean 'failing to take care' (i.e. negligent); it means 'not caring less whether . . .' (i.e. indifferent to the truth): see *Angus* v. *Clifford* [1891] 2 Ch. 449, 471; *Le Lievre* v. *Gould* [1893] 1 QB 491, 501.

(ii) Misrepresentations by Agents

It may happen that the defendant does not make a misrepresentation himself, but uses an agent. The problem is in what circumstances the tort of deceit can be held to have been committed. Consider three different situations:

(1) The defendant, D, authorizes a statement to be made by his agent, A, and knows that it is false. A is, however, innocent of the falsehood.

(2) D does not know that the statement is being made; A deliberately makes a misrepresentation.

(3) D does not know that the statement is being made by A, but (if he did know) would know that it was false; A does not realize that his statement is false.

The first two cases are straightforward. In each, one party is clearly fraudulent, within the meaning of *Derry* v. *Peek*.[19] In case 1, D uses A to make a statement which he knows to be false; he is therefore committing the tort himself, through the medium of A.[20] A is not a tortfeasor.

In case 2, A is himself a tortfeasor, since he fraudulently makes a misrepresentation; D's liability will depend on the application of the rules of vicarious liability: broadly, D will be liable if A had actual authority to make the statement, or if D had by his words or conduct held him out as having such authority in the circumstances.[21]

Case 3, however, presents a problem. Both D and A are innocent; but if their knowledge were to be added together, the requirements of the tort would be made out. Does the doctrine of principal and agent require such an adding together? Because the tort of deceit is strict in requiring fraud, the courts have refused to add together innocent states of mind: 'you cannot add an innocent state of mind to an innocent state of mind and get as a result a dishonest state of

---

[19] (1889) 14 App. Cas. 337.

[20] *Cornfoot* v. *Fowke* (1840) 6 M. & W. 358, 370, 371.

[21] *Armagas Ltd.* v. *Mundogas SA* [1986] AC 717; *Briess* v. *Woolley* [1954] AC 333; *Lloyd* v. *Grace, Smith & Co.* [1912] AC 716. It is not necessary that A's conduct should in fact benefit D: ibid. For the situation where a principal who instructs an agent to achieve a particular end is liable for any fraudulent misrepresentation by the agent in achieving that end, see *Kings North Trust Ltd.* v. *Bell* [1986] 1 WLR 119, 124, quoted at p. 189, below.

mind'.[22] If a defendant, acting alone, makes a misrepresentation which, if he applied his mind to the question, he would realize is false, he may still be innocent of fraud: for example, if he has forgotten facts which would show him that his statement is false, but he makes the statement honestly. There is then an innocent division within a single person—the means of knowledge of the falsehood are present, but not used. The same is the case of the innocent principal and agent, and there too the conclusion must be that there is no deceit.[23]

(iii) The Timing of the Fraud

One problem which can arise is that the defendant is honest when he makes his false statement, but he later discovers the truth. If he fails to alert the plaintiff to his discovery, can he become fraudulent?[24]

The courts have taken the view that it is dishonest to remain silent in such circumstances, and that the defendant is therefore guilty of fraud.[25]

(iv) Standard of Proof

Fraud is a serious allegation; it must be pleaded with sufficient particularity,[26] and the courts are strict in their requirement of proof. Since deceit is a civil action, the basic requirement is similar to all civil actions: that the plaintiff should establish his case on the balance of probabilities. However, this is tailored to the requirements of the particular tort; to establish such a serious allegation as

---

[22] *Armstrong* v. *Strain* [1951] 1 TLR 856, 872 (Devlin J.), affd. [1952] 1 KB 232; *Cornfoot* v. *Fowke* (1840) 6 M. & W. 358.

[23] Ibid.

[24] This can only be an issue if the defendant discovers the truth before the plaintiff relies on the representation, i.e. when the action would crystallize. Later discovery by the defendant must on principle be irrelevant. For the different case, where the statement, though true when made, later becomes false (or vice versa), see p. 113, below.

[25] *Brownlie* v. *Campbell* (1880) 5 App. Cas. 925, 950; *Reynell* v. *Sprye* (1852) 1 De G. M. & G. 660, 709. Presumably the defendant must appreciate that he has misled the plaintiff—i.e. he must choose deliberately not to disabuse the plaintiff of the falsehood.

[26] *Garden Neptune Shipping Ltd.* v. *Occidental Worldwide Investment Corp.* [1989] 1 Lloyd's Rep. 305, 306.

fraud, the courts require a higher degree of probability than, say, for negligence.[27]

(c) Action upon the Misrepresentation

The defendant must have intended that the plaintiff would act in reliance upon the representation; there must also have been actual reliance by the plaintiff.

(i) The Defendant's Intention

The cases have stressed that the plaintiff[28] must have been intended by the defendant to rely upon the representation.[29] If the plaintiff is the direct recipient of the representation, it will generally be easier to establish this; if he is a third party who indirectly receives the representation, it will be necessary to show more particularly that the plaintiff was an intended recipient.[30]

(ii) Materiality and Reliance

The requirements of materiality and reliance for deceit are similar to those for the remedy of rescission.[31] The misrepresentation must be material: it must be (objectively) relevant to the action taken by the plaintiff which causes him loss (entering into the contract), and it must not be trivial.[32]

Once it is established that the misrepresentation was capable of influencing the plaintiff, it is the defendant who must prove that the plaintiff did *not* act in reliance upon it.[33] Furthermore, the fraudulent misrepresentation need be only *one* of the factors which induced the plaintiff to enter into the contract.[34]

[27] *Hornal* v. *Neuberger Products Ltd.* [1957] 1 QB 247; *Bater* v. *Bater* [1951] P. 35.

[28] Or a class of persons which will include the plaintiff: *Bradford Third Equitable Benefit Building Society* v. *Borders* [1941] 2 All ER 205, 211.

[29] *Peek* v. *Gurney* (1873) LR 6 HL 377, 413.

[30] *Barry* v. *Croskey* (1861) 2 J. & H. 1, 23.

[31] See pp. 81 ff., above. For the view that materiality is not required to be proved for fraudulent misrepresentations, see p. 81 n. 68, above.

[32] *Angus* v. *Clifford* [1891] 2 Ch. 449; *Attwood* v. *Small* (1838) 6 Cl. & Fin. 232, 445; and see p. 82 nn. 69 and 70, above.

[33] *Smith* v. *Chadwick* (1884) 9 App. Cas. 187, 196.

[34] *Attwood* v. *Small* (1838) 6 Cl. & Fin. 232, 502; *Reynell* v. *Sprye* (1852) 1 De G. M. & G. 660, 708.

The plaintiff is therefore clearly favoured over the defendant—which is to be expected, given that there is fraud on the part of the defendant. And if the defendant attempts to reverse the effects of his fraud, and to explain the truth to the plaintiff, the onus will be on him to ensure that his explanation is clear, and reaches the plaintiff.[35]

(iii) Change of Circumstances

As with rescission, there may be a change in circumstances between the making of the statement and the plaintiff's action upon it (that is, usually, his entering into the contract). The statement, false when made, may have become true: this prevents the tort being committed, since deceit is complete not when the representation is made, but when it is acted upon.[36] Tested at that moment, therefore, there is no misrepresentation.

However, a statement which was true when made may, by the time of the plaintiff's acting upon it, have become false. For deceit to be committed, the defendant will have to know of the subsequent falsehood, so as to become fraudulent in his failure to communicate the truth. But, assuming that he is fraudulent, it seems that the failure to disabuse the plaintiff could, on the analogy of the cases[37] which dealt with this point in relation to rescission for misrepresentation, constitute the tort of deceit.

(d) Loss: The Damages Recoverable[38]

The basic measure of damages recoverable in the tort of deceit is the tort measure.[39] This means that, in the context of pre-contractual fraudulent misrepresentations, the measure of damages will generally be designed to compensate the plaintiff for the loss he has sustained by entering into the contract, and so to put him back into the financial position in which he was immediately before he entered into the contract in reliance on the misrepresentation.[40]

---

[35] *Arnison* v. *Smith* (1889) 41 Ch. D. 348.

[36] *Briess* v. *Woolley* [1954] AC 333, 353.

[37] *Traill* v. *Baring* (1864) 4 De G. J. & S. 318; *With* v. *O'Flanagan* [1936] Ch. 575, pp. 84 ff., above.

[38] *McGregor on Damages*, 15th edn., 1988, §§1718–38.

[39] *Doyle* v. *Olby (Ironmongers) Ltd.* [1969] 2 QB 158.

[40] *Holmes* v. *Jones* (1907) 4 CLR 1692. See p. 106, above.

Because fraud is necessary for deceit, one would expect that the courts would apply the harshest rules relating to recoverable damages; and this is indeed so. In other areas, there has been a reluctance to award damages to cover all consequential losses suffered by a plaintiff; and to award exemplary damages, or damages to compensate for distress; but these are recoverable in the tort of deceit.

(i) Remoteness of Damage

In deceit, the courts have taken the view that the defendant should pay for all the consequential losses suffered by the plaintiff. The courts will not[41] regard as too remote losses which were not reasonably foreseeable by the defendant. In *Doyle* v. *Olby (Ironmongers) Ltd.*, Lord Denning MR said,[42]

The defendant is bound to make reparation for all the actual damages directly flowing from the fraudulent inducement. The person who has been defrauded is entitled to say:

'I would not have entered into this bargain at all but for your representation. Owing to your fraud, I have not only lost all the money I paid you, but, what is more, I have been put to a large amount of extra expense as well and suffered this or that extra damages.'

All such damages can be recovered: and it does not lie in the mouth of the fraudulent person to say that they could not reasonably have been foreseen.

Winn LJ said[43] that the recoverable damage was that which flowed directly from the fraud. The only limit was that the plaintiff could not recover in respect of losses where he had not himself behaved with reasonable prudence, reasonable common sense, or could in any true sense be said to have been the author of his own misfortune.

The court therefore allowed the plaintiff to recover all the costs incurred in attempting to run a business which he had been induced to buy by the defendant's fraudulent misrepresentations.

(ii) Exemplary Damages[44]

Exemplary damages, otherwise known as punitive damages, are

---

[41] Unlike in the tort of negligence, for example: see p. 125, below.

[42] [1969] 2 QB 158, 167.

[43] Ibid., at p. 168.

[44] Burrows, *Remedies for Torts and Breach of Contract*, pp. 238–50.

designed not to compensate a plaintiff for his loss, but to punish, or to make an example of, the defendant. There is a general reluctance to award such damages in tort,[45] and there has been dispute over whether they can ever be recovered in the tort of deceit.[46] The most recent case on the subject[47] has left the matter open, and it must at least be arguable that, in principle, the fraudulent nature of deceit justifies exemplary damages in an appropriate case.

(iii) Damages for Distress

It now appears that damages are recoverable in the tort of deceit for injured feelings. This is an established head of damages in contract,[48] and the courts have extended it to deceit.[49]

3. THE TORT OF NEGLIGENCE

(a) Introduction: The Development of the Tort

There has been a reluctance to impose liability in tort for misrepresentations which are not fraudulent.[50] Lord Reid's discussion in *Hedley Byrne & Co. Ltd.* v. *Heller & Partners Ltd.*[51] of particular

---

[45] The House of Lords restricted the circumstances in which they are recoverable in *Rookes* v. *Barnard* [1964] AC 1129: see at pp. 1226–8 (Lord Devlin). Exemplary damages are not available for breach of contract: *Perera* v. *Vandiyar* [1953] 1 WLR 672; *Kenny* v. *Preen* [1963] 1 QB 499, 513.

[46] For recovery: *Mafo* v. *Adams* [1970] 1 QB 548, 558–9 (Widgery LJ). Against: ibid., at pp. 554–5 (Sachs LJ); *Cassell & Co. Ltd.* v. *Broome* [1972] AC 1027, 1076, 1080 (Lord Hailsham LC); 1131 (Lord Diplock).

[47] *Archer* v. *Brown* [1985] QB 401, 418–23.

[48] Although only where the contract is intended to give pleasure (such as a holiday: *Jarvis* v. *Swans Tours Ltd* [1973] QB 233) or to avoid distress (such as a contract with a solicitor to obtain a non-molestation order: *Heywood* v. *Wellers* [1976] QB 446): *Bliss* v. *South East Thames Regional Health Authority* [1987] ICR 700, 717–18.

[49] Although not limited, apparently, to pleasure or avoidance of distress cases: *Archer* v. *Brown* [1985] QB 401; *Shelley* v. *Paddock* [1979] QB 120; *Saunders* v. *Edwards* [1987] 1 WLR 1116.

[50] Particularly where the loss caused to the plaintiff by his reliance on the misrepresentation is economic. If direct physical injury is caused, the test is less strict: *Clayton* v. *Woodman & Son (Builders) Ltd.* [1962] 2 QB 533; *Caparo Industries plc* v. *Dickman* [1990] 2 WLR 358, 382. In the context of pre-contractual misrepresentations it is generally economic loss which is at issue; the discussion in this chapter will therefore be limited to negligent misrepresentations which cause economic loss.

[51] [1964] AC 465, 482–3, quoted at p. 63, above. See also ibid., at p. 534 (Lord Pearce): 'Words are more volatile than deeds. They travel fast and far afield.'

problems associated with attaching liability to statements has already been quoted. That case concerned the tort of negligence, and, although there have been many statements in the cases that there is no difference in principle between negligent words and negligent acts,[52] the courts have been very cautious in imposing liability in negligence for statements.[53]

We have seen that the House of Lords in *Derry* v. *Peek*[54] took a restrictive approach to the tort of deceit. In that case, the Court of Appeal had imposed liability on the directors for their misrepresentations which the directors honestly believed to be true, although they had no reasonable grounds for so believing. In effect, this was a liability for negligence, since the directors were unreasonable in their belief of the truth—so a reasonable man would have realized that the statements were untrue. The House of Lords rejected this test; they required *fraud*, not merely negligence.[55]

For some time this decision was regarded as having precluded a liability in tort for negligent statements. In *Le Lievre* v. *Gould*,[56] for example, Bowen LJ relied on *Derry* v. *Peek* as showing that there was no liability for negligent statements:

the law of England . . . does not consider that what a man writes on paper is like a gun or other dangerous instrument, and, unless he intended to deceive, the law does not, in the absence of contract,[57] hold him responsible for drawing his certificate carelessly.

However, it was realized that simply to exonerate a careless (but not fraudulent) representor was not acceptable, because sometimes the *position* held by the representor *vis-à-vis* the representee required the

[52] See e.g. *Hedley Byrne & Co. Ltd.* v. *Heller & Partners Ltd.* [1964] AC 465, 496, 503 (Lord Morris); 508, 510 (Lord Hodson); 517 (Lord Devlin).

[53] It is not possible to describe here in detail the development of the tort of negligence generally. For such a description up to 1989, see *Winfield & Jolowicz on Tort*, 13th edn., 1989, ch. 5 (and the tort continues to develop: see also *Caparo Industries plc* v. *Dickman* [1990] 2 WLR 358; *Murphy* v. *Brentwood District Council* [1990] 3 WLR 414).

[54] (1889) 14 App. Cas. 337.

[55] See p. 109, above.

[56] [1893] 1 QB 491, 502. See also *Angus* v. *Clifford* [1891] 2 Ch. 449, 463–4, 470; *Low* v. *Bouverie* [1891] 3 Ch. 82.

[57] i.e. liability for breach of contract, if there is in the contract a term which guarantees the statement or an implied term of care: *Nocton* v. *Lord Ashburton* [1914] AC 932, 956. It should be noted that, at the time Bowen LJ delivered this judgment, the tort of negligence had not yet developed to allow generalized duties in relation even to negligent acts: this came in the wake of *Donoghue* v. *Stevenson* [1932] AC 562. As we shall see, it took even longer—until *Hedley Byrne & Co. Ltd.* v. *Heller & Partners Ltd.* in 1963—for a generalized duty in relation to negligent words to be developed.

representee to be protected by a remedy in damages. The first sign of this new approach came in *Nocton* v. *Lord Ashburton*,[58] where the House of Lords held that Nocton, a solicitor, was liable to compensate Lord Ashburton, his client, for losses incurred in reliance on the solicitor's negligent (but not fraudulent) advice.

The key to this case—and so to the development of the tort of negligence in relation to misrepresentations—was the position of Nocton *vis-à-vis* Lord Ashburton; it was a relationship of solicitor and client, which was therefore a fiduciary relationship.[59] The House of Lords dismissed the argument that *Derry* v. *Peek* precluded a remedy in damages for non-fraudulent misrepresentations: it dealt only with the tort of deceit, and left untouched other remedies which might be available for misrepresentations.[60] There had, earlier than *Derry* v. *Peek*, been a jurisdiction exercised by the Courts of Equity, to deal with persons who were not fraudulent in the narrow sense, as settled by *Derry* v. *Peek*, but who were in breach of a 'special duty'.[61] It was the fiduciary relationship between Nocton and Lord Ashburton which imposed upon the former such a duty towards the latter—a duty to make a full and not misleading disclosure of relevant facts; and, this duty having been broken, the remedy was granted.[62] The importance of the relative positions of the parties was emphasized by Lord Shaw of Dunfermline:[63]

---

[58] [1914] AC 932.

[59] The advice given by Nocton was not simply in the context of the normal relationship of solicitor and client, but was in relation to a transaction in which he himself had a financial interest.

[60] This is in fact all that was expressly said in *Derry* v. *Peek*; for example, Lord Herschell said ((1889) 14 App. Cas. 337, 373) 'I cannot assent to the doctrine that a false statement made through carelessness, and which ought to have been known to be untrue, of itself renders the person who makes it liable to an action *for deceit*' (italics added). See also *Robinson* v. *National Bank of Scotland Ltd.* (1916) SC (HL) 154, 157.

[61] See [1914] AC 932, 952–6 (Viscount Haldane LC).

[62] The judgments are not altogether clear on some points. It appears that the remedy sought was not damages, but compensation in equity for the breach of the equitable obligations imposed by the fiduciary relationship: see [1914] AC 932, 939. However, the Court of Appeal ordered a remedy in *damages*—a common law remedy: see [1914] AC 932, 940. This was commented upon, but not examined in detail, in the House of Lords: see [1914] AC 932, 958, 965. Moreover, there is no clear and consistent analysis amongst the judgments about the level of duty which was imposed on Nocton—whether it was really a duty *of care*. It seems that the House of Lords thought that they were simply applying existing equitable rules, rather than developing the *common law* of negligence. However, their judgments were taken more widely in *Candler* v. *Crane, Christmas & Co.* [1951] 2 KB 164, n. 65, below, and *Hedley Byrne & Co. Ltd.* v. *Heller & Partners Ltd.* [1964] AC 465.

[63] [1914] AC 932, 972. See also at pp. 968–9.

the principle to be found running through this branch of the law is, in my opinion, this: That once the relations of parties have been ascertained to be those in which a duty is laid upon one person of giving information or advice to another upon which that other is entitled to rely as the basis of a transaction, responsibility for error amounting to misrepresentation in any statement made will attach to the adviser or informer, although the information and advice have been given not fraudulently but in good faith.

This approach, of examining the position of the representor *vis-à-vis* the representee, allowed the development of liability for negligence. It was used by Salmon J in *Woods* v. *Martins Bank Ltd.*,[64] to hold a bank liable for negligent advice given to a potential customer. *Nocton* v. *Lord Ashburton* was authority that a fiduciary relationship could give rise to a duty; Salmon J therefore examined the particular dealings between the bank manager and the potential customer, the plaintiff, to see whether they could be characterized as giving rise to such a relationship:[65]

the limits of a banker's business cannot be laid down as a matter of law. The nature of such a business must in each case be a matter of fact and, accordingly, cannot be treated as if it were a matter of pure law.

Since the bank manager had told the plaintiff that the bank would take charge of his financial affairs, and knew that the customer was looking to him for advice, a fiduciary relationship existed between the bank and the plaintiff:[66] 'as [the manager] chose to advise him, the law in these circumstances imposes an obligation on him to advise with reasonable care and skill'. In order to find the bank liable, Salmon J had to find a fiduciary relationship. This is perhaps placing 'a strained interpretation on the word "fiduciary" which is based on the idea of trust',[67] and it is now no longer necessary to find

---

[64] [1959] 1 QB 55.

[65] Ibid., at p. 70. *Nocton* v. *Lord Ashburton* itself was not cited. However, the Court of Appeal in *Candler* v. *Crane, Christmas & Co.* [1951] 2 KB 164 had recognized that *Nocton* v. *Lord Ashburton* had widened the situations where a duty was owed to those where the parties were in a contractual *or fiduciary* relationship. *Candler* v. *Crane, Christmas & Co.* was cited in *Woods* v. *Martins Bank Ltd.*

[66] [1959] 1 QB 55, 72. Here we see a principle similar to that of the 'assumption of responsibility': see below, p. 121. The analysis of the *particular* dealings between the banker and the plaintiff to see what duties arise is similar to the search for a relationship which gives rise to a presumption of undue influence: see *National Westminster Bank plc* v. *Morgan* [1985] AC 686; pp. 179 ff., below.

[67] *Hedley Byrne & Co. Ltd.* v. *Heller & Partners Ltd.* [1964] AC 465, 511 (Lord Hodson). In effect, Salmon J was saying: because the relationship between the parties is such that one ought to owe the other a duty, we can attach the label 'fiduciary'. *Hedley Byrne*

a fiduciary relationship in order to establish a duty of care. In 1963 the House of Lords, building upon such narrow, specific categories of duty as that laid down in *Nocton* v. *Lord Ashburton*, generalized the test for a duty of care in negligence, in *Hedley Byrne & Co. Ltd.* v. *Heller & Partners Ltd.*[68]

In that case, the defendant bank made a statement to the plaintiff about the financial standing of a company with which the plaintiff was doing business. The statement, which was made through the plaintiff's bankers, in response to a request by the plaintiff, was expressly said by the defendant to be given 'without responsibility'. The House of Lords held that, but for the disclaimer of responsibility, the defendant would have owed a duty of care to the plaintiff in its making of the statement.

All their Lordships took the view that a duty of care in making statements could arise without the need for a fiduciary relationship or a contractual relationship to be established between the parties. However, the formulation of the test for the existence of such a duty of care differs in the various speeches. The tests laid down in *Hedley Byrne & Co. Ltd.* v. *Heller & Partners Ltd.* have also been developed in later cases.[69]

(b) Requirements of the Tort

To establish liability for negligent misrepresentations it is necessary—as in the tort of negligence generally[70]—to show three things: that the defendant owed the plaintiff a duty of care; that the

---

& Co. Ltd. v. *Heller & Partners Ltd.* abandoned the use of this reverse logic, by denying that a fiduciary relationship was necessary to give rise to a duty. For a similar example of reverse logic because of the need to find a fiduciary relationship in order to give rise to a remedy, see Birks, *An Introduction to the Law of Restitution*, 1985, rev. 1989, pp. 383–4, commenting on *Chase Manhattan Bank NA* v. *Israel-British Bank (London) Ltd.* [1981] Ch. 105.

[68] [1964] AC 465. Denning LJ, in a dissenting judgment in the Court of Appeal in *Candler* v. *Crane, Christmas & Co.* [1951] 2 KB 164 had earlier attempted unsuccessfully to establish such a generalized duty. In *Robinson* v. *National Bank of Scotland Ltd.* (1916) SC (HL) 154 the House of Lords, referring to *Nocton* v. *Lord Ashburton*, had said that there was no duty of care owed by a bank making representations of creditworthiness of its customers in response to a request of another bank.

[69] In particular the decisions of the House of Lords in *Smith* v. *Eric S. Bush* [1990] AC 831 and *Caparo Industries plc* v. *Dickman* [1990] 2 WLR 358; see also the decision of the Court of Appeal in *James McNaughton Papers Group Ltd.* v. *Hicks Anderson & Co.* [1991] 1 All ER 134.

[70] See *Winfield & Jolowicz on Tort*, 13th edn., 1989, p. 72.

duty was broken; and that the plaintiff suffered damage which both was caused by the breach of duty and was not too remote.

(i) Duty of Care

The judgments in *Hedley Byrne & Co. Ltd.* v. *Heller & Partners Ltd.*[71] must be the starting-point to determine the test for the existence of a duty of care in relation to statements. We have already seen that, before 1963, a duty of care had been accepted in relation to statements only in narrowly defined circumstances—where there was a contract between the parties, or where there was a fiduciary relationship which imported a duty to be careful in making the statements. The significance of *Hedley Byrne & Co. Ltd.* v. *Heller & Partners Ltd.* is that it broke away from these specific circumstances, and enunciated a more general test. However, because of the difficulties which are encountered in imposing liability for statements, the House of Lords was concerned to state the test quite cautiously.[72]

Perhaps the most useful general statement is found in the speech of Lord Morris of Borth-y-Gest:[73]

if someone possessed of a special skill undertakes, quite irrespective of contract, to apply that skill for the assistance of another person who relies upon such skill, a duty of care will arise. The fact that the service is to be given by means of or by the instrumentality of words can make no difference. Furthermore, if in a sphere in which a person is so placed that others could reasonably rely upon his judgment or his skill or upon his ability to make careful inquiry, a person takes it upon himself to give information or advice to, or allows his information or advice to be passed on to, another person who, as he knows or should know, will place reliance upon it, then a duty of care will arise.

This statement of principle imposes a duty where a representor who is in a position in which it is reasonable for the representee to rely upon him 'takes it upon himself' to make the statement, or where he

---

[71] [1964] AC 465.

[72] It often said that a duty arises only if there is a 'special relationship' between the representor and the representee: see [1964] AC 465, 486 (Lord Reid); 505 (Lord Hodson); 525 (Lord Devlin); 539 (Lord Pearce). This language, building upon the language used in *Nocton* v. *Lord Ashburton* [1914] AC 932, serves to emphasize that the test is narrow, and also distinguishes it from the (even narrower) test of fiduciary relationships.

[73] [1964] AC 465, 502–3. This formulation was accepted and in part repeated by Lord Hodson at p. 514.

ought to realize that the representee will receive the statement and rely upon it. The representee may therefore be either a direct recipient of the words or a person whom the representor ought to realize will be a secondary recipient; and it is irrelevant whether or not there is a contract between the representor and the representee.[74]

An idea which was contained in all the speeches in *Hedley Byrne & Co. Ltd.* v. *Heller & Partners Ltd.* was that the representor must *assume a responsibility* to the representee in relation to his statement.[75] This concept has caused some difficulty in subsequent cases. It can be seen that the reason for the emphasis on the assumption of responsibility in *Hedley Byrne* was the disclaimer of responsibility in that case: the plaintiff failed to establish a duty of care only because the defendant had expressly disclaimed responsibility at the time of making the statement. As Lord Pearce said,[76] 'If both parties say expressly . . . that there shall be no liability, I do not find it possible to say that a liability was assumed.'

However, it is quite clear from the judgments in *Hedley Byrne & Co. Ltd.* v. *Heller & Partners Ltd.* that an *express* assumption of responsibility by the defendant is not required for a duty of care to arise. An objective test is applied to determine whether the defendant ought to have realized that he was being relied upon, and it is therefore the making of a statement in circumstances where the representor knows or ought to know that reliance is being placed on his skill in making the statement which might be called the acceptance of a responsibility for the statement.[77]

The problems of the phrase 'assumption of responsibility' were

[74] It was held by a majority of the Privy Council in *Mutual Life and Citizens' Assurance Co. Ltd.* v. *Evatt* [1971] AC 793, 805–6 that a duty of care will arise only if the advice is given in the course of a business or profession involving the giving of advice of the kind in question, or if the adviser holds himself out as being in a comparable position to one in such a business or profession. The Court of Appeal has declined to follow this: *Esso Petroleum Co. Ltd.* v. *Mardon* [1976] QB 801, 827; *Howard Marine and Dredging Co. Ltd.* v. *A. Ogden & Sons (Excavations) Ltd.* [1978] QB 574, 591, 600. The point has not yet been decided by the House of Lords: *Caparo Industries plc* v. *Dickman* [1990] 2 WLR 358, 383.

[75] It may be seen in the statement of Lord Morris, quoted above, in the words 'a person takes it upon himself to give information or advice . . .'; and Lord Morris said, [1964] AC 465, 494, 'If A assumes a responsibility to B to tender him deliberate advice, there could be a liability if the advice is negligently given.' See also Lord Reid at pp. 483, 486; Lord Devlin at p. 529; Lord Pearce at pp. 539–40.

[76] [1964] AC 465, 540.

[77] Ibid., at p. 486 (Lord Reid). See also *Ministry of Housing and Local Government* v. *Sharp* [1970] 2 QB 223, 268 (Lord Denning MR).

also discussed at length in *Smith* v. *Eric S. Bush*,[78] in which the House of Lords rejected the argument that an express, voluntary assumption of responsibility is required for a duty of care. If there is such an express assumption, there will of course be a duty; but short of that (and it must be rare that representors will expressly accept responsibility so clearly) what gives rise to a duty on the part of the defendant is that the defendant makes a statement within the context of a relationship with the plaintiff in which the defendant knows or ought to know that the particular plaintiff will probably rely upon it and will suffer loss if it is negligently made.[79]

(ii) Liability for Failure to Speak

It has been held by the Court of Appeal in *Banque Keyser Ullmann SA* v. *Skandia (UK) Insurance Co. Ltd.*[80] that a failure to speak is capable of giving rise to liability in negligence under the principles of *Hedley Byrne & Co. Ltd.* v. *Heller & Partners Ltd.*, that is, that the duty can be a duty to take care to speak, as well as to take care in what one actually says. It should be noted that the case was decided before *Smith* v. *Eric S. Bush*, and so used 'voluntary assumption of responsibility' as the touchstone of the existence of a duty of care. However, there seems to be no reason why the relationship between the parties should not, in an appropriate case, give rise to a duty to speak, provided that the defendant knows or ought to know that the plaintiff is placing reliance on his advice. An adviser may sometimes be expected to volunteer advice, not merely to respond to questions.[81]

---

[78] [1990] AC 831.

[79] Ibid., at pp. 847 (Lord Templeman); 862 and 864–5 (Lord Griffiths); 870–1 (Lord Jauncey). If the plaintiff is not the direct recipient of the statement, it will be more difficult to establish the necessary relationship: ibid., at pp. 865 (Lord Griffiths), 871 (Lord Jauncey); *James McNaughton Papers Group Ltd.* v. *Hicks Anderson & Co.* [1991] 1 All ER 134. For a further statement of the test, see *Caparo Industries plc* v. *Dickman* [1990] 2 WLR 358, 367–8, 383–4, 405.

[80] [1990] QB 665, 794. The House of Lords, sub nom. *Banque Financière de la Cité SA* v. *Westgate Insurance Co. Ltd.* [1990] 2 All ER 947 did not comment on this aspect of the judgment of the Court of Appeal; they simply decided that, on the facts, there was no misstatement, and the silence of one party did not amount to a representation: see Lord Templeman, [1990] 2 All ER 947, 955.

[81] See also *Van Oppen* v. *Clerk to the Bedford Charity Trustees* [1990] 1 WLR 235, 259–60; *Cornish* v. *Midland Bank plc* [1985] 3 All ER 513, 516–17, 520, 521.

(iii) Duty of Care between Parties to a Contract

Having ascertained the basic requirements for the existence of a duty of care in negligence, it is necessary for our purposes to consider how those requirements apply where there is a contract between the parties, and the misrepresentation is made at, or leading up to, the time of the contract, on a matter which is relevant to the contract.

The test for a duty of care under *Hedley Byrne & Co. Ltd.* v. *Heller & Partners Ltd.*[82] will often[83] be satisfied in a situation where one party negotiating a contract makes to the other statements which are relevant to the second party's decision to enter into the contract. The key question is whether the representor knows or ought to know that the representee will rely on his skill in making the statement. If the representor makes a statement with a view to encouraging the representee to enter into the contract, he will generally expect the representee to rely on the statement. So, provided that the statement relates to a matter within the skill or knowledge of the representor, rather than the representee, the necessary relationship is likely to exist between them to impose a duty of care.

However, there remains the question of whether the existence of the contract between the representor and the representee precludes, as a matter of policy, the finding of a duty of care in tort: in other words, should the fact that the parties have chosen to enter into a contract mean that their remedies in damages should lie exclusively under the contract?

Hedley Byrne & Co. Ltd. v. *Heller & Partners Ltd.* was a case between persons who were not parties to a contract. Much of the language in the case is directed to determining when, *in the absence of a contract*, there should be an obligation of care in making a statement.[84] It was not until 1976 that a duty of care under *Hedley Byrne* was sought to be established between contracting parties. In *Esso Petroleum Co. Ltd.* v. *Mardon*,[85] Mr Mardon was told by an experienced employee of Esso, during negotiations for the lease of a newly built petrol station, that the estimated throughput of the station was 200,000 gallons a

---

[83] As long as the test is not restricted to business or professional activities: see n. 74, above.
[84] See particularly Lord Devlin, [1964] AC 465, 525–6, 529, 530.
[85] [1976] QB 801.

year. This was wrong—the figure was based on an earlier design of
the garage which had been superseded. The statement was therefore
a misrepresentation made on behalf of one party to the contract, to
the other party, on a matter on which the representor ought to have
had skill, and upon which the representee would be expected to rely.
The Court of Appeal applied *Hedley Byrne*, and said that a duty of
care in negligence could exist between parties to a contract in
relation to pre-contractual statements.

That is not, however, the end of the matter. More recently, there
have been some indications that the courts[86] are more cautious in
allowing duties in tort to coexist with duties in contract. This may at
least have the effect of precluding the finding of a duty of care in tort
which is in any way wider than, or inconsistent with, the duties
under the contract. It remains to be seen whether the courts will take
this any further, so as to deny the existence of duties in tort where
the parties are in a contractual relationship.[87]

(iv) Breach of Duty

It is important to remember that the tort of negligence imposes a
duty *of care*—not a duty *of truth*. It is quite possible to make a false
statement but still not be negligent. The essence of the tort is
therefore not that the defendant made a misrepresentation; only that
he failed to take care in making the (false) statement. Once it is

---

[86] Taking the lead particularly from a dictum of Lord Scarman in *Tai Hing Cotton Mill
Ltd.* v. *Liu Chong Hing Bank Ltd.* [1986] AC 80, 107: 'Their Lordships do not believe that
there is anything to the advantage of the law's development in searching for a liability
in tort where the parties are in a contractual relationship.' See e.g. *Greater Nottingham
Co-operative Society Ltd.* v. *Cementation Piling and Foundations Ltd.* [1989] QB 71; *Bank of
Nova Scotia* v. *Hellenic Mutual War Risks Association (Bermuda) Ltd.* [1990] QB 818;
National Bank of Greece SA v. *Pinios Shipping Co. No. 1* [1989] 3 WLR 185; *Reid* v. *Rush &
Tompkins Group plc* [1990] 1 WLR 212, 229. However, all these cases may perhaps be
distinguished, on the basis that *Esso* v. *Mardon* imposes liability in tort for something
done *before* the contract was entered into—a pre-contractual statement—rather than
for something done during the currency of the contract (which more naturally falls to
be covered, if at all, by the terms of the contract itself).

[87] In *Lee* v. *Thompson* [1989] 2 EGLR 151, 153 the Court of Appeal left open the
question whether a solicitor could be liable in tort to his client, in the light of *Tai Hing
Cotton Mill Ltd.* v. *Liu Chong Hing Bank Ltd.*, above, n. 86. However in *Murphy* v.
Brentwood District Council [1990] 3 WLR 414, 427 Lord Keith assumed that a duty of
care in tort can arise out of a contractual relationship with a professional person.

established that the defendant owed the plaintiff a duty of care, the *content* of that duty—the standard of care—is measured by the standard of the reasonable man. The question essentially is, did the defendant, in making the statement, exercise that level of skill and care that a reasonable man in his position would have done?[88] If he did, he was not negligent. If he did not, he was negligent.

(v) Damage

The tort of negligence is not complete until actionable damage has been suffered by the plaintiff.[89] As with the tort of deceit, discussed earlier,[90] the basic measure of damages recoverable is the 'out-of-pocket' tort measure, which in the context of pre-contractual statements will put the plaintiff into the financial position in which he was immediately before he entered into the contract in reliance on the misrepresentation. However, the rule relating to remoteness of damage in the tort of negligence is different from that in the tort of deceit. We have seen[91] that, in deceit, a defendant must pay for all the consequential losses suffered by the plaintiff, whether or not the defendant could have foreseen them. The courts are not so harsh on a defendant who is not fraudulent, but only negligent. The basic rule in negligence is that the defendant is liable for those losses of the plaintiff which are of a kind which he could reasonably have foreseen at the time of his breach of duty.[92]

This means that if the plaintiff has some out-of-pocket expenses, or other consequential losses, which the defendant would not know about, he will not recover them in negligence, and he will need to establish a claim to damages on the deceit measure in order to hold the defendant liable for them.

[88] *Esso Petroleum Co. Ltd.* v. *Mardon* [1976] QB 801, 820.
[89] *East Suffolk Rivers Catchment Board* v. *Kent* [1941] AC 74, 86–7.
[90] See p. 113, above.
[91] See p. 114, above. In *Swingcastle Ltd.* v. *Gibson* [1990] 3 All ER 463, 469–70, Neill LJ left open the question whether any valid distinction can be drawn between damages awarded for a negligent misstatement and damages awarded in deceit.
[92] *Overseas Tankship (UK) Ltd.* v. *Morts Dock & Engineering Co. Ltd., The Wagon Mound* [1961] AC 388 (Privy Council). The extent of the damage, and the precise way in which it comes about consequent upon the breach of duty, need not be foreseeable: *Hughes* v. *Lord Advocate* [1963] AC 837.

4. DAMAGES UNDER SECTION 2(1) MISREPRESENTATION ACT 1967

(a) The Act and its Origins

The Misrepresentation Act 1967 was enacted in response to recommendations of the Law Reform Committee,[93] which had been asked in 1959 to consider whether any alterations were necessary or desirable in the law relating to innocent[94] misrepresentation and the remedies available for such misrepresentation. The Law Reform Committee reported in 1962, and the Report covered a number of topics. For our present purposes we are concerned with the following recommendation about remedies in damages:[95]

27. (5) Where a person has, either by himself or his agent, induced another to enter into a contract with him (including a contract relating to land) by an untrue representation made for the purpose of inducing the contract he should be liable in damages for any loss suffered in consequence of the representation unless he proves that up to the time the contract was made he (or his agent, if the representation was made by him) believed the representation to be true and had reasonable grounds for his belief.

The Act responded to this recommendation in section 2(1), as follows:[96]

2. (1) Where a person has entered into a contract after a misrepresentation has been made to him by another party thereto and as a result thereof he has suffered loss, then, if the person making the misrepresentation would be liable to damages in respect thereof had the misrepresentation been made fraudulently, that person shall be so liable notwithstanding that the misrepresentation was not made fraudulently, unless he proves that he had reasonable ground to believe and did believe up to the time the contract was made that the facts represented were true.

(b) The Requirements of Section 2(1)

(i) What the Plaintiff has to Prove

Under the terms of the subsection, the plaintiff must prove four things: that he entered into a contract; that the defendant made a

[93] 10th Report (Innocent Misrepresentation) 1962, Cmnd. 1782. For an early account of the Act, see Atiyah and Treitel, (1967) 30 MLR 369.

[94] That is, non-fraudulent: see pp. 64–5, above.

[95] 10th Report (Innocent Misrepresentation) 1962, Cmnd. 1782, para. 27(5).

[96] The Law Reform Committee did not draft the Act.

misrepresentation to him before the contract; that he suffered loss as a result; and that the defendant would be liable to damages if he had been fraudulent.

(A) A Contract

This is self-evident. However, it serves to emphasize that the remedy is linked to contracts, unlike the torts of deceit and negligence, which apply to statements irrespective of whether they are made between contracting parties.

(B) Misrepresentation by the Defendant

Two points require consideration here: what is meant by a 'misrepresentation' in the subsection? And must the misrepresentation be made by the other contracting party personally, or can an agent either be liable himself or impose liability on his principal?

(I) 'Misrepresentation'

The subsection does not explicitly state whether the word 'misrepresentation' is limited to statements of *fact*, or whether it can extend to statements of law, opinion, or intention—nor did the Law Reform Committee deal with this point. We have seen that a *fraudulent* statement of law, opinion, or intention is actionable,[97] on the basis that, as a matter of policy, the presence of the fraud overrides the reluctance to allow remedies for misrepresentations which do not relate to fact. It may well be, therefore, that the Law Reform Committee was silent on this because they assumed that, given that they were discussing innocent—that is, non-fraudulent—misrepresentation, the limited meaning of 'misrepresentation' would be applied. The Act introduced a complication, however, by referring to fraud, which might have led to the argument that it covered all those representations which are actionable if fraudulent—and so including misrepresentations of law, opinion, and intention. This argument was discussed, but rejected, by Geoffrey Lane LJ in *André & Cie. SA* v. *Ets. Michel Blanc & Fils*:[98]

by virtue of s. 2(1) [counsel] submits that that section equates the present case to a fraudulent misrepresentation of law pre-1967 and would, he

---

[97] See pp. 71 ff. (rescission) and 107 (deceit), above.
[98] [1979] 2 Lloyd's Rep. 427, 435 (*obiter*, since the Court of Appeal held that the misrepresentation, being one of foreign law, was in any case to be treated as a misrepresentation of fact: see p. 76, above).

suggests, on its own entitle the victim . . . to damages. Is that right? It would involve ignoring the opening words of s. 2(1):

> Where a person has entered into a contract after a misrepresentation has been made to him.

To put it more accurately, it would be ascribing to the word 'misrepresentation' there a meaning which at common law it did not have because it would have to include a misrepresentation of law as well as one of fact. In my view, that is not justified.

It is also implicit in the subsection that the statement must be factual—the closing words of the subsection, referring to the defence available, talk of the defendant believing that 'the facts represented were true'.

One should also notice that the subsection refers to misrepresentations 'made' by another contracting party. This implies that the remedy is to be granted only in respect of positive statements, and that the subsection does not impose a liability for omissions to speak.[99] However, it may be assumed that a misrepresentation by conduct, and a statement which is literally true but which can be characterized as a misrepresentation by virtue of a misleading omission (a 'half-truth'), will each be a 'misrepresentation made' for the purposes of the section, and so may give rise to liability.

(II) Misrepresentations by Agents   The subsection is not absolutely clear about how representations by agents are to be treated. It says that 'where a *person* has entered into a contract after a misrepresentation has been made by another *party* thereto . . . the *person making the misrepresentation*' is liable.

This, if taken literally, might suggest that, if the misrepresentation is made by an agent of the contracting party, it is the agent who is liable, since he is the 'person making the misrepresentation'. This would, however, be odd, since it would presumably exonerate the principal, since he is not (on that analysis) the 'person making the misrepresentation', and there is no other mechanism under the section to make him liable.[100]

---

[99] *Banque Keyser Ullmann SA* v. *Skandia (UK) Insurance Co. Ltd.* [1990] QB 665, 790 (not discussed on appeal to the House of Lords, sub nom. *Banque Financière de la Cité SA* v. *Westgate Insurance Co. Ltd.* [1990] 2 All ER 947).

[100] Of course, if one thinks of the liability under s. 2(1) as a statutory tort, one would expect the agent to have primary liability, and the principal to be liable only vicariously.

The alternative view is that the word 'person' in the subsection is used in the sense, not of the physical human being making the statement, but the *legal person* acting in the circumstances—that is, the contracting party acting through his agent. On this view, the section is simply assuming the principles of agency.

The latter interpretation seems the more likely, and has been accepted by the courts. In *Resolute Maritime Inc.* v. *Nippon Kaiji Kyokai*[101] Mustill J took the view that, since section 2(1) was concerned with representations made in the particular context of a contract, it should be read as aimed at the particular position of parties to a contract: 'common sense' suggests that if anyone is liable under a statute concerned with representations inducing a contract it ought to be a principal as party to the contract. He therefore rejected the view that an agent could be personally liable under section 2(1).[102] This interpretation appears to be in accordance with the intentions of the Law Reform Committee, who wished the principal to be liable for his agent's misrepresentations.[103]

If the *misrepresentee* uses an agent—and so the statement is made to the agent, rather than the contracting party personally—the principal will be able to rely on the statement as a misrepresentation made to him for the purposes of section 2(1). And if the defendant corrects the misrepresentation to the agent, the principal will be unable to rely on the statement as a misrepresentation even if his agent fails to communicate the correction to him; any remedy will be against the agent, rather than the other contracting party.[104]

(C) *Loss Suffered by the Plaintiff*

Since section 2(1) gives a remedy in damages, it is natural to expect that the plaintiff must prove his loss. However, this raises the wider question of the *nature* of the recoverable loss—the measure of

---

[101] *The Skopas* [1983] 2 All ER 1.

[102] Mustill J also said that the Act was not intended to impose a liability on an agent because there was already a personal liability under the tort of negligence: [1983] 2 All ER 1, 3–4. This is, however, doubtful, since *Hedley Byrne & Co. Ltd.* v. *Heller & Partners Ltd.* [1964] AC 465 had not at the time of the passing of the Act been extended to pre-contractual statements: see pp. 123–4, above; and in any event the Act appears to have been passed without regard for the developments in negligence embodied in *Hedley Byrne*: see Cartwright, 'Damages for Misrepresentation' [1987] Conv. 423, 431–3.

[103] 10th Report (Innocent Misrepresentation) 1962, Cmnd. 1782, para. 27(5), quoted above, p. 126.

[104] *Strover* v. *Harrington* [1988] Ch. 390.

damages prescribed by the subsection—which will be discussed below.[105]

(D) 'Fiction of Fraud'

The subsection has a curious concept: that, for the defendant to be liable, it must be the case that he *would* have been liable to pay damages *if* he had been fraudulent—that is, he would have been liable in the tort of deceit. This is sometimes referred to as a 'fiction of fraud'.[106] In effect, it means that the plaintiff must establish all the requirements of the tort of deceit *except* for fraud on the part of the defendant.

This does not impose a difficult task upon the plaintiff, since, as we have seen, it is the requirement of fraud which makes the tort of deceit difficult to prove: the other requirements are relatively easy to establish in most cases. Those other requirements are:[107]

(1) that the defendant made a material misrepresentation;
(2) that the misrepresentation was intended by the defendant to be acted upon by the plaintiff; and was in fact acted upon by the plaintiff; and
(3) that the plaintiff suffered loss.

Section 2(1) itself explicitly requires that the defendant should have made a misrepresentation and that the plaintiff should have suffered loss; the remaining requirements for the plaintiff to prove to establish a claim under section 2(1) are therefore the materiality of the statement, that he was intended to act upon it,[108] and his action in reliance upon it.[109]

(ii) What the Defendant has to Prove

If the plaintiff succeeds in establishing the points which he has to prove, the defendant will be liable 'unless he proves that he had reasonable ground to believe and did believe up to the time the contract was made that the facts represented were true'. The burden of proof is therefore on the defendant: he is required to prove that he

---

[105] pp. 131–2.   [106] Treitel, p. 268.   [107] See p. 107, above.

[108] *Banque Keyser Ullmann SA* v. *Skandia (UK) Insurance Co. Ltd.* [1990] QB 665, 790.

[109] p. 112, above, for the requirement of reliance in the tort of deceit. For the view that materiality is not required to be proved for fraudulent misrepresentations, see p. 81, n. 68, above. In *Gosling* v. *Anderson* [1972] EGD 709, 714–15, Lord Denning MR applied the presumption of reliance from *Redgrave* v. *Hurd* (1881) 20 Ch. D. 1 (above, p. 82) in a claim under s. 2(1) Misrepresentation Act 1967. See also *Strover* v. *Harrington* [1988] Ch. 390.

in fact believed what he said, and had reasonable ground for that belief—that he was both *honest* and *reasonable*—throughout the period from the statement to the contract. This is not an easy burden to discharge.[110]

(c) The Nature of the Remedy

The remedy is damages; but on what measure? There has been some discussion of this in the cases. Initially, there were some indications that the damages were to be assessed on a *contract* measure;[111] but more recently it has been accepted that the *tort* measure is correct.[112]

The main reason for concluding that the tort measure is intended by the subsection is the reference to fraud. In *Chesneau* v. *Interhome Ltd.*,[113] Eveleigh LJ said,

The subsection itself says: '. . . if the person making the misrepresentation would be liable to damages in respect thereof had the misrepresentation been made fraudulently, that person shall be so liable . . .' By 'so liable' I take it to mean liable as he would be if the misrepresentation had been made fraudulently.

If, however, the subsection is to be regarded as imposing tort measure damages by its reference to fraud, one must be driven to the view that it is the *fraud* measure of damages which are intended— that is, damages identical to the tort of deceit. Indeed, this does appear to be what was intended by the Law Reform Committee who proposed the remedy.[114] We have already seen[115] that there is a

---

[110] *Howard Marine and Dredging Co. Ltd.* v. *A. Ogden & Sons (Excavations) Ltd.* [1978] QB 574, 596 (Bridge LJ).

[111] *Jarvis* v. *Swans Tours Ltd.* [1973] QB 233, 237C; *Gosling* v. *Anderson* [1972] EGD 709, 717.

[112] *F & B Entertainments Ltd.* v. *Leisure Enterprises Ltd.* (1976) 240 EG 455; *André & Cie. SA* v. *Ets. Michel Blanc & Fils* [1977] 2 Lloyd's Rep. 166, 181; *Chesneau* v. *Interhome Ltd.* [1983] CAT 238, *The Times*, 9 June 1983; *Sharneyford Supplies Ltd.* v. *Edge* [1986] Ch. 128, 149 (Ch. D.), [1987] Ch. 305, 323 (CA); *CEMP Properties (UK) Ltd.* v. *Dentsply Research & Development Corporation (No. 2)* [1989] 2 EGLR 196, 200. For a detailed discussion, see Cartwright, [1987] Conv. 423.

[113] Above, n. 112.

[114] 10th Report (Innocent Misrepresentation) 1962, Cmnd. 1782, para. 22, and *F & B Entertainments Ltd.* v. *Leisure Enterprises Ltd.* (1976) 240 EG 455 (Walton J, who had been a member of the Law Reform Committee). The Committee used the analogy of s. 43 Companies Act 1948 (now ss. 67(1) and 68(2)(a) Companies Act 1985) in formulating its proposal for the remedy which is enacted in s. 2(1) Misrepresentation Act 1967; that provision of the companies legislation was originally (in the form of the Directors Liability Act 1890) passed to reverse the effect of *Derry* v. *Peek* (1889) 14 App. Cas. 337 in relation to misrepresentations in company prospectuses: see n. 15, above.

[115] p. 125, above.

difference between the calculation of the damages in the tort of
deceit and in the tort of negligence; deceit is treated more harshly—
for example, recoverable consequential losses are not restricted to
those which the defendant could reasonably have foreseen. It might
be thought odd that section 2(1) can be held, by its reference to
fraud, to carry the deceit rule of remoteness of damage, since the
subsection is designed to cover specifically the situation where the
defendant is *not* fraudulent—and it was the presence of fraud which
prompted the harsher rule.[116] However, this is exactly what the
Court of Appeal has now decided;[116a] and the intention of the
legislature in 1967 does seem to have been to import the deceit
rules.[117]

(d) Section 2(1) and the Tort of Negligence Contrasted

Clearly section 2(1) Misrepresentation Act 1967 and the tort of
negligence cover similar ground. The statutory action is designed to
cover exactly the area with which we are concerned—pre-
contractual misrepresentations—whereas negligence is a general tort
which applies irrespective of whether the plaintiff and defendant are
parties to a contract. However, sometimes they may both be
invoked, and it is useful to contrast them.

Section 2(1) does not use the word 'negligence'; but it covers
broadly the same area as negligence.[118] It holds liable a person who
makes a false statement, and who cannot show that he was both
honest and reasonable in his belief that it was true. The use of the
concept of reasonableness pulls the statutory cause of action close to
negligence, which is based on the conduct of the reasonable man.[119]

What the plaintiff and defendant have to prove in each action is,
however, very different. For a representor to be liable in negligence,[120] he must owe a duty of care to the representee (which,
essentially, means that he must make the statement in circumstances

---

[116] *Doyle* v. *Olby (Ironmongers) Ltd.* [1969] 2 QB 158, 167.

[116a] *Royscot Trust Ltd.* v. *Rogerson* (1991) 141 NLJ 493.

[117] Although *Hedley Byrne & Co. Ltd.* v. *Heller & Partners Ltd.* [1964] AC 465 had been
decided in 1963, its extension to the area covered by s. 2(1) Misrepresentation Act
1967—pre-contractual statements—was not yet developed: see Cartwright, [1987]
Conv. 423 at pp. 431–3.

[118] *Garden Neptune Shipping Ltd.* v. *Occidental Worldwide Investment Corp.* [1989] 1
Lloyd's Rep. 305, 306.

[119] See pp. 124–5, above.   [120] pp. 119–20, above.

where he knows, or ought reasonably to know, that the representee will rely on his skill), break the duty (fail to do what the reasonable man would have done in the circumstances), and cause damage. All these things must be proved by the plaintiff.

In the statutory action, however, the plaintiff's task is much easier: he does not have to prove negligence; it is the defendant who must prove that he was honest and reasonable—broadly, the equivalent of proving that he was *not* negligent. Nor need the plaintiff prove a duty of care—under section 2(1) he must simply prove the factual requirement that the plaintiff and defendant entered into a contract subsequent to the misrepresentation—which is easy to establish. Of course, the existence of a duty of care in the tort of negligence may often be clear, when one considers the relative positions of skill and knowledge of the parties; but it is never as easy as proving the requirements of section 2(1).

A plaintiff is therefore likely to prefer using section 2(1) rather than the tort of negligence, even if both are technically available on a single set of facts.[121]

5. DAMAGES FOR BREACH OF CONTRACT

If the representation is incorporated as a term of the contract, it may give rise to damages for breach of contract.[122] The essence of a contractual term is that a party binds himself to performance of his promise. In the context of misrepresentation, there are two ways in which a contracting party may become liable for breach of contract:

(1) by promising in the contract that his statement is true—a guarantee of truth;

(2) by promising that the statement is made in the exercise of reasonable care and skill.

---

[121] There is also another possible advantage of the statutory action—that the measure of damages (based on deceit) may be greater: see pp. 131–2, above. A plaintiff who is the victim of a pre-contractual misrepresentation is therefore likely in practice to rely on the tort of negligence only if s. 2(1) is not technically available—e.g. to impose personal liability on an agent of the other contracting party. In *Esso Petroleum Co. Ltd.* v. *Mardon* [1976] QB 801 Mr Mardon had to rely on claims other than the statute because the relevant misrepresentation was made in 1963—and the Act applies only to misrepresentations made after it came into force: see s. 5.

[122] And termination of the contract, if the term broken is a condition of the contract, or if it is an intermediate term and the breach is fundamental: *Bunge Corporation, New York* v. *Tradax Export SA, Panama* [1981] 1 WLR 711; *Photo Production Ltd.* v. *Securicor Transport Ltd.* [1980] AC 827, 849.

Not every statement made in the course of pre-contractual negotiations can be a term of the contract. It would impose contractual
liability over too wide an area.[123] Just because a party says something
with a view to inducing the other party to enter into the contract
does not mean that he includes the truth of it *as part of the bargain*.
The basic test of whether a statement has become a term of the
contract is whether the representor can be held to have intended to
be bound to the truth of it, so as to open himself to liability in
damages if it is discovered to be false.

(a) Incorporation of Pre-contractual Misrepresentations as Contractual Terms[124]

Discerning the intention to be bound to the truth of a statement can
be difficult; but an analysis of two cases can assist to see one way in
which the courts approach the question.

In *Oscar Chess Ltd.* v. *Williams*,[125] the defendant's mother bought a
second-hand Morris car in 1954 for £300, on the basis that it was a
1948 model. This date was reflected in the log-book of the car. The
defendant later sold the car to the plaintiff for £290, describing it as a
1948 model. Eight months later, the plaintiff discovered that it was in
fact a 1939 model[126] and claimed damages for breach of contract. The
question therefore was: was the defendant's pre-contractual statement regarding the age of the car a term of the contract? If so, it was
broken simply by being false.

A majority of the Court of Appeal held that it was not a term of
the contract. Even though both parties assumed that the car was a
1948 model, and that assumption was fundamental to the contract,
the statement of its age was not necessarily a term of the contract:
the question was whether it was so *intended*.[127] However, here, as

---

[123] For some arguments about the undesirability of imposing contractual liability so
widely, see p. 66, above. And see *Heilbut, Symons & Co.* v. *Buckleton* [1913] AC 30, 48–
51.

[124] Lewison, *The Interpretation of Contracts*, 1989, §2.09; CFF, pp. 120–6.

[125] [1957] 1 WLR 370.

[126] This was not obvious, since there had been no change of style between such a car
produced in 1939 and one produced in 1948: see [1957] 1 WLR 370, 372.

[127] Morris LJ dissented, on the basis that the statement was an essential term of the
contract: 'The promise to pay £290 for that particular car (a figure arrived at by
reference to the value of 1948 cars) was the counterpart of a term of the contract that
that particular car was a 1948 model', [1957] 1 WLR 370, 380.

generally in the law of contract,[128] intention is determined objectively, rather than subjectively. Denning LJ said,[129]

The question whether a warranty was intended depends on the conduct of
the parties, on their words and behaviour, rather than on their thoughts. If
an intelligent bystander would reasonably infer that a warranty was
intended, that will suffice. . . .

It is instructive to take some recent instances to show how the courts have
approached this question. When the seller states a fact which is or should be
within his own knowledge and of which the buyer is ignorant, intending
that the buyer should act on it, and he does so, it is easy to infer a warranty:
see *Couchman* v. *Hill*,[130] where the farmer stated that the heifer was
unserved, and *Harling* v. *Eddy*,[131] where he stated that there was nothing
wrong with her. So also if he makes a promise about something which is or
should be within his own control: see *Birch* v. *Paramount Estates (Liverpool)
Ltd.*,[132] . . . where the seller stated that the house would be as good as the
show house. But if the seller, when he states a fact, makes it clear that he has
no knowledge of his own but has got his information elsewhere, and is
merely passing it on, it is not so easy to imply a warranty. Such a case was
Routledge v. *McKay*,[133] where the seller 'stated that it was a 1942 model and
pointed to the corroboration found in the [log-]book,' and it was held that
there was no warranty. . . .

The judge seems to have thought that there was a difference between
written contracts and oral contracts. He thought that the reason why the
buyer failed in *Heilbut, Symons & Co.* v. *Buckleton*[134] and *Routledge* v. *McKay*[135]
was because the sales were afterwards recorded in writing, and the written
contracts contained no reference to the representation. I agree that that was
an important factor in those cases. If an oral representation is afterwards
recorded in writing, it is good evidence that it was intended as a warranty. If
it is not put into writing, it is evidence against a warranty being intended.
But it is by no means decisive. There have been many cases where the courts
have found an oral warranty collateral to a written contract such as *Birch* v.
Paramount Estates (Liverpool) Ltd.[136] But when the purchase is not recorded in
writing at all it must not be supposed that every representation made in the
course of the dealing is to be treated as a warranty. The question then is still:
Was it intended as a warranty?

[128] See Ch. 1, above. [129] [1957] 1 WLR 370, 375–6.
[130] [1947] KB 554. [131] [1951] 2 KB 739.
[132] Reported only at (1956) 16 EG 396. It was there held that a 'serious question and
answer' between the purchaser of a new house and a representative of the vendor, in
which the representative promised that the house would be equivalent in quality to a
show house, gave rise to a collateral contract, because the negotiations went forward
and the sale was concluded on the faith of the promise.
[133] [1954] 1 WLR 615, 621. [134] [1913] AC 30.
[135] [1954] 1 WLR 615. [136] (1956) 16 EG 396; n. 132, above.

There are therefore various criteria by which to judge the intention of the parties, but there is no single rule. One must consider what the parties said, did, and wrote, to see whether—objectively—the representor can be said to have intended to promise that his statement was true. This is simply a specific example of the enquiry to ascertain the terms of the contract. We have seen[137] that the basic approach in such an enquiry—in the absence of actual (subjective) agreement between the parties—is to ask whether the representor so conducted himself that the representee was reasonably entitled to assume, and did in fact assume, that the representor was intending to bind himself to the term in question.[138]

However, it is clear that Denning LJ saw the crucial factor in *Oscar Chess Ltd.* v. *Williams* as being the balance of skill and knowledge of the parties. The seller had no personal knowledge, and could only rely on the log-book; whereas the buyer held itself out as having a skill, and had the means of checking the date of the car with the manufacturer. Hodson LJ took the same view:[139]

The defendant was stating an opinion on a matter of which he had no special knowledge or on which the buyer might be expected also to have an opinion and to exercise his judgment.

A case which contrasts with *Oscar Chess Ltd.* v. *Williams* is *Dick Bentley Productions Ltd.* v. *Harold Smith (Motors) Ltd.*,[140] which again involved a car sale. In this case, however, the seller, who made a misrepresentation about the mileage of a car, was a dealer in cars who had told the purchaser that he was in a position to find out about the history of the cars which he sold. The Court of Appeal held that the representation about the mileage of the car was a term of the contract. Lord Denning MR referred to the guide-lines which he set out in *Oscar Chess Ltd.* v. *Williams*,[141] but added a further test:[142]

if a representation is made in the course of dealings for a contract for the very purpose of inducing the other party to act upon it, and actually inducing him to act upon it, by entering into the contract, that is prima facie ground for inferring that it was intended as a warranty. . . . But the maker of

---

[137] Ch. 1, above.
[138] Lord Denning, in the passage quoted, adopts a different test—'detached objectivity'. For this, see pp. 21 ff., above.
[139] [1957] 1 WLR 370, 378.
[140] [1965] 1 WLR 623.
[141] Above, p. 135.
[142] [1965] 1 WLR 623, 627–8.

the representation can rebut this inference if he can show that it really was an innocent misrepresentation, in that he was in fact innocent of fault in making it, and that it would not be reasonable in the circumstances for him to be bound by it.

This principle tends towards holding more readily pre-contractual statements to be terms of the contract, since it shifts to the representor the burden of proving that the representation was *not* intended to be incorporated. Lord Denning MR held that the inference in *Oscar Chess Ltd.* v. *Williams* had been rebutted; but that *Dick Bentley Productions Ltd.* v. *Harold Smith (Motors) Ltd.* was different in that there the representor was in a position to know or find out about the history of the car, and he had no reasonable foundation for the misrepresentation. Here again, therefore, it is the respective skills of the representor and representee which are taken into account to determine the binding force of the representation.[143]

(b) Contractual Duties of Care

Even if, however, the misrepresentation is not held to be a term of the contract in the sense that its truth is guaranteed, there may still be liability for breach of contract. It may be that there is a contractual term that the statement is made in the exercise of reasonable care and skill.

This is in effect a contractual duty of care: it is broken—and therefore damages may be awarded for breach of contract—not simply by showing that the statement is false, but by showing that the care required was not taken. This is similar to the breach of a duty of care in the tort of negligence: it is possible to make a false statement, without being negligent.[144]

An example of such a contractual duty of care can be found in *Esso Petroleum Co. Ltd.* v. *Mardon*,[145] which has already been discussed in the context of negligence. Mr Mardon claimed—and succeeded— against Esso on two grounds: negligence and breach of contract.

---

[143] Cf. *Harlingdon and Leinster Enterprises Ltd.* v. *Christopher Hull Fine Art Ltd.* [1990] 3 WLR 13, 21: for a statement by a seller of goods to become an essential term of the contract, so that the contract can be said to be 'by description' within s. 13 Sale of Goods Act 1979, there must be *reliance* (objectively tested) by the buyer on the seller (Nourse LJ). Slade LJ at pp. 30–1 emphasized that reliance is relevant to establish the parties' intentions.

[144] See pp. 124–5, above.

[145] [1976] QB 801; pp. 123–4, above.

There was, however, no contractual promise that the throughput of the garage would be 200,000 gallons a year; but the Court of Appeal held that there was a contractual promise that the estimate of the throughput was being made with care. Lord Denning MR said,[146]

It was a forecast made by a party—Esso—who had special knowledge and skill. . . . They knew the facts. They knew the traffic in the town. They knew the throughput of comparable stations. They had much experience and expertise at their disposal. They were in a much better position than Mr. Mardon to make a forecast. It seems to me that if such a person makes a forecast, intending that the other should act upon it—and he does act upon it, it can well be interpreted as a warranty that the forecast is sound and reliable in the sense that they made it with reasonable care and skill.

Again, we here see the importance of the relative positions of skill and knowledge of the parties.

(c) The Damages Recoverable

The basic measure of damages recoverable for breach of contract has already been discussed.[147] The purpose of an award of damages for breach of contract is to put the plaintiff in the position in which he would have been had the promise been performed, rather than broken: this generally means an award of money equivalent to the cost of the failed performance. In the context of a misrepresentation which is guaranteed to be true, it means putting the plaintiff in the financial position in which he would have been if the misrepresentation had been true.[148]

If the nature of the contractual term is not a guarantee of the truth of the statement, however, but a promise that the statement is made with care,[149] the same measure of damages cannot apply. Since the defendant has not promised that the statement is true, it is not appropriate that he should have to pay damages to place the plaintiff in the position in which he would have been had the statement been true. Instead, the courts have taken the view that the measure of damages for breach of such a term of a contract should be similar to

---

[146] Ibid., at p. 818.

[147] Above, pp. 105–6.

[148] There are general rules in the law of contract limiting the amount of damages recoverable for breach in certain circumstances: e.g. remoteness of damage and mitigation. See Treitel, ch. 21.

[149] As in *Esso Petroleum Co. Ltd.* v. *Mardon* [1976] QB 801, above.

the measure of damages in negligence, since, as in the tort of negligence, the damages are essentially to compensate for the consequences of a failure to take care. The measure of damages is therefore similar to the tort measure: to compensate the plaintiff for the out-of-pocket losses he has sustained by reason of entering into the contract.[150]

6. OTHER MONEY REMEDIES FOR MISREPRESENTATION

(a) Indemnity

An indemnity is a money remedy which is sometimes granted to compensate for a misrepresentation, although its use is narrowly confined. It is not, strictly, a damages remedy; it is an order for compensation in equity which may accompany rescission of a contract.

If a contract is rescinded for misrepresentation, it is avoided *ab initio*; and the performance which has been completed under the contract is reversed. In theory, therefore, the parties are returned to their respective starting-points. However, it may be that the innocent party, who has exercised his right to rescind the contract for the misrepresentation, has some losses which the reversal of performance does not cancel out. And, more particularly, some of those losses may have been necessarily incurred in the performance of the obligations under the contract which has been rescinded. It is such losses which can be remedied by an indemnity.

For example,[151] if there is a contract for the occupation of a building for the purposes of poultry breeding, and the landlord or licensor makes a misrepresentation that the premises are in a sanitary condition and a good state of repair, suitable for poultry breeding, the representee may be able to rescind the contract. His losses may include such things as:

(1) the value of poultry stock lost as a result of the insanitary state of the premises;
(2) the costs of removing and storing his equipment;
(3) the rates which he has paid to the local authority, and which he was obliged to pay under the terms of the contract;

---

[150] Ibid., at pp. 820–1.
[151] *Whittington* v. *Seale-Hayne* (1900) 82 LT 49.

(4) the cost of repairs which he has undertaken to the premises pursuant to his specific repairing obligations under the contract.

If the contract is rescinded, the representee will be able to recover (3) and (4) as an indemnity, since they are losses incurred in performing obligations contained in the contract itself. (1) and (2) are not recoverable as an indemnity, since the representee was not obliged under the contract to use the premises for poultry breeding: they can be recovered only if one of the remedies in damages is available.[152]

The indemnity is a natural adjunct to the remedy of rescission, since compensating the plaintiff for expenditure which he has incurred—albeit in dealings with third parties—under the obligations contained in the contract is a necessary part of erasing those obligations retrospectively, which is what rescission in effect involves. However, the indemnity is not very commonly used nowadays. If a damages remedy on the tort measure (which involves compensating the representee for his out-of-pocket losses) is available, then the losses which are recoverable by way of an indemnity will be included in the recoverable damages—but other losses may also be included as damages. The indemnity was developed by equity before the damages remedies for non-fraudulent misrepresentations were available; but now that there are remedies in the tort of negligence and under section 2(1) Misrepresentation Act 1967, the usefulness of the indemnity is limited to those cases where there is *no* damages remedy available: that is, where the defendant was wholly innocent. In such a case, although he has made a misrepresentation which justifies rescission of the contract, the representor cannot be held liable even under section 2(1) Misrepresentation Act 1967 because he can establish that he was both honest and reasonable in his belief in the truth of what he said.[153]

(b) Damages in lieu of Rescission under Section 2(2) Misrepresentation Act 1967

For the sake of completeness, this remedy in damages must be noted here, although it has been discussed already.[154]

---

[152] Ibid.
[153] See pp. 130–1, above.
[154] See pp. 99–101, above.

6

Cumulation of Remedies and Underlying Principles

1. CUMULATION OF REMEDIES FOR MISREPRESENTATION

We have seen that there is a bewildering variety of remedies for misrepresentation, some of which may be available concurrently on a single set of facts: for example, if there is a fraudulent pre-contractual misrepresentation, the requirements both of the tort of deceit and of rescission may be satisfied. A final question to consider is whether the plaintiff may ever be granted more than one remedy at the same time.

Perhaps the best way to approach this question is to consider which remedies are logically *inconsistent*, so as to eliminate certain combinations of remedies. The following combinations are, on this basis, *not* possible:

(a) Tort Measure Damages and Contract Measure Damages

Put very simplistically, tort measure damages are backward-looking, and put the plaintiff in the position in which he was before the contract—they give him back his capital investment (plus consequential losses); contract measure damages are forward-looking, and put the plaintiff in the position in which he should have been under the properly completed contract—they give him his expected return.[1] If both contract and tort measure damages are given, it is allowing the plaintiff to have his capital back, but to get his return on that capital too—that is having his cake and eating it.[2]

Damages for breach of contract cannot therefore be obtained concurrently with those remedies which are measured on a tort

---

[1] pp. 105–6, above.
[2] Cf. *Cullinane* v. *British 'Rema' Manufacturing Co. Ltd.* [1954] 1 QB 292. However, it ought to be possible in principle to recover *net* profit as well as capital: see Beale, *Remedies for Breach of Contract*, 1980, p. 156.

basis—the torts of deceit and negligence, and the statutory claim under section 2(1) Misrepresentation Act 1967.

Nor will termination of the contract[3] be awarded with tort measure damages, since it always goes hand-in-hand with damages for breach: termination involves putting an end to the outstanding obligations of performance ('primary obligations') under the contract, and the obligation on the contract-breaker to pay damages for breach of contract then arises.[4]

(b) Rescission and Remedies for Breach of Contract

Rescission involves avoiding the contract *ab initio*: the contract is thereafter treated as if it had never existed. The award of damages (or termination) for breach of contract requires there to be an existing contract upon which the remedy can hinge; rescission and remedies for breach of contract are therefore logically inconsistent.[5]

For the same reasons, remedies for breach cannot be obtained concurrently with either an indemnity (since the indemnity is itself a remedy which goes hand-in-hand with rescission[6]) or damages under section 2(2) Misrepresentation Act 1967, since such damages are designed to be an equivalent to rescission, and will be awarded only where 'it is claimed . . . that the contract ought to be or has been rescinded'.[7]

(c) Rescission and Damages under Section 2(2) Misrepresentation Act 1967

This is impossible precisely because the statute provides that damages under section 2(2) are an alternative to rescission. Similarly, an indemnity (which is awarded with rescission) and damages under section 2(2) will not be available together.[8]

(d) Section 2(2) Damages and Damages in the Tort of Deceit

These cannot be awarded together because damages under section 2(2) are available only if the representation is made 'otherwise than fraudulently'.

---

[3] p. 133 n. 122, above.

[4] *Photo Production Ltd.* v. *Securicor Transport Ltd.* [1980] AC 827, 849.

[5] *Alati* v. *Kruger* (1955) 94 CLR 216, 222.

[6] p. 139, above.   [7] p. 99, above.

[8] Contrast the statutory discretion contained in s. 50 Supreme Court Act 1981, which allows damages to be awarded in substitution for *or in addition to* the equitable remedies of specific performance and injunction.

Certain other combinations of remedies are, however, possible.

(e) More than One Head of Tort Measure Damages

It may be possible, as a matter of law, for claims to be established on a single set of facts under more than one of the causes of action which give tort measure damages (deceit, negligence, and section 2(1) Misrepresentation Act 1967: the most likely combination is negligence and section 2(1), since both cover similar ground[9]). And there is no inconsistency in awarding damages concurrently under two heads of tort. However, damages in tort are compensatory,[10] and the plaintiff must not be allowed to recover twice in respect of the same loss. So, if damages are awarded under two heads of tort, one award must be deducted from the other to avoid double recovery. This means that, in practice, the award will simply be of the larger measure—usually, the deceit measure[11]—rather than a double award.

(f) Rescission and Tort Measure Damages

These two types of remedy pull in the same direction—they are both backward-looking; rescission reversing the performance of the contract to avoid it *ab initio*, and tort measure damages returning the plaintiff to the financial position in which he was immediately *before* the contract. There is therefore no logical inconsistency in allowing these remedies to be cumulated. However, if rescission is effected, the plaintiff may (as part of the reversal of performance of the defendant's obligations) recover some of what he has lost. For example, if the buyer of a car, who has paid over the purchase price, rescinds the contract of purchase, he will recover from the seller the purchase price. He will not therefore be able to claim this as an element in his tort damages. However, if he has other losses which are recoverable in tort, there is no reason why he should not be able to recover them in addition to rescinding the contract (provided, of course, that he can establish a tort).

For example, in *Archer* v. *Brown*,[12] Peter Pain J held that damages in the tort of deceit were recoverable in addition to rescission; and

---

[9] p. 132, above.

[10] *McGregor on Damages*, 15th edn., 1988, §9.

[11] Since there is a wider recovery in deceit for consequential losses, for example; see p. 125, above. The deceit measure appears also to be the measure used also by s. 2(1) Misrepresentation Act 1967: see pp. 131–2, above: *Royscot Trust Ltd.* v. *Rogerson* (1991) 141 NLJ 493.   [12] [1985] QB 401, 415.

that damages under section 2(1) Misrepresentation Act 1967 would similarly be recoverable in conjunction with rescission.

(*g*) *Damages under Section 2(1) Misrepresentation Act 1967 or in the Tort of Negligence, and Damages under 2(2) Misrepresentation Act 1967*

The award of damages under both section 2(1) and section 2(2) Misrepresentation Act is possible because section 2(3) specifically envisages it; however, it provides that there will be no double recovery, since damages recoverable under section 2(2) are deducted from those recoverable under section 2(1):[13]

2. (3) Damages may be awarded against a person under subsection (2) of this section whether or not he is liable to damages under subsection (1) thereof, but where he is so liable any award under the said subsection (2) shall be taken into account in assessing his liability under the said subsection (1).

Similarly, damages could be recovered in negligence and under section 2(2), but with an appropriate set-off to avoid double recovery. In practice, this means that only the larger measure is likely to be awarded.

(*h*) *Rescission and Indemnity*

These are certainly available together—the indemnity was developed precisely in order to accompany rescission and give compensation for obligations incurred under the contract.[14]

(*i*) *Indemnity and Tort Measure Damages*

Strictly, these may be ordered together (but with a deduction of one from the other in so far as there would be double recovery); however, since the losses which would be comprised in an indemnity will usually be recoverable within the tort measure damages, there is in practice little point in claiming separately the indemnity.[15]

(*j*) *Termination and Damages for Breach of Contract*

If a contract is terminated for breach, the right to damages for the

---

[13] It is generally assumed that this shows that an award of damages under s. 2(1) will be greater than an award under s. 2(2): see e.g. Treitel, p. 279. This is not, however, necessarily so: see Cartwright, [1987] Conv. 423, 428–9.

[14] p. 139, above.

[15] p. 140, above.

	Indemnity	S. 2(2) M.A. 1967	S. 2(1) M.A. 1967	Negligence damages	Deceit damages	Breach of contract damages	Termination of contract
Rescission	✓(h)	✗(c)	✓(f)	✓(f)	✓(f)	✗(b)	✗(b)
Termination of contract	✗(b)	✗(b)	✗(a)	✗(a)	✗(a)	✓(j)	
Breach of contract damages	✗(b)	✗(b)	✗(a)	✗(a)	✗(a)		
Deceit damages	(✓)(i)	✗(d)	(✓)(e)	(✓)(e)			
Negligence damages	(✓)(i)	(✓)(g)	(✓)(e)				
S. 2(1) M.A. 1967	(✓)(i)	(✓)(g)					
S. 2(2) M.A. 1967	✗(c)						

✓ possible combination

✗ impossible combination

(✓) theoretically possible combination, but not awarded in practice

(a)–(j) refer to the discussion in the respective sections in Chapter 6

FIG. 6.1. Cumulation of remedies for misrepresentation.

breach arises automatically.[16] These two remedies—both being remedies for breach of contract—can therefore certainly be awarded concurrently.

These various combinations are represented in Fig. 6.1.

2. UNDERLYING PRINCIPLES

Perhaps the most striking thing about misrepresentation in the law of contract is the remarkable range of remedies available. We have seen that these remedies—in equity, in tort, in contract, and under statute—have been built up over the years, and without any concerted attempt to reduce them to a coherent body of rules: they all fit in their own pigeon-holes.

But are there any principles which unite the remedies? The first point to be borne in mind is that the state of mind of the representor is an important factor to determine his liability for his statements. If he is fraudulent, then remedies have long been accepted as being available against him. For misrepresentations made by a contracting party who is not fraudulent, remedies have still been developed, but more cautiously: in particular, the courts were reluctant to allow remedies in damages for non-contractual, non-fraudulent misrepresentations. However, even a wholly innocent misrepresentation can give rise to the remedy of rescission.

Another theme which runs through the remedies is that the relative positions of the parties—the representor and the representee—are crucial to determine the liability which attaches to the representation. In particular, the balance of skill and knowledge of the parties is used as a factor to determine whether the representor should be liable for his statement.

In relation to the remedy of rescission, we saw that an overriding rule is that the statement must be one of fact; and this was (*inter alia*) contrasted with statements of opinion. In order to ascertain whether a particular statement is to be regarded as factual, the courts look to see whether the representor was in a superior position: whether he was, or was to be taken to be, in a position where he ought to know what he was talking about. If he was in such a superior position, *vis-à-vis* the other party, he will be responsible for his statement (even if

---

[16] *Photo Production Ltd.* v. *Securicor Transport Ltd.* [1980] AC 827, 849.

he phrased it in terms simply of opinion—and even if he genuinely did believe what he said).[17] And even if the statement is not of fact—for example, if it is a statement of law—there may still be liability. If the statement is honest, it will not give rise to rescission, because the parties are in an equal position to find out the law; and there are policy reasons in favour of sanctity of contract which militate against allowing recovery. But if the misrepresentation is fraudulent, the fraud overrides all other considerations: one contracting party cannot be allowed deliberately to take advantage of the other.[18]

In the law of tort, we saw similar principles at work. The language of the cases is different, because the various torts have been developed without particular regard to misrepresentations made between contracting parties. So the cases do not use as a criterion of liability that the misrepresentation must have been factual. A fraudulent misrepresentation has long been given a remedy in the tort of deceit:[19] deliberate falsehood is firmly dealt with. But we have seen that, since 1963, negligent misrepresentations have also been remedied.[20] And when we look at the principles which are applied in the tort of negligence to determine whether one party owes a duty of care to the other in making his statement, we see that there is a similarity to the law of rescission. Although different terminology is used—in negligence it is not a distinction between statements of 'fact' and 'opinion', but the search for a duty of care—the underlying principle is similar. What gives rise to a duty of care is a 'special relationship' between the parties:[21] one party being, or being taken to be, in a superior position of skill or knowledge at the time of making the statement so that a duty attaches to him to be careful in his statement.

Moreover, even in the cases concerning the remedy of damages for breach of contract we have seen the same idea. The crucial question there is whether the representor can be said to have promised in the contract either that the representation was true; or that he was exercising care in making the statement.[22] We saw that

---

[17] *Smith* v. *Land and House Property Corporation* (1884) 28 Ch. D. 7; p. 80 above.

[18] See pp. 77–9, above.   [19] See p. 109, above.

[20] See p. 120, above. The remedy of damages under s. 2(1) Misrepresentation Act 1967 falls between the torts of deceit and negligence: the statute applies where there is in fact no fraud, but on the basis of a fictitious *assumption* of fraud; and, in effect, it covers negligent misrepresentations: see p. 132, above. The statute simply assumes that in the specific situation of pre-contractual negotiations, a duty should attach to one party who makes a representation to justify his honesty and the reasonableness of his belief in his statement.

[21] See p. 120 n. 72, above.   [22] See p. 133, above.

the courts will hold more readily that there is implied into the contract a term that care is being taken; but the circumstances in which such an implied term will be found are precisely the same as those in which a duty of care will be found in the tort of negligence, based on a 'special relationship'.[23] And although the courts are more cautious in holding that a pre-contractual representation was incorporated into the contract so as to guarantee its truth, one factor to which they look to determine such incorpoation is whether the representor was in a better position than the representee to know the truth of the statement.[24] They are here inquiring into the intentions of the parties—whether they intended, or can be taken to have intended, that the representor would guarantee in the contract the truth of his statement. But the test which they apply looks again to the relative positions of the parties—the balance of their knowledge and skill.

So we can see that one key factor which links together the law of misrepresentation is the responsibility which attaches to a superior position of one party over the other at the time of the contract. Deliberately taking advantage, by fraudulent representations, cannot in any circumstances be permitted. But even short of such deliberate misrepresentations, mere position, or holding out of position, carries responsibility. It is therefore vital, when considering the liability of a party to a contract for a statement which he made leading up to the contract, to analyse carefully not only what the parties said and did at the time of the contract, but also their relative and respective positions, skill, and knowledge as regards the subject-matter of the statement.

Furthermore, the fact that even a wholly innocent misrepresentation can give rise to the remedy of rescission shows that a degree of responsibility attaches simply to the making of a representation which causes the representee to misunderstand the factual basis of the contract. Although damages cannot be awarded for such an innocent misrepresentation, the contract itself is vitiated. The misrepresentee, whose misunderstanding has been induced by the other party, is allowed to escape from the contract if he so wishes. The fact that the misrepresentor has taken it upon himself to make a relevant statement which was false—even though he did not realize the falsehood—means that the balance of the negotiations has been disturbed.

---

[23] *Esso Petroleum Co. Ltd.* v. *Mardon* [1976] QB 801; pp. 137–8, above.
[24] *Oscar Chess Ltd.* v. *Williams* [1957] 1 WLR 370; p. 136, above.

III
PRESSURE AND ABUSE
OF POSITION

7

Duress

1. THE ESSENCE OF DURESS AND UNDUE INFLUENCE

We have seen that misrepresentation involves one party inducing the other to contract by misleading him about some fact or facts relevant to his decision to enter into the contract. This interferes with the representee's freedom to form an independent judgment about whether, and on what terms, to enter into the contract: he is acting on a wrong set of assumptions, caused by the representor.

Duress and undue influence are in a sense similar to misrepresentation, in that they too involve conduct by one party which interferes with the other party's freedom to form an independent judgment about the contract. However, they are different from misrepresentation, in that they do not involve a party being misled about the circumstances of the contract; instead, they involve one party putting unfair pressure, or exerting unfair influence, on the other party in the course of the negotiations leading up to the contract. Two points need to be borne in mind from the outset in relation to duress and undue influence: their one-sided nature; and the difficulty of defining the types of pressure or influence which will vitiate a contract.

(a) One-Sided Remedies

Duress and undue influence involve one party putting pressure, or exerting influence, on the other party, to persuade him to contract. One party disturbs the balance of the negotiations; consequently the remedy will be one-sided. Only the party on whom the pressure has been applied will be able to use it as a reason for obtaining a remedy.

Moreover, this one-sidedness helps to point to the remedy granted for duress and undue influence: since the contract is vitiated from the very beginning, it is natural that the remedy is that the contract is avoided *ab initio*. However, since the essence is pressure put on one party, it is in the power of that pressurized party to decide whether or not to invoke the remedy—that is, the contract is not void, but *voidable* at the instance of the pressurized party.[1]

(b) Defining actionable pressures

During the negotiations leading up to the conclusion of a contract, there are many pressures to which the parties may be subject: they may be making the contract for a variety of reasons which they would say give them 'no choice'. And it is quite natural that one party would attempt to put some degree of pressure on the other to obtain the contract. The question which must be considered in some detail is: what sort of pressure can the courts hold to be illegitimate? There must come a point when the pressure, judged by such criteria as its degree, or the circumstances in which it is exercised, has become illegitimate so as to allow the pressurized party to avoid the contract. Such an avoidance is, however, clearly a drastic remedy, and we must look hard at the policy decisions which underlie the rules developed by the courts in this area.

2. DURESS

We shall first consider the law of duress, which was developed by the common law.[2] There has been a steady development in this area. We shall see that the common law has long recognized that a contract which was procured by pressure applied to the person of the plaintiff is vitiated; it was more cautious in the case of pressure

---

[1] In this, duress and undue influence are similar to misrepresentation; but we have seen (Part II, above) that the remedies for misrepresentation are complicated by being numerous. There is no remedy in damages for duress or undue influence as such: an independent cause of action, such as a tort, must be established if damages are sought: see *Banque Keyser Ullmann SA* v. *Skandia (UK) Insurance Co. Ltd.* [1990] QB 665, 780. However, duress will generally involve a tort—particularly the tort of intimidation: *The Universe Sentinel* [1983] 1 AC 366, 400. Curiously, however, Dillon LJ in *Alec Lobb (Garages) Ltd.* v. *Total Oil (Great Britain) Ltd.* [1985] 1 WLR 173, 177 went so far as to refer to 'the *tort* of economic duress'. The remedy for duress is avoidance of the contract, and restitution of property or money exacted under such duress: *The Universe Sentinel*, above, at p. 385.

[2] *Barton* v. *Armstrong* [1976] AC 104, 118, 121. Cf. *Banque Keyser Ullmann SA* v. *Skandia (UK) Insurance Co. Ltd.* [1990] QB 665, 780.

applied not to the person, but to the property of the plaintiff; and more cautious still in cases of pressure in relation to the plaintiff's economic interests. These different areas will be discussed in turn.

(a) Duress to the Person

Duress to the person involves a threat by one party to the life, health, liberty, or physical comfort of the other,[3] to persuade him to enter into the contract.

The leading modern case is *Barton* v. *Armstrong*,[4] in which Barton sought to avoid a contract by which he had agreed to buy Armstrong's shares in a company. The trial judge found[5] that on many occasions Armstrong had threatened Barton with death, and that Barton was justified in taking and did take these threats seriously. The threats found to have been proved included:

(1) A statement by Armstrong to Barton that 'the city is not as safe as you may think between office and home. You will see what I can do against you . . .'

(2) Telephone calls made by Armstrong to Barton in the middle of the night, for four or five nights at a time; the calls consisted generally of heavy breathing, with sometimes a voice saying, 'you will be killed'.

(3) A public statement made by Armstrong to Barton, that 'you stink; you stink. I will fix you'—followed by a conversation in which Armstrong claimed that he was in a position to procure police officers to do his bidding, and that for $2,000 one could have someone killed. After this incident, Barton hired a bodyguard. Later, Barton was approached by a Yugoslav man 'with a bad criminal record', who claimed that Armstrong had hired him to kill Barton— although the trial judge was not satisfied that the Yugoslav was actually employed by Armstrong.

In spite of such threats as these, the trial judge refused to declare the contract voidable for duress. He took the view[6] that 'Armstrong was

---

[3] Or, perhaps, of a close relative: 1 Roll. Abr. 687(B)5: 'un fits avoidera son fait per dures al son pere'; cf. (B)6: 'Home n'avoidera un fait per dures al estranger.' But now such situations would be covered in any event by the equitable doctrine of undue influence: p. 172, below.

[4] [1976] AC 104.

[5] Ibid., at pp. 112–15.

[6] Ibid., at p. 116.

. . . a "reluctant vendor" and that his threats were not intended and were not thought by Barton to be intended to induce him to enter into the agreement but were simply manifestations of blind malevolence.' The threats had therefore not coerced Barton into signing the contract: it was 'sheer commercial necessity that was the real and quite possibly the sole motivating factor'.[7]

The majority of the Privy Council[8] overturned this, and held that the contract was voidable: the evidence, they thought, did not justify the judge concluding that the threats were not an operating factor in Barton's entering into the contract. The minority,[9] by contrast, took the view that the judge's findings of fact were so clear that it was not open to an appeal court to review them. They therefore held the contract valid. However, the majority and minority in the Privy Council did not differ in their views of the law to be applied in relation to duress to the person.

One question which had given rise to difficulties in the lower courts was the nature of the causal link required to establish duress. Must the pressure be the *only* reason for the plaintiff having entered into the contract? Or the *predominant* reason? Or the *clinching* reason? Or just *a* reason? The Privy Council was clear that the last of these was the test: a contract is vitiated by duress to the person, provided only that the pressure was at least *a* reason for the contract.[10] '[H]is reason for acting must . . . be a conscious reason so that the complainant can give evidence of it: "I acted because I was forced."'[11] And, once it is shown that there has been unlawful pressure, the burden is on the defendant to show that the pressure did not cause the plaintiff to enter into the contract.[12] This is similar to the test of causation in misrepresentation,[13] and it is presumably

---

[7] Ibid., at p. 113.

[8] Lord Cross of Chelsea, Lord Kilbrandon, and Sir Garfield Barwick.

[9] Lord Wilberforce and Lord Simon of Glaisdale.

[10] [1976] AC 104, 118–19. This was on the analogy of fraudulent misrepresentation, where the rule is that, 'Once make out that there has been anything like deception, and no contract resting in any degree on that foundation can stand': *Reynell* v. *Sprye* (1852) 1 De G. M. & G. 660, 708 (Lord Cranworth LJ); see p. 83, above. The minority of the Privy Council were prepared to accept this test for the purposes of the present case, although they reserved their opinion on cases which may arise in other contexts: [1976] AC 104, 121. On the question of whether the same, narrow test is appropriate in other categories of duress—e.g. economic duress—see p. 168, below.

[11] [1976] AC 104, 122.

[12] Ibid., at p. 120.

[13] pp. 82–3, above.

adopted for a similar reason: because it is so difficult to establish why one entered into a contract. Once it is shown that the defendant acted wrongly in applying unlawful pressure, he ought to have the (very difficult) burden of disproving the causal relationship between the pressure and the contract; the law favours the innocent party over the wrongdoer.

Barton v. *Armstrong* is also very helpful in its discussion of the concept of duress generally. In their dissenting judgment, Lord Wilberforce and Lord Simon of Glaisdale said,[14]

The basis of the plaintiff's claim is . . . that though there was apparent consent there was no true consent to the agreement: that the agreement was not voluntary.[15]

This involves consideration of what the law regards as voluntary, or its opposite; for in life, including the life of commerce and finance, many acts are done under pressure, sometimes overwhelming pressure, so that one can say that the actor had no choice but to act. Absence of choice in this sense does not negate consent in law: for this the pressure must be one of a kind which the law does not regard as legitimate.

Therefore, in order to establish that a contract is voidable for duress, one must establish two things:

(1) that the pressure was illegitimate; and
(2) the necessary relationship between the illegitimate pressure and the action of the plaintiff in entering into the contract.

In the case of duress to the person, we know from *Barton* v. *Armstrong*[16] that

(1) pressure which consists of threats to the life, health, or physical comfort of the plaintiff is of itself illegitimate; and
(2) the necessary relationship is that the pressure should have constituted *a* reason for the plaintiff having entered into the contract; no higher degree of causation is required.

The question which we must consider, however, is whether similar answers should be given in relation to other categories of duress.

---

[14] [1976] AC 104, 121.
[15] On the question of the sense in which it can be said that duress involves absence of consent, see pp. 160 ff., below.
[16] [1976] AC 104, 118–19, 121.

(*b*) Duress to Property

In duress to property, the pressure is of a different kind from duress to the person. As the name suggests, it involves threats to damage property, or an interference with property (for example, the actual or threatened detention or seizure of property) which is designed to induce the owner of the property to enter into a contract.

This is an area where there has been some confusion in the cases in the past. Two authorities suggested that the rule is that if a person has *agreed* to pay money, under duress to his property, then he cannot avoid the contract to pay; however, if he has actually *paid* money, or transferred property, under such duress, then he can recover it—the transaction is unwound.

In the case of a completed transaction, *Astley* v. *Reynolds*[17] held that, where a plaintiff had been compelled to pay an amount in excess of the legal rate of interest to secure the return of plate which he had pawned with the defendant, he was entitled to recover the excess on the ground of duress. This was said by the Court[18] to be because

the plaintiff might have such an immediate want of his goods, that an action of trover would not do his business: where the rule volenti non fit injuria is applied,[19] it must be where the party had his freedom of exercising his will, which this man had not: we must take it he paid the money relying on his legal remedy to get it back again.

That is, he was under pressure which took away his freedom of choice in making the payment of money; and he had no alternative and suitable remedy at the time he made the payment, which justified his action at the time.

Astley v. *Reynolds* was, however, a case of a payment, rather than a contract to pay. In the later case of *Skeate* v. *Beale*,[20] the plaintiff landlord distrained to put pressure on the defendant to pay arrears of rent. The defendant promised to pay the arrears claimed, in

[17] (1731) 2 Str. 915.

[18] Ibid., at p. 916. The absence of alternative remedies is used in modern cases as an important criterion for holding that *economic* duress has been applied: see e.g. *Pao On* v. *Lau Yiu Long* [1980] AC 614, 635; n. 45, below.

[19] i.e. the rule that whenever a man pays money, knowing what he does, he shall never recover it back again: see the report of *Astley* v. *Reynolds* at 2 Barn. KB 40, 41.

[20] (1841) 11 Ad. & E. 983.

consideration of the plaintiff withdrawing the distress. Later, however, he refused to pay the full amount which he had promised, on the ground of duress to his property—that is, that he had made the promise only in order to obtain the release of the property taken by way of distress.

Lord Denman CJ took a firm view that duress of goods—although it may be sufficient to vitiate an actual payment of money, as in *Astley* v. *Reynolds*[21]—cannot vitiate a contract.[22] He said that there is a fundamental difference between duress to the person (which can avoid a contract) and duress to property (which cannot):[23]

The former is a constraining force, which not only takes away the free agency, but may leave no room for appeal to the law for a remedy . . . but the fear that goods may be taken or injured does not deprive any one of his free agency who possesses that ordinary degree of firmness which the law requires all to exert.

This appears to have been a decision of policy: contracting parties can be expected to resist duress to their property, and to use the alternative remedies which the law provides.[24] However, one would not expect there to be a different rule for payments and agreements to pay; in the case of an actual payment, there must have been at least a split second when there was an agreement to pay. It is odd that the fact that a contract is executed is a reason for favouring its avoidance over a contract which is still executory.[25]

However, it is not profitable to dwell on this difficulty now. *Skeate* v. *Beale* was decided in 1841; the common law of duress has moved on since then, in another area: duress to economic interests. We shall

---

[21] See above, n. 17.

[22] An alternative interpretation of *Skeate* v. *Beale* is that 'Lord Denman CJ was dealing with either a compromise of, or a submission to, a claim': Beatson, [1974] CLJ 97, 105 (see now also Beatson, 'Duress, Restitution and Contract Renegotiation', in *The Use and Abuse of Unjust Enrichment*, 1991). Lord Denman certainly regarded the agreement in *Skeate* as 'voluntarily entered into': (1841) 11 Ad. & E. 983, 991. However, this is the logical conclusion of his view that duress to goods can never vitiate a contract because the availability of alternative remedies gives a *choice* of courses of action. Lord Denman's statement that 'an agreement is not void because made under duress of goods' ((1841) 11 Ad. & E. 983, 990) is categoric; if the case is to be seen as compromise of, or submission to, a claim, Lord Denman must be saying that there will be such a compromise or submission in *all* cases of duress to goods.

[23] (1841) 11 Ad. & E. 983, 990.

[24] For a different policy decision in relation to the defence of duress to a charge of murder, see *R.* v. *Howe* [1987] AC 417, 432 (Lord Hailsham of St Marylebone LC).

[25] Beatson, [1974] CLJ 97, 106–8.

see that the courts have now accepted that pressure exerted not even against property, but simply against economic interests, can in certain circumstances avoid a contract. *Skeate* v. *Beale* and the cases on duress to property must therefore now be read in the light of the cases on 'economic duress'. In *The Alev*,[26] for example, Hobhouse J held a contract voidable for duress where the facts showed duress of goods, but following the principles of the economic duress cases: 'The principle that agreements can be avoided if entered into under duress of goods or economic duress is now well established.' *Skeate* v. *Beale* and the earlier cases on duress to property were not cited; the economic duress cases were assumed to set out all the necessary principles.

(c) Economic Duress

(i) The Nature of Economic Duress

Economic duress is the situation where the defendant coerces the plaintiff into entering into a contract by exerting *economic* pressure on him. The threat is to harm not his person nor even his property, but other interests such as rights he has under a contract.[27] A typical case is where one party to a contract threatens to break the contract in order to extract some advantage from the other party—often a contractual variation of the original contract.

For example, in *The Atlantic Baron*,[28] the defendants contracted to build a tanker for the plaintiffs, for a price fixed in US dollars. When the dollar was later devalued by 10 per cent, the defendants sought a corresponding increase in the contract price, threatening to refuse to perform the contract if their demand was not met. The plaintiffs paid, but it was later held that the circumstances under which they had paid amounted to economic duress.[29]

---

[26] [1989] 1 Lloyd's Rep. 138, 145.

[27] Notice that there can be overlap between categories. For example, a contract for the sale of land may give rise to proprietary rights, and hence a threat by the vendor not to complete could be categorized as duress to property: cf. *Nixon* v. *Furphy* (1925) 25 SR(NSW) 151.

[28] *North Ocean Shipping Co. Ltd.* v. *Hyundai Construction Co. Ltd.*, *The Atlantic Baron* [1979] QB 705.

[29] They failed in their action to recover the excess paid, however, since, although they made it clear at the time of the payment that they were paying 'without prejudice' to their rights, they had not taken any action by way of protest after the duress had ceased to be applied by the defendants. This amounted, therefore, to an affirmation of the variation to the contract. See pp. 168–9, below. One point which should be borne

Clearly the concept of economic duress will be difficult. We are here in the area of commercial activity where pressure is put as a matter of course upon those with whom a person is dealing or is proposing to deal. A key difficulty will therefore be to establish the circumstances in which such pressure is *illegitimate*. Recognizing this, the courts have developed a distinction: between pressure which is sufficient to constitute economic duress; and pressure which is merely 'commercial pressure' (and which does not amount to economic duress).

This distinction was made in the first English case to acknowledge that economic duress might vitiate a contract; *The Siboen and the Sibotre*.[30] Kerr J there said,[31]

But even assuming, as I think, that our law is open to further development in relation to contracts concluded under some form of compulsion not amounting to duress to the person, the Court must in every case at least be satisfied that the consent of the other party was overborne by compulsion so as to deprive him of any animus contrahendi. This would depend on the facts of each case. One relevant factor would be whether the party relying on duress made any protest at the time or shortly thereafter. Another would be to consider whether or not he treated the settlement as closing the trans-action in question and as binding upon him, or whether he made it clear that he regarded the position as still open. . . . But the facts of the present case fall a long way short of the test which would in law be required to make good a defence of compulsion or duress. . . . [The agent of the party alleging duress] was acting under great pressure, but only commercial pressure, and

in mind in a situation such as that in *The Atlantic Baron*, where it is a variation to an existing contract which is sought to be challenged on the ground of duress, is that the issue of duress is relevant only if the variation is in any event binding as a contract. There may be difficulty in such a case in establishing consideration for the promise to vary the original contract, since a promise to perform in accordance with the original terms is not of itself sufficient consideration for a promise to increase the price: *Stilk* v. *Myrick* (1809) 2 Camp. 317. In *The Atlantic Baron*, it was found that there was consider-ation for the promise to pay the additional 10% purchase price, in the form of an increase in the credit arrangements by the defendant. Moreover, the Court of Appeal in *Williams* v. *Roffey Bros. & Nicholls (Contractors) Ltd.* [1990] 2 WLR 1153 took a relaxed view of the rule in *Stilk* v. *Myrick*: if one party's promise to increase his obligations under a contract is not given as a result of economic duress, it may be binding; the consideration being any 'practical benefit' obtained by the other, such as having the promisor continue to perform his contract, without therefore needing to go to the trouble and expense of finding a replacement.

[30] *Occidental Worldwide Investment Corp.* v. *Skibs A/S Avanti, The Siboen and the Sibotre* [1976] 1 Lloyd's Rep. 293.

[31] Ibid., at p. 336.

not under anything which could in law be regarded as a coercion of his will so as to vitiate his consent.

This statement of principle is, however, problematic. Kerr J used the terminology of 'commercial pressure' to mark off those forms of economic pressure which must be endured without the contract being vitiated; however, he contrasted 'commercial pressure' with 'coercion of the will so as to vitiate consent'. The phrase 'coercion of the will which vitiates consent' can be misleading, for two reasons; first, because it is not true that duress involves absence of consent; and, second, because it fails to emphasize that a key criterion for duress is the *illegitimacy* of the pressure.

(ii) 'Vitiation of Consent'

The idea that duress operates by vitiating consent, which was stated by Kerr J in *The Siboen and the Sibotre*, was used in other cases which accepted and developed the concept of economic duress. For example, in *Pao On* v. *Lau Yiu Long*[32] Lord Scarman, giving the judgment of the Privy Council, said,

Duress, whatever form it takes, is a coercion of the will so as to vitiate consent. . . . In their Lordships' view, there is nothing contrary to principle in recognising economic duress as a factor which may render a contract voidable, provided always that the basis of such recognition is that it must amount to a coercion of will, which vitiates consent. It must be shown that the payment made or the contract entered into was not a voluntary act.

The problem with duress is to understand why a party who now claims that he entered into a contract under coercion did in fact decide to contract. It is not surprising that the language of voluntary or involuntary actions was used. In *Maskell* v. *Horner*[33] Lord Reading CJ said,

If a person with knowledge of the facts pays money, which he is not in law bound to pay, and in circumstances implying that he is paying it voluntarily

---

[32] [1980] AC 614, 635–6. See also *Syros Shipping Co. SA* v. *Elaghill Trading Co., The Proodos C* [1981] 3 All ER 189, 192; *Alec Lobb (Garages) Ltd.* v. *Total Oil (Great Britain) Ltd.* [1983] 1 WLR 87, 93. The test of 'coercion of the will' which 'vitiates' consent was also adopted by the Court of Appeal in *Hirani* v. *Hirani* (1983) 4 FLR 232, 234, in relation to duress as rendering a *marriage* voidable.

[33] [1915] 3 KB 106, 118, dealing with a claim for the return of tolls paid by a trader to the owner of a market under threat of seizure of his property.

to close the transaction, he cannot recover it. Such a payment is in law like a gift, and the transaction cannot be reopened. If a person pays money, which he is not bound to pay, under the compulsion of urgent and pressing necessity or of seizure, actual or threatened, of his goods he can recover it as money had and received. . . . Payment under such pressure establishes that the payment is not made voluntarily to close the transaction.

Such language—of duress being constituted by the involuntary nature of the payment—naturally led to the language of absence of consent; it was a common view, and was even used in *Barton* v. *Armstrong*.[34] However, it is now clear that duress does not involve an absence of consent in the sense that the contracting party does not know what he is doing. In the case of misrepresentation,[35] a party enters into a contract on a false assumption about a matter of fact; in a sense, he could therefore be said to be consenting only to a different situation from that in which he is actually placed. But even in the context of misrepresentation it is not usual to say that a misled party's 'consent is vitiated' when he contracts. Duress is different from misrepresentation, in that the coerced party does know what he is doing; but he has no choice but to do it. It might be said that his freedom of choice is vitiated; his eventual consent is not.

The essence of duress can be seen from statements in *Director of Public Prosecutions for Northern Ireland* v. *Lynch*.[36] Lord Simon of Glaisdale, for example, said,[37]

Similarly with duress in the English law of contract. Duress again deflects, without destroying, the will of one of the contracting parties. There is still an intention on his part to contract in the apparently consensual terms; but there is coactus volui on his side. . . . The contract procured by duress is therefore not void: it is voidable—at the discretion of the party subject to duress.

[34] [1976] AC 104, 121. See *Chitty*, §501.

[35] See Part II, above.

[36] [1975] AC 653. The case concerned the availability of duress as a defence to a charge of murder in the criminal law, but the judgments contain some discussion of the juridical basis of duress generally. *Director of Public Prosecutions for Northern Ireland* v. *Lynch* was overruled by *R.* v. *Howe* [1987] AC 417, but no doubt was cast on the discussions in *Lynch* about the basis of duress; indeed, Lord Hailsham ([1987] AC 417, 428) specifically approved statements in the judgments of Lord Kilbrandon and Lord Edmund-Davies which had emphasized that duress involves knowingly doing something that one would not wish to do.

[37] [1975] AC 653, 695. See also at pp. 680 (Lord Wilberforce), 703 (Lord Kilbrandon), and 709–10 (Lord Edmund-Davies).

The inaccuracy of the phrase 'vitiation of consent' in the context of duress was discussed by the House of Lords in *The Universe Sentinel*.[38] Lord Diplock, in explaining the rationale of duress, said,[39]

It is not that the party seeking to avoid the contract which he has entered into with another party, or to recover money that he has paid to another party in response to a demand, did not know the nature or the precise terms of the contract at the time when he entered into it or did not understand the purpose for which the payment was demanded. The rationale is that his apparent consent was induced by pressure exercised upon him by that other party which the law does not regard as legitimate, with the consequence that the consent is treated in law as revocable unless approbated either expressly or by implication after the illegitimate pressure has ceased to operate on his mind.

Lord Scarman took a similar line:[40]

The authorities upon which [*Barton* v. *Armstrong*[41] and *Pao On* v. *Lau Yiu Long*[42]] were based reveal two elements in the wrong of duress: (1) pressure amounting to compulsion of the will of the victim; and (2) the illegitimacy of the pressure exerted. There must be pressure, the practical effect of which is compulsion or the absence of choice. Compulsion is variously described in the authorities as coercion or the vitiation of consent. The classic case of duress is, however, not the lack of will to submit[43] but the victim's intentional submission arising from the realisation that there is no other practical choice open to him. This is the thread of principle which links the early law of duress (threat to life or limb) with later developments when the law came also to recognise as duress first the threat to property and now the threat to a man's business or trade.

It is clear, therefore, that the emphasis has shifted. The test for duress is not whether the coerced party's action in entering the

---

[38] *Universe Tankships Inc. of Monrovia* v. *International Transport Workers' Federation, The Universe Sentinel* [1983] 1 AC 366. The point had earlier been forcefully made by Atiyah in (1982) 98 LQR 197 and (1983) 99 LQR 353. See also, in Australia, *Crescendo Management Pty. Ltd.* v. *Westpac Banking Corporation* (1988) 19 NSWLR 40, 45–6.

[39] [1983] 1 AC 366, 384.

[40] Ibid., at p. 400.

[41] [1976] AC 104.

[42] [1980] AC 614.

[43] 'I wonder whether this passage may not contain a typographical error. . . . I wonder whether "the lack of will to submit" should not have been "the lack of will to resist" or "the lack of will in submitting"': *B & S Contracts and Design Ltd.* v. *Victor Green Publications Ltd.* [1984] ICR 419, 428 (Kerr LJ).

contract was involuntary; or whether his consent was vitiated;[44] but, more generally, it must be established that there was pressure which was so great that it effectively gave him no choice but to act as he did.[45] However, that is not enough: it must also be shown that the pressure was *illegitimate*.

(iii) Illegitimacy of the Pressure

In *The Siboen and the Sibotre*,[46] Kerr J had contrasted 'commercial pressure' (which is not sufficient to vitiate a contract) with 'coercion of the will so as to vitiate consent'. We have seen that it is misleading to say that duress involves a vitiation of consent. Moreover, 'coercion of the will' (which concentrates on the quantity or effect of the pressure) is not appropriate as the antithesis of 'commercial pressure' (which refers to the quality of the pressure). For duress to be established, there must of course be coercion of the will, in the sense that the plaintiff is made to do something he would not otherwise have done; but even the fact that the plaintiff was put under extreme pressure so that he had no choice but to submit is not enough to establish duress. In addition, the *circumstances* of the pressure need to be considered; some pressures—even over-whelming pressures—must be borne without the pressurized party having the choice later of avoiding the contract. For example, if one party to a contract threatens to exercise a power in the contract to terminate it, knowing that the other party would be placed in a

[44] However, in *Hennessy* v. *Craigmyle & Co. Ltd.* [1986] ICR 461, 468, Sir John Donaldson MR applied Lord Scarman's dictum from *Pao On* v. *Lau Yiu Long*, and said that the coerced party's will must be overborne, and his consent vitiated. *The Universe Sentinel* was not cited. See also *Atlas Express Ltd.* v. *Kafco (Importers and Distributors) Ltd.* [1989] QB 833, 841 (where Tucker J used the language of vitiation of consent) and *The Alev* [1989] 1 Lloyd's Rep. 138, 145 (where Hobhouse J thought that 'The consent of the defendants was overborne. There was a coercion of their will. They neither in law nor in fact entered into the agreement voluntarily').

[45] Relevant questions, in determining whether the pressure was so great, will be whether the person alleged to have been coerced did or did not protest; whether he had an alternative course open, such as an adequate legal remedy; whether he was independently advised; and whether he later took steps to avoid the contract: *Pau On* v. *Lau Yiu Long* [1980] AC 614, 635; *Maskell* v. *Horner* [1915] 3 KB 106; *The Siboen and the Sibotre* [1976] 1 Lloyd's Rep. 293, 336, quoted at p. 159, above. The adequacy of alterna-tive remedies appears to be tested objectively; *quaere* whether this is the best approach: see Chandler, [1989] LMCLQ 270, 275–7.

[46] [1976] 1 Lloyd's Rep. 293. See p. 159, above.

disastrous financial position if he lost the contract, the first party is acting quite lawfully: he has obtained during the bargaining process leading up to the contract the right to terminate at will. Such pressure—although constituting overwhelming pressure—would not amount to duress, precisely because it could not be described as illegitimate.[47]

The problem, then, is to draw the line between pressures which are legitimate and those which are illegitimate; and it is in the case of economic duress that such a task is most difficult and most important, because of the multitude of pressures which are exerted in commercial situations.

The only serious discussion in the cases of the concept of legitimacy of pressure is found in *The Universe Sentinel*.[48] The plaintiffs in that case owned a vessel, the *Universe Sentinel*, which was 'blacked' by the defendant union. In order to obtain the lifting of the blacking, the plaintiffs acceded to the defendant's demand for payment of $US80,000, in respect of arrears of pay for the crew and including a sum of $6,480 by way of contribution to the union welfare fund. The plaintiffs later sought to recover the $6,480.

A key factor in the decision in *The Universe Sentinel* was the context in which it arose: an alleged trade dispute. The House of Lords was divided over whether the plaintiffs were entitled to the return of the $6,480; they were not, however, divided over the principles relating to economic duress. The majority held that there was no trade dispute; this was crucial in determining that the pressure exerted by the union was illegitimate, and that the $6,480 was therefore recoverable on the ground of economic duress. Had there been a trade dispute (as the minority of the House of Lords held), the pressure would have been legitimate, and the money would have been irrecoverable.

The reason that the existence of a trade dispute was so important was because, under the Trade Union and Labour Relations Act 1974,[49] immunity is granted in tort to certain activities (which would include the blacking of vessels) conducted in the contemplation or furtherance of a trade dispute. Strictly, this immunity only applies to liability in tort; but the House of Lords regarded the statute as showing a point of public policy: the fact that immunity was granted in tort for certain actions affords

---

[47] See, however, n. 59, below.　　　　[48] [1983] 1 AC 366.
[49] See ss. 13, 14, and 29.

an indication . . . of where public policy requires that the line should be drawn between what kind of commercial pressure by a trade union upon an employer in the field of industrial relations ought to be treated as legitimised despite the fact that the will of the employer is thereby coerced, and what kind of commercial pressure in that field does amount to economic duress that entitles the employer victim to restitutionary remedies.[50]

There is little general discussion in *The Universe Sentinel* of the meaning of 'illegitimate' for the purpose of economic duress.[51] However, Lord Scarman discussed[52] the requirement:

In determining what is legitimate two matters may have to be considered. The first is as to the nature of the pressure. In many cases this will be decisive, though not in every case. And so the second question may have to be considered, namely, the nature of the demand which the pressure is applied to support.

The origin of the doctrine of duress in threats to life or limb, or to property, suggests strongly that the law regards the threat of unlawful action as illegitimate, whatever the demand. Duress can, of course, exist even if the threat is one of lawful action: whether it does so depends upon the nature of the demand.

It therefore appears that pressure may be illegitimate *either*

1. because the thing threatened is unlawful: such as a threat to injure someone, or damage their property. Presumably this category may extend, for example, to a threat to commit any crime or tort; *or*

2. because, even though the thing threatened is lawful, the way in which the pressure is exerted is illegitimate: for example, the application of the pressure itself constitutes a tort or the advantage which is sought to be obtained by the threat is illegitimate. Indeed, Lord Scarman in *The Universe Sentinel*[53] used the analogy of the crime of blackmail, where[54]

The ordinary blackmailer normally threatens to do what he has a perfect right to do—namely, communicate some compromising conduct to a person whose knowledge is likely to affect the person threatened. . . . What he has

---

[50] [1983] 1 AC 366, 385 (Lord Diplock).

[51] No doubt because the parties had agreed that, in the circumstances of the case, the Trade Union and Labour Relations Act 1974 could be used as a guide for the determination of the legitimacy of the pressure exerted by the union: see Lord Cross of Chelsea at [1983] 1 AC 366, 391

[52] Ibid., at p. 401.

[53] Ibid.

[54] *Thorne* v. *Motor Trade Association* [1937] AC 797, 806–7.

to justify is not the threat, but the demand of money. The gravamen of the charge is the demand without reasonable or probable cause: and I cannot think that the mere fact that the threat is to do something a person is entitled to do either causes that threat not to be a 'menace' within the Act[55] or in itself provides a reasonable or probable cause for the demand.

So we have only limited guidance on the circumstances in which economic pressure will be illegitimate for the purposes of duress. If the thing threatened, or the circumstances in which the pressure is exerted, amount to a crime or a tort, it appears from *The Universe Sentinel* that the coercion will be illegitimate; if the pressure was overwhelming, so as to give the coerced party no choice but to submit, then economic duress is likely to be held to have been established. Moreover, the threat of a breach of contract may be 'illegitimate', and so the question will be whether the threat was sufficiently overwhelming to constitute duress. For example, in *B & S Contracts and Design Ltd.* v. *Victor Green Publications Ltd.*[56] Kerr LJ said,

a threat to break a contract unless money is paid by the other party can, but by no means always will, constitute duress. It appears from the authorities that it will only constitute duress if the consequences of a refusal would be serious and immediate so that there is no reasonable alternative open, such as by legal redress, obtaining an injunction, etc.

This statement may imply that a threat to break a contract will always be 'illegitimate'; whether duress is established will therefore depend on the *quantum* of pressure (did it overbear the pressurized party's will?). However, it is not clear that a threat to break a contract ought of itself to be illegitimate: the way in which the threat is made ought to be highly relevant. Many proposed renegotiations of commercial contracts may be entirely reasonable, even if the party

---

[55] See now Theft Act 1968, s. 21.

[56] [1984] ICR 419, 428. See also at p. 425 (Griffiths LJ). And see *The Atlantic Baron* [1979] QB 705, 719; *The Siboen and the Sibotre* [1976] 1 Lloyd's Rep. 293, 334–5; *Atlas Express Ltd.* v. *Kafco (Importers and Distributors) Ltd.* [1989] QB 833. A threat to break a contract can constitute the tort of intimidation; indeed, 'Threatening a breach of contract may be a much more coercive weapon than threatening a tort': *Rookes* v. *Barnard* [1964] AC 1129, 1169 (Lord Reid). See also at pp. 1185–8 (Lord Evershed); 1206–7 (Lord Devlin). At p. 1209, Lord Devlin said, 'All that matters to the plaintiff is that, metaphorically speaking, a club has been used. It does not matter to the plaintiff what the club is made of—whether it is a physical club or an economic club, a tortious club or an otherwise illegal club.'

resisting renegotiation will suffer severe consequences if he refuses to consent.[57]

The cases[58] since *The Universe Sentinel* have, however, declined to lay down any further general rules relating to the meaning of 'illegitimate'.[59]

(d) The Development of the Categories of Duress

We have seen that there has been a progressive development of the law relating to duress as a vitiating factor in contract. Duress was first recognized in the form of duress to the person; then it was—more cautiously—accepted in relation to property; finally, and only recently, it has been accepted that duress to economic interests can vitiate a contract.

The courts have here been following a natural pattern of development. The physical integrity of the person has long been recognized as deserving protection; protection of property follows; commercial interests are lower down the list, and are now protected, but with considerably more caution.[60] In relation to duress to the person, it has been so obvious that such pressure cannot be tolerated, that there has been little discussion of the reason why. When we come to

[57] Cf. the facts of *Williams* v. *Roffey Bros. & Nicholls (Contractors) Ltd.* [1990] 2 WLR 1153. Birks, [1990] LMCLQ 342, 346 favours a test that a threatened breach of contract is illegitimate only if it is 'accompanied by bad faith or malice—the deliberate exploitation of difficulties of the other party'.

[58] *B & S Contracts and Design Ltd.* v. *Victor Green Publications Ltd.* [1984] ICR 419, 423 (Eveleigh LJ), 425 (Griffiths LJ); *Hennessy* v. *Craigmyle & Co. Ltd.* [1986] ICR 461; *The Alev* [1989] 1 Lloyd's Rep. 138, 145; *Atlas Express Ltd.* v. *Kafco (Importers and Distributors) Ltd.* [1989] QB 833, 841.

[59] For the question of whether a threat not to enter into a contract ought to be regarded as illegitimate, see *Restatement*, §176 Comment (f) and illustrations 13, 14; Goff and Jones, pp. 236–8; and cf. *Allen* v. *Flood* [1898] AC 1, 121 (inducing A not to contract with B is not actionable in tort because no legal right of B is infringed). Phillips J in *Dimskal Shipping Co. SA* v. *International Transport Workers' Federation, The Evia Luck (No. 2)* [1989] 1 Lloyd's Rep. 166, 180 held, in the context of industrial action, that the legitimacy of a person's conduct falls to be determined according to the law of the country in which it took place, and not on the assumption that the conduct took place in England. However, this was reversed by the Court of Appeal (Neill LJ dissenting): [1990] 1 Lloyd's Rep. 319. See also *Kaufman* v. *Gerson* [1904] 1 KB 591, 597–9.

[60] Compare, for example, the tort of negligence, which willingly protects persons and property, but has been traditionally much more reluctant in relation to economic interests: see e.g. *D & F Estates Ltd.* v. *Church Commissioners for England* [1989] AC 177; and the greater protection afforded to damage to the person than damage to property under the Unfair Contract Terms Act 1977, s. 2.

duress to economic interests, however, the effort is concentrated on why such pressure ought to vitiate a contract; and in particular on distinguishing between those pressures which can, and those which cannot, constitute duress. The emphasis has therefore in this area fallen on the concept of *legitimacy* of the pressure as a criterion for judging its legal effect.

One further issue which is not fully considered in the cases is the necessary causative link between the pressure and the contract, in the case of economic duress. We have seen[61] that in the case of duress to the person, the pressure need be only *a* reason; it need not even be the predominant reason for the coerced party entering into the contract. Duress to the person cannot, however, be tolerated at any cost, and it is natural that such a generous rule of causation should have been adopted in that context. It is not, however, clear that the same rule would be applied by the courts in the case of economic duress. Since the courts are taking a restrictive approach to economic duress, and have emphasized the requirement that the pressure should be overwhelming, giving the coerced party no choice but to act as he did, it may be that they would hold that the pressure must be more than simply *a* reason for the contract.[62]

(e) Limits to Duress

Duress makes a contract only voidable at the instance of the coerced party.[63] He may therefore affirm the contract, rather than avoid it.

---

[61] p. 154, above.

[62] Birks, *An Introduction to the Law of Restitution*, 1985, rev. 1989, pp. 179–84. *Contra, Crescendo Management Pty. Ltd.* v. *Westpac Banking Corporation* (1988) 19 NSWLR 40, 46, where McHugh JA thought that 'the proper approach . . . is to ask whether any applied pressure induced the victim to enter into the contract and then ask whether that pressure went beyond what the law is prepared to countenance as legitimate? Pressure will be illegitimate if it consists of unlawful threats or amounts to un-conscionable conduct. But the categories are not closed. Even overwhelming pressure, not amounting to unconscionable or unlawful conduct, however, will not necessarily constitute economic duress. . . . It is unnecessary, however, for the victim to prove that the illegitimate pressure was the sole reason for him entering into the contract. It is sufficient that the illegitimate pressure was one of the reasons for the person entering into the agreement.' This approach does not regard the *quantity* of pressure as having of itself any significance in economic duress. As such, it is very different from the English cases.

[63] *Director of Public Prosecutions for Northern Ireland* v. *Lynch* [1975] AC 653, 695; *The Atlantic Baron* [1979] QB 705, 719; *The Universe Sentinel* [1983] 1 AC 366, 383–4, 400. For a view that duress should render a contract void, rather than voidable, see Lanham, (1966) 29 MLR 615. The order in *Barton* v. *Armstrong* [1976] AC 104, 120 was that 'the

Affirmation in this context[64] means expressly or impliedly consenting to the continuing validity of the contract after the illegitimate pressure has ceased to operate.[65] Affirmation may be implied when the coerced party fails to protest or take any other action to avoid the contract for some time after the pressure is withdrawn.[66]

Also, since the contract is voidable after the pressure has ceased to apply, the fact that a bona fide third party has without notice of the duress obtained rights in the subject-matter of the contract will preclude rescission.[67]

deeds in question were executed by Barton under duress and are void so far as concerns him'. However, this appears only to be stating the consequence of the avoidance: i.e. after the avoidance the deeds are void; before the avoidance they were voidable (capable of being declared void, but—for the moment—valid).

[64] For affirmation in relation to misrepresentation, see pp. 95–6, above.

[65] *The Universe Sentinel* [1983] 1 AC 366, 384; *The Atlantic Baron* [1979] QB 705, 720.

[66] *The Atlantic Baron* [1979] QB 705, 720.

[67] There appears to be no authority. For such a rule in misrepresentation, see pp. 98–9, above. In the case of duress the contract is voidable at common law, rather than in equity; but the same rule relating to third party rights applies to contracts voidable at common law: *White* v. *Garden* (1851) 10 CB 919.

8

Undue Influence

We have seen in Chapter 7 that, under the category of duress, the common law allowed a remedy for wrongful pressure exerted on a contracting party, but that (until the recent development of economic duress) the remedy was limited to cases of direct pressure to the person (and, perhaps, the property) of the victim. Long before the recent extension of the law of duress into the field of pressure to economic interests, it was recognized that other pressures exerted by one contracting party on the other deserved a remedy:

what does it matter what particular form of coercion is used, so long as the will is coerced? Some persons would be more easily coerced by moral pressure ... than by the threat of physical violence. It seems to me impossible to say that it is not coercion to threaten a wife with the dishonour of her husband and children.[1]

As its name suggests, undue influence, which is a creation of equity, involves the wrongful exercise of influence by one contracting party over the other. This raises the major question: what sort of influence is wrongful, or 'undue'? We shall see that, in considering this question, equity looked primarily at the relationship between the parties: if one party was in a position of being able to exert influence over the other, his actions were scrutinized most carefully to ensure that he had not abused his position. In examining these actions, the Courts of Equity[2] developed a distinction between two categories of undue influence: *actual* influence, where the evidence demonstrated the exercise of influence; and what has often been called *presumed* influence, where the circumstances of the contract, in the context of the relationship between the parties, enabled a court to presume that influence had been exerted, although it could not be affirmatively proved on the evidence.

---

[1] *Kaufman* v. *Gerson* [1904] 1 KB 591, 597.
[2] The classic exposition is in *Allcard* v. *Skinner* (1887) 36 Ch. D. 145: see Cotton LJ at p. 171 and Lindley LJ at p. 181.

It should be noted that the equitable rules relating to undue influence are not confined to cases of contracts; the doctrine applies also to other transactions, such as gifts. Many of the cases which will be discussed in this chapter concerned gifts, rather than contracts.[3] The width of application of the doctrine of undue influence has led to some difficulties of language in expressing its underlying basis; but it has been accepted by the House of Lords that the principles of undue influence discussed in cases involving gifts do apply equally to contracts.[4]

1. 'ACTUAL' INFLUENCE

The category of 'actual' undue influence was stated by Lindley LJ in *Allcard* v. *Skinner*[5] as follows:

First, there are cases in which there has been some unfair and improper conduct, some coercion from outside, some overreaching, some form of cheating, and generally, though not always, some personal advantage obtained by a donee[6] placed in some close and confidential relation to the donor.

This makes it clear that the essence of undue influence is improper pressure or taking of advantage. The requirements of actual undue influence were stated by the Court of Appeal in *Bank of Credit and Commerce International SA* v. *Aboody*:[7]

Leaving aside proof of manifest disadvantage,[8] we think that a person relying on a plea of actual undue influence must show that (a) the other party to the transaction (or someone who induced the transaction for his own benefit) had the capacity to influence the complainant; (b) the influence was exercised; (c) its exercise was undue; (d) its exercise brought about the transaction.

A number of areas therefore need to be covered. What sort of influences can give rise to a remedy? What is meant by 'undue' in this context? Is there a requirement that the transaction, to be

---

[3] For example, the leading case of *Allcard* v. *Skinner* (1887) 36 Ch. D. 145 involved a gift, rather than a contract.

[4] *National Westminster Bank plc* v. *Morgan* [1985] AC 686, 707, 708.

[5] (1887) 36 Ch. D. 145, 181.

[6] Lindley LJ used the language of gift, because *Allcard* v. *Skinner* involved a gratuitous transaction entered into under undue influence: see text to n. 3, above.

[7] [1990] QB 923, 967.   [8] As to which, see pp. 174 ff., below.

vitiated by actual undue influence, should be 'manifestly disadvantageous' to the party seeking to set it aside? What degree of
causation is required between the influence and the entering into the
contract? The last of these—causation—will be discussed later[9] in
relation to undue influence generally. However, the other three areas
will be considered here.

(a) What Sort of Influences Vitiate a Contract?

Duress at common law was limited to direct pressure to the person
(or property). There was no remedy if the pressure was not aimed at
the person of the other contracting party (for example, a threat to
prosecute, rather than to cause physical harm to, the other party[10])
or was not even aimed directly at him (for example, a threat to
prosecute the other party's son[11]). However, such cases are covered
under the category of undue influence.

In several cases, for example, the influence has consisted of a
threat to prosecute a member of the coerced party's family;[12] it is
even enough if there is no such direct threat, but both parties know
that the purpose of entering into the contract is to prevent a
prosecution.[13] There have also been cases of actual undue influence
outside the context of threats to prosecute; for example, where a
secretary and companion obtained gifts totalling nearly £28,000 from
an 84-year-old widower;[14] or where a wife, under pressure and to get
peace from her husband, signed a charge over her home, to secure
the liabilities to a bank of a family company.[15] It is not possible to
generalize, beyond saying that the facts of each case must be considered in detail to ascertain whether one party was able to, and did,
exert some influence or pressure on the other party to enter into the
contract.

---

[9] p. 187, below.

[10] *Flower* v. *Sadler* (1882) 10 QBD 572, 576.

[11] *Williams* v. *Bayley* (1866) LR 1 HL 200. But cf. p. 153 n. 3, above.

[12] *Kaufman* v. *Gerson* [1904] 1 KB 591 (husband); *Williams* v. *Bayley* (1866) LR 1 HL
200 (son); *Mutual Finance Ltd.* v. *John Wetton & Sons Ltd.* [1937] 2 KB 389 (brother).

[13] *Mutual Finance Ltd.* v. *John Wetton & Sons Ltd.* [1937] 2 KB 389, 395. The principle
may apply outside family relationships, provided that the person coerced was in
substance influenced by the desire to prevent the prosecution of a person, and was
known and intended to be so influenced by the person exercising the influence: ibid.,
at p. 396.

[14] *Re Craig, decd.* [1971] Ch. 95.

[15] *Bank of Credit and Commerce International SA* v. *Aboody* [1990] QB 923.

(b) 'Undue'

In undue influence, as much as in the law of duress,[16] there is a problem in distinguishing between pressures which are legitimate and so must be endured by the pressurized party without his being able to escape from the contract, and pressures which are illegitimate. Much can depend on the precise way in which the pressure is applied. In *Williams* v. *Bayley*,[17] for example, a son had forged his father's signature by way of endorsement of some promissory notes. The bankers who had received the notes insisted on a settlement from the father, and the father executed a mortgage of certain property in their favour. The mortgage agreement was declared invalid on the ground of undue influence. Lord Cranworth LC explained the distinction between legitimate pressure and undue influence in that context:[18]

> it is not pressure in the sense in which a Court of equity sets aside transactions on account of pressure, if the pressure is merely this: 'If you do not do such and such an act I shall reserve all my legal rights, whether against yourself, or against your son.' If it had only been, 'if you do not take on yourself the debt of your son, we must sue you for it,' I cannot think that that amounts to pressure, when the parties are at arms' length, and particularly when, as in this case, the party supposed to be influenced by pressure had the assistance of his solicitor . . . But if what really takes place is this: If you do not assist your son, by taking on yourself the payment of these bills and notes on which there are signatures which are said, at least, to be forgeries, you must not be surprised at any course we shall take, meaning to insinuate, if not to say, we shall hold in our hands the means of criminally prosecuting him for forgery.

A threat to sue to enforce a claim—even a disputed claim—is therefore legitimate; to use evidence in one's possession of a possible criminal charge in order to exert the pressure is *not* legitimate.[19] It is taking active advantage of a superior position of knowledge, in a way which equity does not regard as fair.

For influence to be 'undue', it is not, however, necessary for it to be accompanied by malign intent: the party exerting the influence may not intend to cause any detriment to the influenced party, and

---

[16] See pp. 163 ff., above.

[17] (1866) LR 1 HL 200.

[18] Ibid., at pp. 209–10.

[19] This is similar to the test for illegitimacy of pressure in economic duress, set out by Lord Scarman in *The Universe Sentinel* [1983] 1 AC 366, 401; p. 165, above.

may believe that the contract which is entered into as a consequence of the influence is justifiable.[20] Moreover, there need be no active coercion or bullying of the sort which tends to characterize the law of duress; undue influence covers more subtle influences, which may even extend to the influence of a husband over his wife, who trusted him without questioning the contents of the documents which he asked her to sign, but where the husband deliberately used his influence and deliberately concealed the risks involved in the transactions and deprived the wife of the free use of her independent and informed judgment.[21] In such circumstances the crucial fact was that the transaction was instigated by the husband, and led to the wife being 'a mere channel through which the will of [the husband] operated'.[22]

(c) 'Manifestly Disadvantageous Transaction'

A further issue which has recently been considered in the cases is whether the transaction which is being set aside for actual undue influence must be a disadvantageous one for the victim. We shall see[23] that the requirement that the transaction be manifestly disadvantageous to the influenced party has been emphasized for the purposes of *presumed* undue influence; there, however, it is used to demonstrate that it is likely that influence has been applied. In a sense, it ought not to be necessary, where the application of influence can *actually* be shown.

However, in *Bank of Credit and Commerce International SA* v. *Aboody*,[24] the Court of Appeal held that there is a requirement of manifest disadvantage in cases of actual undue influence, just as much as in presumed influence. That decision was reached after a long consideration of the authorities and arguments of principle. The previous authorities were not binding, but were weighty. There were a number of dicta in Court of Appeal cases which had assumed that there was a requirement of manifest disadvantage;[25] and a decision

---

[20] *Bank of Credit and Commerce International SA* v. *Aboody* [1990] QB 923, 968, 970.

[21] Ibid., at pp. 967–9.

[22] Ibid., at p. 969, quoting *Tufton* v. *Sperni* [1952] 2 TLR 516, 530, 532.

[23] pp. 183–5, below.

[24] [1990] QB 923.

[25] *Coldunell Ltd.* v. *Gallon* [1986] QB 1184, 1194 (Oliver LJ); *Goldsworthy* v. *Brickell* [1987] Ch. 378, 405 (Nourse LJ); *Midland Bank plc* v. *Johns* (unreported) 30 July 1987 (Nourse LJ); *Midland Bank plc* v. *Shephard* [1988] 3 All ER 17, 22 (Neill LJ); *Bank of Baroda* v. *Shah* [1988] 3 All ER 24, 30 (Neill LJ).

of Hoffmann J to the same effect.[26] The foundation for all of these cases was the decision of the House of Lords in *National Westminster Bank plc* v. *Morgan*,[27] which had been concerned with presumed undue influence, but which contained dicta relating to undue influence generally. Lord Scarman,[28] after consideration of the judgment of Lindley LJ in *Allcard* v. *Skinner*,[29] referred to the 'need to show that the transaction is wrongful in the sense explained by Lindley LJ before the court will set aside a transaction whether relying on evidence or the presumption of the exercise of undue influence'. And he later[30] said that the 'wrongfulness of the trans-action must ... be shown: it must be one in which an unfair advantage has been taken of another'. Lindley LJ had been dis-cussing, in the passages cited by Lord Scarman, the underlying principles of undue influence, which he summed up in the term 'victimization'. Undue influence is concerned with extricating people not from transactions which they have entered into as a result of their own folly, but from transactions into which they have been forced—they have been victimized.

A transaction can of course be 'wrongful' or 'unfair' either in the sense that it has been *procured* unfairly, or in the sense that its *terms* are unfair.[31] It was not clear from Lindley LJ's judgment in *Allcard* v. *Skinner*, nor from Lord Scarman's interpretation of it in *National Westminster Bank plc* v. *Morgan*,[32] that the transaction, if entered into under actual undue influence, had to be manifestly disadvantageous to the 'victimized' party. But the decision in *Bank of Credit and Commerce International SA* v. *Aboody*, in holding that there was such a requirement, has made clear the essence of 'wrongfulness', or 'victimization' in the context of actual undue influence: it is not enough that unfair pressure has been exerted on one contracting

---

[26] *Bank of Credit and Commerce International SA* v. *Kanamia* (unreported) 6 March 1986.

[27] [1985] AC 686.

[28] Ibid., at p. 706.

[29] (1887) 36 Ch. D. 145, 182–5.

[30] [1985] AC 686, 707.

[31] *Hart* v. *O'Connor* [1985] AC 1000, 1017–18, quoted below, pp. 215–16 (Lord Brightman, who there assumed that undue influence involves unfair procurement, rather than unfair terms).

[32] There is, however, an indication in Lord Scarman's judgment ([1985] AC 686, 709) that undue influence may always involve a disadvantageous transaction: 'it is the unimpeachability at law of a disadvantageous transaction which is the starting-point from which the court advances to consider whether the transaction is the product merely of one's own folly or of the undue influence exercised by another'.

party by the other; the doctrine of undue influence is not concerned simply with setting aside contracts procured unfairly; the contract itself must in addition be unfair in its terms.

Clearly this requirement has the effect of narrowing the scope of undue influence. In particular, it narrows the usefulness of the category of actual undue influence, and tends to bring it closer to presumed influence. It is often likely to be more difficult to show that undue influence was in fact exerted than to show that the presumption has arisen.[33] If manifest disadvantage must also be shown for actual undue influence, there will often be little point in trying to establish the exercise of the influence on the evidence: let the presumption suffice.

Moreover, the shift of undue influence from protecting against unfair pressures to protecting only against such pressures which actually cause a manifestly disadvantageous transaction moves away from the rationale of other vitiating factors in the formation of contracts.[34] There is no such requirement in duress or in misrepresentation, where it is enough that the vitiating factor is present, and caused the contract, without looking also at the fairness of the bargain. Undue influence begins, therefore, to sit uncomfortably with these other areas of the law to which it ought to be related.[35]

The Court of Appeal in *Bank of Credit and Commerce International SA* v. *Aboody*[36] realized that there might be an objection that it was wrong to leave without remedy a person whose will has been

[33] See pp. 177 ff., below.

[34] This is particularly so, since the concept of a 'manifestly disadvantageous transaction' appears to be strict. It must be a disadvantage which 'would have been obvious as such to any independent and reasonable persons who considered the transaction at the time with knowledge of all the relevant facts': *Bank of Credit and Commerce International SA* v. *Aboody* [1990] QB 923, 965, approving the formulation of the trial judge. For a different view of the time at which the nature of the disadvantage is tested, see *Midland Bank plc* v. *Phillips, The Times*, 28 March 1986: neither the date of the transaction, nor the date of the result; 'the Court must look primarily at the terms of the transaction into which the parties entered. But it also looks at what has happened as an example, if the result is shown fairly to flow from the transaction, of what might happen having made such an arrangement. . . . this issue is not a pure question of law, but a mixed question of fact and law, and, as concerns the facts, a question of degree' (Ralph Gibson LJ).

[35] Particularly since the development of economic duress has brought duress closer to the ground which has traditionally been covered by actual undue influence: see pp. 158 ff., above; and cf. the facts of *Ormes* v. *Beadel* (1860) 2 Giff. 166—a case treated as undue influence, but which might nowadays be regarded as economic duress; and which was cited in *The Atlantic Baron* [1979] QB 705, 718.

[36] [1990] QB 923, 962–4.

overborne by undue influence into entering a contract, but where the contract could not be shown to be manifestly disadvantageous. Their answer was that some cases would be covered by other areas of the law—in particular, an area of law known as 'abuse of confidence', whereby a person cannot enforce a contract entered into with another with whom he is in a fiduciary or confidential relationship, unless he shows that the transaction was fair.[37] This does not, of course, adequately meet the objection that, in a similar way to duress and misrepresentation, the mere fact of the exercise of undue influence, if actually established, ought to vitiate a contract.

2. 'PRESUMED' INFLUENCE

The second category of undue influence is 'presumed' influence. Here, the circumstances of the contract, and the relative positions of the parties, are scrutinized to ascertain whether it may be presumed that one party has influenced the other; if so, the burden is on the first party to rebut that presumption by showing that there was no such influence. The two questions which must be answered are therefore: when does the presumption arise? and how is the presumption rebutted?

(a) The Presumption

There are two separate hurdles to overcome before the presumption arises: first, it must be shown that one party was in a position to influence the other; second, it must be shown that the contract was prima facie inexplicable unless influence had been exercised.

(i) The Relative Positions of the Parties

No presumption of undue influence will be found unless it appears, on the facts, that one party was in such a position that he *could have* exerted influence over the other party in entering into the contract. Cotton LJ in *Allcard* v. *Skinner*[38] spoke of the situation 'where the relations between the donor and donee have at or shortly before the execution of the gift been such as to raise a presumption that the

---

[37] *Snell's Equity*, 29th edn., 1990, p. 558. See pp. 209–10, below.
[38] (1887) 36 Ch. D. 145, 171.

donee had influence over the donor'. The purpose of the doctrine of undue influence was 'to prevent the relations which existed between the parties and the influence arising therefrom being abused'. This shows that it is crucial to examine closely the relative positions of the parties, to see whether one holds a position *vis-à-vis* the other which is capable of abuse.

There are certain generic relationships where one would expect a presumption to arise. It has even been said[39] that

there are several well defined relationships, such as parent and child, superior and member of a sisterhood, doctor and patient and solicitor and client, to which the presumption is, as it were, presumed to apply unless the contrary is proved. In such relationships it would seem that you only have to look at the relative status of the parties in order to presume that the requisite degree of trust and confidence is there.

It is certainly the case that some such relationships have attracted the presumption, apparently because of the general nature of the relationship concerned,[40] whilst there are certain other relationships which have been said not generally to attract the presumption on this basis.[41] However, it is dangerous to assume that particular relationships will, or will not, attract the presumption of undue influence. 'The relationships which may develop a dominating influence of one over another are infinitely various. There is no substitute in this branch of the law for a "meticulous examination of the facts." '[42]

[39] *Goldsworthy* v. *Brickell* [1987] Ch. 378, 401.

[40] See e.g. *Billage* v. *Southee* (1852) 9 Hare 534 (doctor and patient); *Zamet* v. *Hyman* [1961] 1 WLR 1442 (fiancé and fiancée, aged 79 and 71 respectively. Donovan LJ disagreed: 'one knows that not all engagements are idyllic affairs' (at p. 1452)); *Archer* v. *Hudson* (1844) 7 Beav. 551 (parent (or person standing *in loco parentis*) and child soon after the child reaches the age of majority).

[41] See e.g. *Bank of Montreal* v. *Stuart* [1911] AC 120, 137 (husband and wife); *National Westminster Bank plc* v. *Morgan* [1985] AC 686, 707 (banker and customer).

[42] *National Westminster Bank plc* v. *Morgan* [1985] AC 686, 709 (Lord Scarman, quoting Sir Eric Sachs in *Lloyds Bank Ltd.* v. *Bundy* [1975] QB 326, 347). See also the argument of counsel in *National Westminster Bank Plc.* v. *Morgan*, at p. 696: 'beyond the confines of certain family relationships (e.g. parent and child), it may be doubted whether the existence of a relationship that may be placed in a particular category will, without additional and special features, be treated as confidential. Thus: (i) doctor/patient. Quaere, whether the relationship is confidential as between a man with a broken wrist and the doctor who attends him at a hospital emergency department; contrast the on-going relationship that one may have with one's general practitioner. (ii) Minister of religion/adherent. Quaere, whether this will ever by itself be a relationship that is confidential; more is required, e.g. as in the relationship of confessor/penitent or one of similar "spiritual direction." '

Various phrases have been used to express the nature of the relationship between parties which gives rise to the presumption. It has been said to be where one party has had a *duty to advise* the other, or to manage his property for him,[43] or a 'duty of *fiduciary care*' towards him;[44] or where there is a *confidential relationship* between them, meaning 'a relationship wherein one party has ceded such a degree of *trust and confidence* as to require the other, on grounds of public policy, to show that it has not been betrayed or abused';[45] or where one party stands in such a *special relationship*[46] or *fiduciary relationship*[47] to the other that a presumption of undue influence arises. However, there is a danger of attaching too firm a label. Lord Scarman, in *National Westminster Bank plc* v. *Morgan*[48] criticized the use of such rigid terminology:

I believe that the Lords Justices[49] were led into a misinterpretation of the facts by their use, as is all too frequent in this branch of the law, of words and phrases such as 'confidence,' 'confidentiality,' 'fiduciary duty.' There are plenty of confidential relationships which do not give rise to the presumption of undue influence (a notable example is that of husband and wife . . .); and there are plenty of non-confidential relationships in which one person relies upon the advice of another, e.g. many contracts for the sale of goods.

Lord Scarman went on himself to use a label to describe the necessary relationship: he described it as being where a person has a 'dominating influence' over another.[50] This might appear a very narrow test, and has subsequently been criticized by the Court of Appeal.[51] It appears that Lord Scarman was simply using the phrase

---

[43] *Allcard* v. *Skinner* (1887) 36 Ch. D. 145, 181 (Lindley LJ).

[44] *Lloyds Bank Ltd.* v. *Bundy* [1975] QB 326, 340 (Sir Eric Sachs); *Horry* v. *Tate & Lyle Refineries Ltd.* [1982] 2 Lloyd's Rep. 416, 423 (Peter Pain J).

[45] *Goldsworthy* v. *Brickell* [1987] Ch. 378, 400 (Nourse LJ).

[46] *Tufton* v. *Sperni* [1952] 2 TLR 516, 530 (Jenkins LJ).

[47] *Re Craig, decd.* [1971] Ch. 95, 100 (Ungoed-Thomas J); *Tufton* v. *Sperni* [1952] 2 TLR 516, 530 (Jenkins LJ); *Tate* v. *Williamson* (1866) LR 2 Ch. App. 55, 60–1 (Lord Chelmsford LC). Cf. the obligations of disclosure which also arise in cases of fiduciary relationships: p. 91, above.

[48] [1985] AC 686, 703.

[49] i.e. in the Court of Appeal in *National Westminster Bank plc* v. *Morgan* [1983] 3 All ER 85.

[50] [1985] AC 686, 707, drawing upon *Poosathurai* v. *Kannappa Chettiar* (1919) LR 47 IA 1, a decision of the Privy Council on the Indian Contract Act 1872.

[51] *Goldsworthy* v. *Brickell* [1987] Ch. 378. In *Re Brocklehurst's Estate* [1978] Ch. 14, 41, Bridge LJ used the idea of dominance (but not in so firm a way as Lord Scarman in *Morgan*): 'If one looks at the facts of the decided cases where a presumption of undue

to describe the situation where one party is in a position to exercise influence over the other and that other naturally relies upon the first party for advice or places trust and confidence in him.[52]

The language of 'trust', 'confidence', and 'fiduciary relationship' has become common in this area as a means of expressing the equitable basis of undue influence. One cannot, however, say that, just because there is a fiduciary relationship between two parties, a presumption of influence will arise.

Fiduciary relations are of many different types; they extend from the relation of myself to an errand boy who is bound to bring me back my change up to the most intimate and confidential relations which can possibly exist between one party and another where the one is wholly in the hands of the other because of his infinite trust in him.[53]

Undue influence has often been presumed in cases where there is a fiduciary relationship for the simple reason that the relationship very often involves one person being in a position to influence the other;[54] but simply to find a fiduciary relationship on general equitable principles[55] is not sufficient. The particular facts of the case must be examined to see whether the nature of the fiduciary relationship justifies the interference of the court.[56] It may be helpful to consider some particular cases.

It is obvious that the respective characters of the two parties will be very important in determining the influence which one may be

---

influence has been held to arise, the typical features characterising the relationships are, first, a duty on the donee to advise the donor, secondly, a position of actual or potential dominance of the donor by the donee, and thirdly a measure of confidence and trust reposed by the donor in the donee. This third characteristic is, no doubt, always present and this accounts for frequent reference to relationships giving rise to the presumption as fiduciary relationships.'

[52] [1987] Ch. 378, 416 (Parker LJ). The earlier cases did not require 'domination'—in the sense in which it might commonly be understood; 'it would run contrary to human experience to presume that every patient is dominated by his doctor or every client by his solicitor': [1987] Ch. 378, 404 (Nourse LJ). In *Tufton* v. *Sperni* [1952] 2 TLR 516, 520, for example, Evershed MR said that undue influence 'includes, as a matter of law, both undue influence in the sense of domination of one over another, and also abuse of the duties of care and confidence which may be imposed on one party towards another as a result of the particular relationship which emerges from the special circumstances of their association'.

[53] *Re Coomber* [1911] 1 Ch. 723, 728 (Fletcher Moulton LJ).

[54] *Smith* v. *Kay* (1859) 7 HLC 750, 771.

[55] See Hanbury and Maudsley, *Modern Equity*, 13th edn., 1989, pp. 565 ff.

[56] *Re Coomber* [1911] 1 Ch. 723, 729.

presumed to have over the other. If there is a gift made by a 'strong-willed, autocratic and generous man, whom [the donee] liked, respected and looked up to as a social superior' the court is unlikely to hold that there is a relationship of trust and confidence which gives rise to a presumption of influence by the donee.[57] However, if the donee is 'a middle-aged woman at the height of her powers . . . markedly able and competent, of a managing disposition and strong personality; . . . physically and mentally tough and powerful, and combines these formidable qualities with a charming manner', and the donor is an 84-year-old widower, who is 'dependent on [the donee] for his comforts and emotionally for her companionship and for her participation in his business affairs . . . a failing and vulnerable old man', the relationship will give rise to a presumption of influence by the donee.[58]

Other cases have scrutinized the relationship between the parties to see what opportunity was available to one party to take advantage of the other. For example, where the donee was the lady superior of a sisterhood, and the donor was a member of the sisterhood who had bound herself to observe the rules of the sisterhood, including rules obliging her to regard the voice of the superior as the voice of God, and not to seek advice of any extern without the superior's leave, the relationship gave rise to the presumption of influence.[59] And a doctor was said to be in a relation of confidence with his patient when he extracted a promissory note for an excessive sum 'when the patient's position in life was about to be changed',[60] in that his daughter was to marry a nobleman of high rank, and so would come into a fortune.

Even though certain generic relationships have been said generally not to give rise to the presumption, the courts still scrutinize the facts to ascertain whether the parties have gone beyond the regular confines of the relationship, and put themselves

[57] *Re Brocklehurst's Estate* [1978] Ch. 14, 36.

[58] *Re Craig, decd.* [1971] Ch. 95, 107, 119–20. Indeed, the facts were so strong that the judge would have been prepared to hold that there was *actual* undue influence.

[59] *Allcard* v. *Skinner* (1887) 36 Ch. D. 145. It is too simplistic to say that the presumption arose from the generic relationship of superior and member of a sisterhood; the Court examined closely the *particular* rules by which the member was bound to ascertain the nature of the relationship between the donor and donee: see Lindley LJ at pp. 184–5.

[60] *Billage* v. *Southee* (1852) 9 Hare 534, 540.

into a position of trust or confidence.[61] An area where this has arisen in particular is the relationship of banker and customer. Such a relationship does not ordinarily give rise to the presumption; it is a commercial relationship, where the parties are dealing at arm's length, with their own separate interests to protect. In the ordinary course of banking business, a banker can therefore explain the nature of a proposed transaction to his customer without laying himself open to a charge of undue influence.[62] However, a banker may go further and advise on more general matters germane to the wisdom of the transaction, and he may therefore begin to cross the line into the area of confidentiality; the court must examine all the facts, including the history of the transaction, to ascertain whether or not that line has been crossed.[63]

It is important, however, always to bear in mind that the particular relationship between the parties must be scrutinized to ascertain whether the transaction ought to be regarded as vitiated. Jenkins LJ in *Tufton* v. *Sperni*[64] warned against an inadequate examination of the relationship:

It would, of course, be wrong to work backwards from the undeniable fact of an unconscionable bargain and endeavour to construct some fiduciary

[61] One relationship which is said not to give rise to the presumption is that of husband and wife, because of the special nature of that relationship; 'in the case of husband and wife the burden of proving undue influence lies upon those who allege it': *Bank of Montreal* v. *Stuart* [1911] AC 120, 137. However, in *Simpson* v. *Simpson* [1989] Fam. Law 20, Morritt J held (*obiter*) that, on the facts, a husband was presumed to have been influenced by his wife in certain transfers of property he made in her favour during a serious illness shortly before his death. Morritt J recognized that the relationship of husband and wife did not as such give rise to any presumption of undue influence, but thought that a presumption might arise from special circumstances of illness or dependency, provided that consideration was given to the donor's own likely feelings and intentions as a spouse of the donee, and the extent to which the impugned transactions were disadvantageous to the spouse donor. Crucial facts were: (1) the husband's reducing mental capacity; (2) his increasing dependence on his wife; (3) the effect of the transfers on the dispositions made under his will; (4) the transfers were not in keeping with his normal pattern of behaviour; and (5) he did not consult, or even inform, his solicitor and friend of many years' standing.

[62] *National Westminster Bank plc* v. *Morgan* [1985] AC 686, 707. See also *Horry* v. *Tate & Lyle Refineries Ltd.* [1982] 2 Lloyd's Rep. 416: an insurer was presumed to have influenced a claimant under an insurance policy, where the claimant was known by the insurer to be relying on the insurer's agent in settling the claim, instead of taking separate legal advice.

[63] *Lloyds Bank Ltd.* v. *Bundy* [1975] QB 326, 347 (Sachs LJ), approved in *National Westminster Bank plc* v. *Morgan* [1985] AC 686, 708–9. In the former case it was held that the bank had 'crossed the line'; in the latter, it had not.

[64] [1952] 2 TLR 516, 530.

relationship between the parties on the strength of which to set it aside. That is a temptation which must be firmly resisted. It must be shown that the transaction in question did in fact arise out of some special relationship between the parties and that the relationship was a fiduciary one. Moreover, it must be shown not merely that there was a fiduciary relationship of some sort, but that the fiduciary relationship was of such a character as to warrant the interference of the Court: *Re Coomber*.[65]

(ii) The Nature of the Contract: 'Manifestly Disadvantageous'

Even if the relationship between the parties is such that the presumption of influence arises, the presumption is not perfected until there is a contract entered into, within the context of that relationship, which is of such a nature that it is prima facie explicable only on the basis that the influence was exerted. Although influence might be presumed before such a contract, it is only then that it is presumed to be *undue*.[66]

There have been various expressions used to describe the necessary type of contract. Lindley LJ in *Allcard* v. *Skinner*[67] said that if a small gift is made to a person standing in a confidential relation to a donor, it is not sufficient to presume that the influence has been exerted; what is necessary is a gift 'so large as not to be reasonably accounted for on the ground of friendship, relationship, charity, or other ordinary motives on which ordinary men act'.

Allcard v. *Skinner* involved a gift, rather than a contract.[68] The fact that undue influence embraces gifts, as well as contracts, has given particular problems in the terminology to be used to describe the necessary type of transaction; for example, it cannot be appropriate to require an 'unequal bargain' for the simple reason that in cases of gift there is no bargain.[69] In cases of contract, where *ex hypothesi* there must be some consideration given to the party who seeks to avoid the contract on the ground of undue influence, the relative unfairness to him of the bargain is a natural criterion to consider.

---

[65] [1911] 1 Ch. 723; n. 56, above.

[66] *Goldsworthy* v. *Brickell* [1987] Ch. 378, 401. The emphasis appears to be on *disadvantage* to the person seeking to avoid the contract, rather than *advantage* to the other; undue influence 'is not confined to those cases in which the influence is exerted to secure a benefit for the person exerting it'—it also applies if the benefit is conferred on a third party: *Bullock* v. *Lloyds Bank Ltd.* [1955] Ch. 317, 324.

[67] (1887) 36 Ch. D. 145, 185.

[68] See text to n. 3, above.

[69] *National Westminster Bank plc* v. *Morgan* [1985] AC 686, 708.

And it may be that in contracts the disparity of benefits will need to be more obvious than in the case of gifts, because of the policy rule in the law of contract that the courts are reluctant to enquire into the adequacy of consideration given by each party.[70] However, whether the transaction be a contract or a gift, the underlying principle is the same: does the substance of the transaction suggest that undue influence may have been exerted by one party against the other, given that the parties are in such a relationship that influence could have been exerted?

This test is not objective; the transaction which is alleged to be vitiated must be looked at bearing in mind the particular character and attitudes of the party entering into it. Where, for example, an 87-year-old man, who had been deserted by his wife, made very large gifts to a friend and helper, the gifts were allowed to stand; the old man's character was crucial in determining that there was no influence exerted on him; he was a wealthy man without an heir; he was strong-willed, autocratic, and generous. His character therefore served to explain why so large a gift was made, and the fact that a hypothetical ordinary man would not have been expected to act in such a way was irrelevant.[71]

More recently, the expression used by the House of Lords to describe the nature of the transaction is 'manifestly disadvantageous'. In *National Westminster Bank plc* v. *Morgan*,[72] Lord Scarman made it clear that there is a requirement of manifest disadvantage;[73] and that the purpose of such a requirement is to bridge the evidential gap to establish the exercise of influence:

I know of no reported authority where the transaction set aside was not to the manifest disadvantage of the person influenced. It would not always be a

---

[70] Treitel, pp. 58–9.

[71] *Re Brocklehurst's Estate* [1978] Ch. 14, 39–40. See also *Petrou* v. *Woodstead Finance Ltd.* [1986] FLR 158 (short-term loan at an annual interest rate of 42% was not manifestly disadvantageous because finance was needed urgently and the borrower's payment record was poor).

[72] [1985] AC 686, 704.

[73] For the purpose served by a requirement of 'manifest disadvantage' in *actual* undue influence, see pp. 174 ff., above. Notice that the language of 'manifest disadvantage' is rather stronger than that used by Lindley LJ in *Allcard* v. *Skinner* (a gift 'so large as not to be reasonably accounted for . . .'); the disadvantage has to be obvious: *Bank of Credit and Commerce International SA* v. *Aboody* [1990] QB 923, 965, n. 34, above. In consequence, the House of Lords in *National Westminster Bank plc* v. *Morgan* appeared to be narrowing the law of undue influence—at least in relation to presumed influence.

gift: it can be a 'hard and inequitable' agreement (*Ormes* v. *Beadel*[74]); or a transaction 'immoderate and irrational' (*Bank of Montreal* v. *Stuart*[75]) or 'unconscionable' in that it was a sale at an undervalue (*Poosathurai* v. *Kannappa Chettiar*[76]). Whatever the legal character of the transaction, the authorities show that it must constitute a disadvantage sufficiently serious to require evidence to rebut the presumption that in the circumstances of the relationship between the parties it was procured by the exercise of undue influence.

This emphasizes the purpose of the presumption: although it is not possible to establish actual influence on the evidence, the combination of the relationship between the parties and the nature of the transaction leads one to believe that there must have been some undue influence applied. It is therefore clear that the equitable jurisdiction in relation to undue influence is not aimed simply at preventing unfair bargains, or at preventing transactions between parties in particular types of relationship; it is aimed at preventing the active, wrongful application of pressure or influence: the presumption is simply a tool to be used to establish such pressure or influence. 'It is not a vague "public policy" but specifically the victimisation of one party by the other.'[77]

(b) Rebutting the Presumption

Once the presumption has arisen, the burden is on the person who is presumed to have exerted the influence to show that he did not abuse his position, and that the transaction was not brought about by any undue influence on his part.[78] There have been numerous statements in the cases on what must be shown in order to discharge this burden; in essence, it is that the transaction was the

---

[74] (1860) 2 Giff. 166, 174 (a case, however, of *actual* influence).

[75] [1911] AC 120, 137.

[76] (1919) LR 47 IA 1, 3–4.

[77] *National Westminster Bank plc* v. *Morgan* [1985] AC 686, 705, drawing upon *Allcard* v. *Skinner* (1887) 36 Ch. D. 145, 182–3. See p. 175, above; p. 196, below. The language of 'victimization' may be too strong: cf. the criticism of the language of 'domination' by the Court of Appeal in *Goldsworthy* v. *Brickell* [1987] Ch. 378; p. 179, above. On the presumption as simply 'a tool of the lawyer's trade' in this context, see *Bank of Credit and Commerce International SA* v. *Aboody* [1990] QB 923, 964, quoting Bridge LJ in *Re Brocklehurst's Estate* [1978] Ch. 14, 43.

[78] *Allcard* v. *Skinner* (1887) 36 Ch. D. 145, 181 (Lindley LJ).

spontaneous act of the party concerned, acting under circumstances which enabled him to exercise an independent will.[79]

This burden is not easy to discharge. It will already have been established that the contracting party *could* have been unduly influenced; the party alleged to have exercised the influence is required to prove a negative—that he did *not* influence. It is in general difficult to show what did and did not influence a person in entering into a contract.[80] However, there are certain indications to which one can look in order to demonstrate the absence of influence. In particular, one can see whether the party seeking to avoid the contract obtained independent advice on the transaction before he entered into it; and it may well be prudent for a party who is at risk of being held to be presumed to influence the other to *advise* the other to obtain independent advice.[81]

If a person alleging that he was subject to undue influence obtained independent advice,[82] it may be clear that he was choosing to enter the contract of his own free will, after at least the chance to make an informed decision on its merits. Such advice must, however, be given with the knowledge of all the relevant circumstances and must be such as a competent and honest adviser would give. Where, therefore, a widow, before executing a deed of gift of valuable property in favour of her nephew, consulted an independent lawyer but the lawyer did not know one crucial fact— that the property involved was almost the whole of the property she owned—the presumption that the nephew had exerted undue influence was not rebutted.[83]

---

[79] Ibid., at p. 171 (Cotton LJ). A more concise test is whether the transaction was entered into 'only after full, free and informed thought about it': *Zamet* v. *Hyman* [1961] 1 WLR 1442, 1446 (Lord Evershed MR); *Goldsworthy* v. *Brickell* [1987] Ch. 378, 408.

[80] See p. 83, above.

[81] Cf. *Kings North Trust Ltd.* v. *Bell* [1986] 1 WLR 119, 125. However, it will generally not be appropriate to require the party presumed to exert influence to take steps to ensure that independent advice is actually taken: *Coldunell Ltd.* v. *Gallon* [1986] QB 1184, 1201, 1208–9.

[82] 'Advice' does not mean that the adviser tells the person whether they should or should not do it; 'a solicitor best gives advice when he takes care that the client understands fully the nature of the act and the consequences of that act . . . It is for adult persons of competent mind to decide whether they will do an act, and I do not think that independent and competent advice means independent and competent approval': *Re Coomber* [1911] 1 Ch. 723, 729–30.

[83] *Inche Noriah* v. *Shaik Allie Bin Omar* [1929] AC 127.

Independent legal advice is not the only way in which the presumption can be rebutted; it may be advice which is not from a lawyer, but some other person who is independent and capable of explaining the nature and effect of the proposed transaction;[84] or there may be no advice at all, but evidence which shows that the party in question entered into the transaction freely without being influenced by the other.[85] Moreover, the fact that the party did not *follow* the independent advice does not prevent the presumption from being rebutted; as long as the advice was given, the party had the means of making an informed choice.[86]

3. CAUSATION

A further question is, what test of causation should be used for undue influence? Should the influenced party have to show that the influence caused him to enter into the contract? And should it be, for example, *a* reason? Or the *overriding* reason?

We have seen that it is often difficult to show why one concluded a contract; and that the courts in other contexts have therefore adopted tests favourable to the party seeking to avoid the contract. In misrepresentation, for example,[87] the representor has the burden of disproving reliance by the representee on his statement; and in duress to the person[88] the duress need only be *a* cause and the burden of disproving causation is on the party who has applied the illegitimate pressure.

One would expect the courts to be similarly generous to the person who enters a contract under undue influence. In the case of presumed influence, the question is not generally posed using the language of causation, but in effect the rebutting of the presumption requires the party presumed to have exercised the influence to prove that he did not, by abuse of his position, cause the contract. In relation to actual influence, the Court of Appeal in *Bank of Credit and Commerce International SA* v. *Aboody*[89] took the view that influence

---

[84] Ibid., at p. 135.

[85] *Re Brocklehurst's Estate* [1978] Ch. 14.

[86] *Inche Noriah* v. *Shaik Allie Bin Omar* [1929] AC 127, 135.

[87] pp. 82–3, above.

[88] pp. 154–5, above. There is, however, some doubt whether such a generous test will be used in economic duress: see p. 168, above.

[89] [1990] QB 923, 970–1.

will not vitiate a contract in a case where the evidence establishes that on the balance of probabilities the complainant would have entered into the transaction in any event. But this does not prove that the contract was not made because of the threats.[90] It does not specify the test of causation, nor the burden of proof.

4. UNDUE INFLUENCE AND THIRD PARTIES

Assume that there is a contract between A and B. There is no evidence (nor even any presumption) that A exerted undue influence against B. However, there is evidence (or an unrebutted presumption) that C exerted such influence. Can B use this to avoid the contract with A?

One's first reaction may be that B ought not to be able to avoid the contract. Whatever pressures B was under from other parties was nothing to do with A, and it would be wrong to make A's contract depend on them. This very statement contains, however, the basis of a principle which can be developed. It is right to say that A should not be affected provided that the pressure by C *was nothing to do with him*. The question therefore becomes, in what circumstances ought A to shoulder any responsibility for C's actions?

We shall see that the courts have developed rules to answer this. In the first place, A may be held to be responsible for the influence if C, in applying the influence, was acting as his agent; in the second place he may not have any personal responsibility for the influence, but he may be unable to take advantage of the contract with B if he knows about it, or is a volunteer.

(a) Agency

A number of cases have used the concept of agency to hold a contracting party responsible for the undue influence of a third party. For example, in *Kings North Trust Ltd.* v. *Bell*,[91] a lender's solicitors sent to the borrower's solicitors documents to obtain a charge to secure a loan. The security was to be given not only by the borrower, but also by his wife; the borrower's solicitors were asked

[90] Cf. *Barton* v. *Armstrong* [1976] AC 104, 121H.
[91] [1986] 1 WLR 119.

by the lender's solicitors to arrange for the wife to execute the documents; the solicitors allowed the borrower to take the documents home for his wife's signature. The lender was held to be affected by the influence which the husband exerted against his wife in obtaining her signature on the documents. Dillon LJ said,[92]

On the general law of principal and agent, the principal (the creditor), however personally innocent, who instructs an agent (the husband) to achieve a particular end (the signing of the document by the wife) is liable for any fraudulent misrepresentation[93] made by the agent in achieving that end.

If C is acting generally as A's agent in relation to the transaction, A will be bound on normal principles of agency by C's actions within his actual or ostensible authority. If, however, C is not acting as such a general agent the question is whether C was none the less an agent for the particular purpose of obtaining B's agreement to the contract in question. *Kings North Trust Ltd.* v. *Bell* was an application of a narrow principle established in *Turnbull & Co.* v. *Duval,*[94] that if a creditor, or potential creditor, of a husband desires to obtain, by way of security for the husband's indebtedness, a guarantee from his wife or a charge on property of his wife, and if the creditor entrusts to the husband himself the task of obtaining the execution of the relevant documents by the wife, then the creditor can be in no better position than the husband himself, and the creditor cannot enforce the guarantee or the security against the wife if it is established that the execution of the document by the wife was procured by undue influence of the husband, and the wife had no independent advice.[95] A phrase which was used in *Turnbull & Co.* v. *Duval,*[96] which has been applied in a number of later cases[97] is 'they left everything to [the agent], and must abide the consequences'. If, therefore, in our example, A 'left everything to' C, and it was in the context of action

[92] Ibid., at p. 124.
[93] The undue influence was bound up with misrepresentations, on the facts: the wife knew that she was signing a charge over her home, but the husband misled her about the purpose of the loan. See also *Avon Finance Co. Ltd.* v. *Bridger* [1985] 2 All ER 281.
[94] [1902] AC 429.
[95] *Kings North Trust Ltd.* v. *Bell* [1986] 1 WLR 119, 123.
[96] [1902] AC 429, 435 (Lord Lindley, giving the judgment of the Privy Council).
[97] See e.g. *Chaplin & Co. Ltd.* v. *Brammall* [1908] 1 KB 233, 237–8; *Avon Finance Co. Ltd.* v. *Bridger* [1985] 2 All ER 281, 288; *Bank of Baroda* v. *Shah* [1988] 3 All ER 24, 29; *Bank of Credit and Commerce International SA* v. *Aboody* [1990] QB 923, 973.

taken by C within that authority given by A that C exerted the undue influence, B can use the fact of influence to avoid the contract with A.

This situation appears, however, to have arisen in a fairly narrow factual context. *Kings North Trust Ltd.* v. *Bell* and *Turnbull & Co.* v. *Duval* both concerned the influence of a husband over his wife.[98] The argument that the principle is limited to spouses was rejected in *Avon Finance Co. Ltd.* v. *Bridger*,[99] where it was applied to influence by 'a son in the prime of life' over 'parents in the evening of life'; the basis of the principle was that the relationship was such that it should be appreciated that the possibility of influence exists; therefore the 'principal' ought to realize that the 'agent' may exert influence.[100]

Whether such a relationship exists, and such agency can be established, will depend on the facts. The key question is what the contracting party, A, did to justify holding that the wrongful acts of the third party, C, should affect him.[101] If, therefore, C is not to the knowledge of A involved in obtaining B's consent to the contract, A cannot fairly be said to be affected by C's actions.[102] The cases in which A has been held to be affected all involved conscious acts of, or consent to, delegation by the creditor (or an agent for whom the creditor was responsible) to the fraudulent agent, associated with a subjective intention that he (or his agent) should be involved in obtaining the signature of the debtor or surety.[103]

(b) Notice; Volunteers

It is important to remember that remedies for undue influence were

---

[98] As also did *Chaplin & Co. Ltd.* v. *Brammall*, n. 97, above.

[99] [1985] 2 All ER 281.

[100] Ibid., at p. 288. This presumption of influence contrasts with the usual rule in undue influence that there is no presumption of influence in a transaction *between* husband and wife: *Bank of Montreal* v. *Stuart* [1911] AC 120, n. 61, above; *Midland Bank plc* v. *Shephard* [1988] 3 All ER 17, 21–2; *Barclays Bank plc* v. *Kennedy* [1989] 1 FLR 356, 364.

[101] *Bank of Credit and Commerce International SA* v. *Aboody* [1990] QB 923, 972–3.

[102] *Coldunell Ltd.* v. *Gallon* [1986] QB 1184; *Midland Bank plc* v. *Perry* [1988] 1 FLR 161. However, B may have other remedies against A; for example, for damages in the tort of negligence, if A owed B a duty of care: *Midland Bank plc* v. *Perry*.

[103] *Coldunell Ltd.* v. *Gallon* [1986] QB 1184, 1209. The fact that the debtor/surety signs the document in question in the presence of the creditor does not prevent the principle applying, if the creditor left it to the agent to obtain the presence of the debtor/surety to execute the document, and the meeting is only a formality: *Barclays Bank plc* v. *Kennedy* [1989] 1 FLR 356.

developed by the Courts of Equity; the principles of undue influence have therefore traditionally used the language and concepts of equity. Even in relation to the principles of agency, discussed in the previous section, it has been said that the underlying basis of allowing a party to a contract to rely on influence exerted by the other party's agent is linked to the equitable nature of undue influence, rather than the general principles of the law of agency: 'it would be inconsistent with the equitable nature of the relief for the bank not to be affected by the undue influence exerted by its agent when the transaction would not exist but for the wrongful acts of its agent'.[104]

Similarly, applying the usual principles of equity relating to third parties, the cases have taken the position that—again using the example set out above[105]—if A has notice of the undue influence exerted by C, or if he is a volunteer, he cannot rely on the transaction against B.

Several cases[106] have dealt with notice. The rule is that, if A, at the time of entering into the contract, has actual or constructive notice of the undue influence by C, he cannot enforce the contract against B, if B seeks to rely on the influence as a defence: 'an equity is raised against [A] irrespective of any question of agency'.[107] A must have notice either (in the case of actual influence) of the circumstances alleged to constitute the actual exercise of the undue influence; or (in the case of presumed influence) of the circumstances from which the presumption of undue influence is alleged to arise.[108]

It has also been held, on the usual equitable principles,[109] that a volunteer could not take advantage of the transaction; a bona fide

---

[104] *Bank of Credit and Commerce International SA* v. *Aboody* [1990] QB 923, 972.

[105] p. 188.

[106] e.g. *Lancashire Loans Ltd.* v. *Black* [1934] 1 KB 380; *O'Sullivan* v. *Management Agency and Music Ltd.* [1985] QB 428; *Bank of Credit and Commerce International SA* v. *Aboody* [1990] QB 923.

[107] *Bank of Credit and Commerce International SA* v. *Aboody* [1990] QB 923, 973.

[108] Ibid. The fact that constructive notice is included means that A need not know in fact of these circumstances. The cases have not, however, discussed in detail the degree to which such knowledge will be attributed to him, although the Court of Appeal in *Bank of Credit and Commerce International SA* v. *Aboody* [1990] QB 923, 974, appeared to think that constructive notice would be established if the party had 'any reason to suspect it'. *Lancashire Loans Ltd.* v. *Black* and *O'Sullivan* v. *Management Agency and Music Ltd.*, n. 106 above, both concerned *actual* knowledge of circumstances (actual and presumed influence, respectively).

[109] *Snell's Equity*, p. 47.

purchaser of the subject-matter of the contract for value without notice is therefore not affected:[110]

against whom does this inference of undue influence operate? Clearly it operates against the person who is able to exercise the influence . . . and, in my judgment, it would operate against every volunteer who claimed under him, and also against every person who claimed under him with notice of the equity thereby created, or with notice of the circumstances from which the Court infers the equity. But, in my judgment, it would operate against no others.

5. RESTRICTIONS ON RELIEF

Undue influence makes a contract not void, but voidable.[111] Moreover, it is an equitable principle. The contract is not therefore automatically set aside, and the ability of a party who has been subjected to undue influence to avoid the contract may be restricted by the court. Three particular heads of restriction on the right to avoid a contract for undue influence must be mentioned: affirmation of the contract (with which must be considered delay and estoppel); the intervention of third party rights; and the impossibility of restitution.

(a) Affirmation, Delay, and Estoppel

The essence of undue influence is unfair influence or pressure by one party over the other, at the time of making the contract. If the influenced party is to be allowed to avoid the contract, he must make objection to the contract at the earliest possible moment, otherwise he may be held to have acquiesced in, or affirmed, the contract.

The question is, what is the 'earliest possible moment'? There have been differing expressions of this in the cases. All have, however, taken as their starting-point a principle similar to that employed in the law of duress,[112] that the influenced party is not required to make objection on the ground of undue influence before the influence has ceased to operate.[113] It is not necessary that there should be objection, or that the influenced party should seek to

[110] *Bainbrigge* v. *Browne* (1881) 18 Ch. D. 188, 196–7. See also *Midland Bank plc* v. *Perry* [1988] 1 FLR 161, 167; *Huguenin* v. *Baseley* (1807) 14 Ves. Jun. 273.
[111] *Allcard* v. *Skinner* (1887) 36 Ch. D. 145, 186.
[112] See p. 169, above.
[113] *Mutual Finance Ltd.* v. *John Wetton & Sons Ltd.* [1937] 2 KB 389, 397.

avoid the contract, as soon as it has been made; it is only when he has regained his freedom from the influence that he must act.

Some cases have said that the influenced party must object as soon as the influence ceases to operate;[114] others that the objection must be within a reasonable time thereafter.[115] What all the cases are striving for is a principle under which it would be inequitable to allow the influenced party to set aside the transaction.[116] Nothing which he says or does whilst the influence is still being exerted can affect his ability to avoid the contract. Once he regains his freedom from influence, however, his words and actions must be carefully scrutinized. If he then says unequivocally that he chooses not to take objection to the contract on the ground of undue influence, he will be held to have affirmed the contract, and cannot thereafter change his mind. Short of such an explicit statement, however, the question is whether he can be held to have impliedly affirmed the contract. If it can be shown that he knows of his right to avoid the contract,[117] his failure to object quickly may constitute evidence of affirmation.[118]

One should add that the language simply of delay, or of estoppel, is sometimes used in this context. It may be that delay, if sufficiently long, would prevent avoidance of the contract;[119] or that an influenced party's delay may be so long as reasonably to induce the other party to think, and to act to his detriment upon the belief that, the transaction will not be impugned, so that the influenced party may be estopped from objecting.[120]

---

[114] Ibid.   [115] *Allcard* v. *Skinner* (1887) 36 Ch. D. 145, 187.

[116] *Goldsworthy* v. *Brickell* [1987] Ch. 378, 416.

[117] This is a prerequisite: *Allcard* v. *Skinner* (1887) 36 Ch. D. 145, 174; *Peyman* v. *Lanjani* [1985] Ch. 457. See also pp. 95–6, above. An awareness that one might have rights, coupled with a deliberate decision not to enquire what one's rights are or to act upon them, will also be treated as affirmation: *Allcard* v. *Skinner* (1887) 36 Ch. D. 145, 192.

[118] *Allcard* v. *Skinner* (1887) 36 Ch. D. 145, 187.

[119] Ibid., at p. 186 (Lindley LJ, referring to the analogy of the Statute of Limitations (6 years)); Cotton LJ, however, expressed the view that 'delay in asserting rights cannot be in equity a defence unless the Plaintiff were aware of her rights': ibid., at p. 174. Bowen LJ (at p. 191) expressed the view that delay in itself is not a bar. Cf. delay as a bar to rescission for misrepresentation: pp. 96–8, above.

[120] *Allcard* v. *Skinner* (1887) 36 Ch. D. 145, 192 (Bowen LJ); there must, however, be a representation (by words or conduct) that the right to avoid the contract would not be enforced: *Goldsworthy* v. *Brickell* [1987] Ch. 378, 410–11. It may be that a true estoppel (with detrimental reliance by the representee) ought not to be necessary: simply an 'objective' interpretation of the words or conduct of the influenced party as showing an intention to affirm the contract: cf. *Smith* v. *Hughes* (1871) LR 6 QB 597; *The Hannah Blumenthal* [1983] 1 AC 854; pp. 13–15, above.

(*b*) Third Party Rights

We have seen that, as a general rule, the courts hold that a voidable contract may be avoided only so long as a third party has not bona fide obtained for value rights in the subject-matter of the contract; if such a third party has obtained rights, his rights are preferred over the right of the influenced party to avoid the contract, and the contract is thereafter incapable of avoidance.[121]

In the context of undue influence this bar to avoidance applies. We have already seen[122] that a third party who acquires rights under the contract cannot be in a better position than the influencer—and so takes his rights subject to their being withdrawn if the influenced party wishes to avoid the contract on the ground of undue influence—if the third party is either a volunteer, or has notice of the influence. The corollary of this is that a third party who takes for value, and without notice of the influence, is not subject to his rights subsequently being taken away.

(*c*) Impossibility of Restitution

If the contract is avoided for undue influence, it is rescinded *ab initio*;[123] this involves the unwinding of the transaction, and the restitution by each party of his receipts from the other under the terms of the contract. A problem can therefore arise if it is not possible to restore *in specie* those receipts. It appears, however, that the courts will take a relaxed attitude to the requirement of restitution, and will still order the contract to be rescinded if 'practical justice' can be achieved between the parties.[124] This is because principles of equity are being applied, and in particular because a breach of a fiduciary relationship is involved in many cases of undue influence.[125] In order to achieve 'practical justice' it has been accepted that the courts may impose terms on a decree of

---

[121] See p. 98, above.

[122] pp. 190–2, above.

[123] This is the same as rescission in the case of misrepresentation: see p. 68, above.

[124] *O'Sullivan* v. *Management Agency and Music Ltd.* [1985] QB 428, 458. The law of misrepresentation has been rather more developed in relation to this issue: see pp. 93–5, above.

[125] On the question of whether it is right to use the terminology of fiduciary relationships in undue influence, see p. 180, above.

rescission for undue influence, and that the terms imposed may require the influencer to account to the influenced party for any profits he has made, whilst also awarding him compensation for any work he has performed pursuant to the transaction.[126]

6. RATIONALE OF UNDUE INFLUENCE

There remains the question of what underlying principles may be detected in the law of undue influence. One word which has been used a great deal in the cases is 'unconscionable'. A person who has obtained a contract by influence over the other party which is in fact *undue* influence, cannot *in conscience* be allowed to take advantage of it. Adopting such terminology does not provide an easy solution to an issue of undue influence, because there is no simple meaning to the word 'unconscionable';[127] however, it does show the underlying idea of undue influence. There is perhaps more emphasis than in duress on why the influencer should not be allowed to take advantage of the contract, and less on the impact which the influence had on the consent of the other party. It is clear that the way in which undue influence operates is similar to duress: it does not involve an absence of consent by the influenced party, but because advantage has been—or is presumed to have been—taken the transaction cannot stand, even though the influenced party may have consented. 'The question is, not, whether [the influenced party] knew what [he] was doing, had done, or proposed to do, but how the intention was produced.'[128]

One key point about undue influence is that it is not a doctrine designed to vitiate contracts simply because they are unfair, or are entered into between parties in particular relationships deserving of protection.[129] The essence of undue influence is that the position has

---

[126] *O'Sullivan* v. *Management Agency and Music Ltd.* [1985] QB 428, 458, 464–8, where cases dealing with profits acquired by a fiduciary in breach of his fiduciary duty were relied upon: *Regal (Hastings) Ltd.* v. *Gulliver* [1967] 2 AC 134; *Boardman* v. *Phipps* [1967] 2 AC 46.

[127] 'Definition is a poor instrument when used to determine whether a transaction is or is not unconscionable: this is a question which depends upon the particular facts of the case': *National Westminster Bank plc* v. *Morgan* [1985] AC 686, 709 (Lord Scarman).

[128] *Huguenin* v. *Baseley* (1807) 14 Ves. Jun. 273, 300; applied in *Re Craig, decd.* [1971] Ch. 95, 101.

[129] For a different view, see Birks, *An Introduction to the Law of Restitution*, 1985, rev. 1989, pp. 205–8.

been abused. Even in cases of presumed influence, the search is for cases where, from the relative positions of the parties, and the disadvantageous nature of the contract, a court is prepared to assume that there has been influence. If a court believes that there has been no abuse of position—no undue influence—it cannot say that there is still a presumption of influence and the contract is therefore vitiated.[130] Lindley LJ set out the principles of undue influence in *Allcard* v. *Skinner*:[131]

What then is the principle? Is it that it is right and expedient to save persons from the consequences of their own folly? or is it that it is right and expedient to save them from being victimised by other people? In my opinion the doctrine of undue influence is founded upon the second of these two principles. Courts of Equity have never set aside gifts on the ground of the folly, imprudence, or want of foresight on the part of donors. . . . On the other hand, to protect people from being forced, tricked or misled in any way by others into parting with their property is one of the most legitimate objects of all laws; and the equitable doctrine of undue influence has grown out of and has been developed by the necessity of grappling with insidious forms of spiritual tyranny and with the infinite varieties of fraud.

This shows that the basis of the law of undue influence is the prevention of *active* abuse of a position of influence. The first question is always whether there is an inequality between the parties, such that one party is able by his superior position to influence the other; but undue influence is concerned with the abuse of that position. Lord Chelmsford, speaking in a case of actual undue influence, said,[132]

the case comes within the principles on which a Court of equity proceeds in setting aside an agreement where there is inequality between the parties, and one of them takes unfair advantage of the situation of the other, and uses undue influence to force an agreement from him.

---

[130] *Re Brocklehurst's Estate* [1978] Ch. 14, 41.
[131] (1887) 36 Ch. D. 145, 182–3, applied in *National Westminster Bank plc* v. *Morgan* [1985] AC 686, 705.
[132] *Williams* v. *Bayley* (1866) LR 1 HL 200, 216.

9

Abuse of Bargaining Position

In a sense, the title 'abuse of bargaining position' might be used to describe all the areas with which we have so far been concerned in Parts II and III: the imbalance between the parties which we have highlighted in misrepresentation, duress, and undue influence, coupled with the advantage taken of that imbalance by the inducement of a contract by a false statement, or the pressure exerted, could be said to be an active abuse by one party of his bargaining position *vis-à-vis* the other party. However, there are other cases where a contract may be vitiated, where there is no misrepresentation, and no duress or undue influence, but the relative positions of the parties at the time of contracting is crucial to the analysis of the validity of the contract.

The language which has commonly been used to describe some cases in this area is 'unconscionable bargains'; and some attempt has been made to unite all the cases in the areas with which we are concerned under the banner of 'inequality of bargaining power'. However, it is important to understand that it is not simply the unfairness of the bargain, nor the relative positions of inequality of bargaining power, which affects the validity of a contract. The contract may be vitiated only when the necessary *link* can be shown between the inequality of position and the bargain: it is an *abuse* of the bargaining position which is required.

1. SALES BY 'POOR AND IGNORANT PERSONS'

One particular area where the courts have allowed contracts to be set aside is where one party takes advantage of the poverty or ignorance of the other. The springboard for the development of this area was a series of old cases in which the Courts of Equity had protected expectant heirs—that is, those who were presently in a difficult financial position, but were relying on the fact—or hope—that they would in due course come into a large inheritance.[1] For example, in *Earl of Aylesford* v. *Morris*[2] A, described[3] as foolish and extravagant, had soon after he reached his majority borrowed from M at rates exceeding 60 per cent in order to pay off large debts which he had incurred during his minority. His only present income was an allowance from his father, of less than £500 a year; but he would be entitled on his father's death to large estates producing an annual rental of around £20,000. It is clear that A was here in a difficult position: he required extra money in order to meet his extravagance; and he could be tempted to borrow, even at high rates of interest, in the knowledge that his father was in bad health, and so he might come into his inheritance and be able to pay off what he owed. The courts recognized this temptation, and looked carefully at contracts entered into in such circumstances. Lord Selborne LC,[4] drawing upon an earlier judgment of Lord Hardwicke in *Earl of Chesterfield* v. *Janssen*[5] said that 'the circumstances or conditions of the parties contracting—weakness on one side, usury on the other, or extortion, or advantage taken of that weakness' raised a presumption of fraud. But

Fraud does not here mean deceit or circumvention; it means unconscientious use of the power arising out of these circumstances and conditions; and when the relative position of the parties is such as *prima facie* to raise this presumption, the transaction cannot stand unless the person claiming the benefit of it is able to repel the presumption by contrary evidence, proving it to have been in point of fact fair, just and reasonable.

This makes it clear that the relative positions of the parties are crucial: the facts are to be examined to see whether they are such as 'to give the stronger party dominion over the weaker'.[6] What

---

[1] Lord Selborne LC in *Earl of Aylesford* v. *Morris* (1873) 8 Ch. App. 484, 497 rejected an argument that the jurisdiction was limited to cases where (1) the person seeking to avoid the contract had a mere expectation of succeeding to his father rather than a vested remainder in the family property ; and (2) it was a dealing—such as a mortgage—of that estate in remainder which was impugned. What was required was simply that the 'expectant heir' was trusted upon the credit of his expectations, that is, of his prospect of succeeding on the death of his father to the family estates.

[2] (1873) 8 Ch. App. 484.

[3] Ibid., at p. 488, by his own counsel.

[4] Ibid., at pp. 489–91.

[5] (1751) 2 Ves. Sen. 125, 157.

[6] *Earl of Aylesford* v. *Morris* (1873) 8 Ch. App. 484, 491.

matters, though, is not simply the relative positions of the parties; it is from those positions, coupled with a bargain entered into in the context of those positions which is prima facie oppressive and extortionate,[7] that the 'unconscientious use of power' is presumed: there must be an *abuse* of the position of strength by the stronger party. If the presumption arises, then the stronger party must show that the transaction was 'fair, just and reasonable'.[8]

The principles of *Earl of Aylesford* v. *Morris* were not, however, restricted to expectant heirs. They were generalized—drawing upon other cases[9]—by Kay J in *Fry* v. *Lane*:[10]

The result of the decisions is that where a purchase is made from a poor and ignorant man at a considerable undervalue, the vendor having no independent advice, a Court of Equity will set aside the transaction. . . .

The circumstances of poverty and ignorance of the vendor, and absence of independent advice, throw upon the purchaser, when the transaction is impeached, the onus of proving, in Lord Selborne's words, that the purchase was 'fair, just and reasonable.'

---

[7] Ibid., at p. 495.

[8] Ibid., at p. 491. An early, over-zealous exercise of this jurisdiction, which had allowed certain transactions with expectant heirs to be set aside simply on the ground of undervalue, even if it appeared that there had been fair dealing, was reversed by the Sales of Reversions Act 1867. The provisions are now contained in Law of Property Act 1925, s. 174, which also expressly reserves the jurisdiction of the court to set aside or modify unconscionable bargains. See also *Brenchley* v. *Higgins* (1900) 70 LJ Ch. 788, 790.

[9] *Evans* v. *Llewellin* (1787) 1 Cox 333 (the plaintiff, a poor man, was told of an inheritance and was immediately offered a large sum to relinquish it: he was 'taken by surprise'; an 'undue advantage was taken of his situation': Kenyon MR at p. 340); *Haygarth* v. *Wearing* (1871) LR 12 Eq. 320 (where there was, however, a misrepresentation of the value of the subject-matter of the contract); *Wood* v. *Abrey* (1818) 3 Madd. 417, 423 ('mere inadequacy of price is no more weight in equity than at law. If a man who meets his purchaser on equal terms, negligently sells his estate at an under value, he has no title to relief in equity. But a Court of Equity will inquire whether the parties really did meet on equal terms; and if it be found that the vendor was in distressed circumstances, and that advantage was taken of that distress, it will avoid the contract': Leach V-C); *Longmate* v. *Ledger* (1860) 2 Giff. 157 (the vendor, a poor man advanced in years and known to be of weak and eccentric disposition, contracted to sell property to a creditor at a wholly inadequate price); *Clark* v. *Malpas* (1862) 4 De G. F. & J. 401 (a vendor, a man in humble life and imperfectly educated, was induced during an illness to sell the only cottages he owned, at an undervalue: the contract was voidable, as being obtained by advantage being taken of the vendor's position and circumstances, and executed without sufficient deliberation and without sufficient advice: Turner LJ at p. 405); *Baker* v. *Monk* (1864) 4 De G. J. & S. 388 (sale at an undervalue to a substantial tradesman by a single woman in humble life, of slender education, between 60 and 70 years of age, unprotected and unaided).

[10] (1888) 40 Ch. D. 312, 322.

Following this test, there are therefore three points which must be established by the plaintiff:

(1) that he was poor and ignorant;
(2) that he had no independent advice; and
(3) that the sale was at a considerable undervalue.

If these are established, the onus shifts to the purchaser to show that the transaction was fair, just, and reasonable.

(a) 'Poor and Ignorant'

In *Fry* v. *Lane* itself the plaintiffs, who succeeded in their claim to have their transactions set aside, were described[11] as 'poor persons in a humble position'. The concepts of poverty and ignorance have, however, been developed, and in *Cresswell* v. *Potter*[12] Megarry J held that a lady who had been a van driver for a tobacconist and was currently a Post Office telephonist, and who wished to avoid a conveyance to her husband of her rights in the matrimonial home, was poor and ignorant.[13]

I think that the plaintiff may fairly be described as falling within whatever is the modern equivalent of 'poor and ignorant'. Eighty years ago, when *Fry* v. *Lane* was decided, social conditions were very different from those which exist today. I do not, however, think that the principle has changed, even though the euphemisms of the 20th century may require the word 'poor' to be replaced by 'a member of the lower income group' or the like, and the word 'ignorant' by 'less highly educated.' The plaintiff has been a van driver for a tobacconist and is a Post Office telephonist. The evidence of her means is slender. The defendant told me that the plaintiff probably had a little saved, but not much; and there was evidence that her earnings were about the same as the defendant's, and that these were those of a carpenter. The plaintiff also has a legal aid certificate.

In those circumstances, I think that the plaintiff may properly be described as 'poor' in the sense used in *Fry* v. *Lane*, where it was applied to a laundryman who, in 1888, was earning £1 a week. In this context, as in others,[14] I do not think that 'poverty' is confined to destitution. Further,

---

[11] Ibid., at p. 313. For example, one was a laundryman, earning £1 a week.

[12] Decided in 1968 but not reported until [1978] 1 WLR 255, after attention had been drawn to the case by Balcombe J in *Backhouse* v. *Backhouse* [1978] 1 WLR 243; Balcombe J had appeared as counsel for the defendant in *Cresswell* v. *Potter*.

[13] [1978] 1 WLR 255, 257–8.

[14] Cf. *Re Niyazi's Will Trusts* [1978] 1 WLR 910, where Megarry V-C held, with some hesitation, that a trust for 'the construction of or as a contribution towards the cost of the construction of a working mens hostel' was charitable as being a trust for the relief of the poor.

although no doubt it requires considerable alertness and skill to be a good telephonist, I think that a telephonist can properly be described as 'ignorant' in the context of property transactions in general and the execution of conveyancing documents in particular.

It appears from this that 'poverty' is not a narrow concept—simply being less well off than the average seems to qualify. 'Ignorance', however, has quite a particular meaning: it is to be judged in relation to the transaction in question. What was crucial in *Cresswell* v. *Potter* was not the general educational skills of the plaintiff, but her skills in relation to the particular conveyancing transaction: 'The document [abounded] in terms which, though speaking to the conveyancer in language of precision, can hardly be expected to speak to a van driver and telephonist lucidly or, indeed, at all.'[15]

(b) No Independent Advice

Cresswell v. *Potter* also explained the requirement that the plaintiff should have entered into the transaction without independent advice. The argument was raised that the plaintiff could easily have consulted a solicitor. This is clearly not sufficient, and Megarry J rejected it. What matters is not whether the plaintiff could as a matter of fact have obtained advice; nor even whether she did or did not in fact obtain advice. The key point is whether her attention has been drawn to the nature of the transaction, and the advisability of taking some independent advice.[16]

(c) 'Considerable Undervalue'

The requirement that the sale be at a considerable undervalue must be a question of fact. In *Cresswell* v. *Potter*, the undervalue was evident: the wife gave up her rights in the home in return only for an indemnity against liabilities under the mortgage of the property—in effect, for nothing. In *Fry* v. *Lane*, £170 was paid for the sale of a reversionary interest under a will which ultimately proved to be worth £730.[17] It is important to bear in mind, however, that the

---

[15] [1978] 1 WLR 255, 260.

[16] Ibid., at p. 259. The advice must be *independent*: in *Fry* v. *Lane*, the solicitor for the purchaser also acted for the vendors: (1888) 40 Ch. D. 312, 323. Cf. undue influence, where independent advice is a relevant criterion—but not a substantive requirement—to rebut the presumption: p. 186, above.

[17] There was, however, actuarial evidence that the value of the interest at the date of the purchase was £475: (1888) 40 Ch. D. 312, 318, 322–3.

purpose of this requirement is to assist in raising the presumption that an active advantage has been taken of the weaker party. It is therefore understandable that the courts have required that there must be a *considerable* undervalue. Although there must be something of a sliding scale and it is not possible to specify precisely how great the undervalue must be, a lesser test of the discrepancy between the price paid and the price which ought to have been paid would not lead one to think that there had been any abuse of position.[18]

2. OTHER CASES OF ABUSE OF BARGAINING POSITION

(a) Development of *Fry* v. *Lane*

There have been signs of further development of this area. Megarry J in *Cresswell* v. *Potter*[19] said that the three requirements set out by Kay J in *Fry* v. *Lane* were not the only circumstances which would suffice to vitiate a contract; he referred to the possibility of other 'circumstances of oppression or abuse of confidence which will invoke the aid of equity'. This might have been referring to other heads of equity, such as undue influence; but Michael Wheeler QC in *Watkin* v. *Watson-Smith*[20] took it as an indication that the doctrine of *Fry* v. *Lane* itself was not restricted to the three requirements of Kay J. There, it was held[21] that a frail old man of 80 who signed a contract to sell his bungalow for £2,950 (instead of the real price of £29,500) would have been able to rely on the *Fry* v. *Lane* rule: although he was not poor and ignorant, these requirements could be substituted by a desire for a quick sale, and old age with its accompanying diminution of physical and mental capacity.

The line of authority which derives from *Earl of Aylesford* v. *Morris*[22] has also been developed in Canada, Australia, and New Zealand, to a more general concept of 'unconscionable bargains'. In *Morrison* v. *Coast Finance Ltd.*[23] Davey JA described the requirements as

---

[18] Cf. the requirement that the transaction be *manifestly* disadvantageous, in undue influence: pp. 174 ff., 183 ff., above.

[19] [1978] 1 WLR 255, 257.

[20] *The Times*, 3 July 1986.

[21] *Obiter*, since it was found that the contract was vitiated by mistake.

[22] (1873) 8 Ch. App. 484.

[23] (1965) 55 DLR (2d) 710, 713. See also, in Canada, *Knupp* v. *Bell* (1968) 67 DLR (2d)

proof of inequality in the position of the parties arising out of the ignorance, need or distress of the weaker, which left him in the power of the stronger, and proof of substantial unfairness of the bargain obtained by the stronger. On proof of those circumstances, it creates a presumption of fraud which the stronger must repel by proving that the bargain was fair, just and reasonable . . . or perhaps by showing that no advantage was taken.

This shows a shift in emphasis: it is not so much that there must be poverty and ignorance, but that there must be *inequality* between the parties; this inequality *arises out of* such factors as poverty and ignorance.

The concept of the unconscionable bargain was also explained by the Privy Council in *Hart* v. *O'Connor*.[24] There, the question was whether an agreement for the sale of land could be set aside either (1) on the ground of the vendor's lack of mental capacity, or (2) as an unconscionable bargain, when the sale was alleged to have been at an undervalue, and the vendor was of unsound mind at the time of entering into the contract. The Privy Council refused to set aside the transaction on either ground. In relation to the plea of mental incapacity, the crucial fact was said to be that the purchaser did not know, nor should he reasonably have known, of the vendor's incapacity at the time of the contract; he therefore could not be said to have victimized, or taken advantage of, the vendor.[25] The Privy Council clearly thought that the basis of the jurisdiction of equity to

256; in Australia, *Blomley* v. *Ryan* (1954–6) 99 CLR 362; and in New Zealand, *K* v. *K* [1976] 2 NZLR 31; *Moffat* v. *Moffat* [1984] 1 NZLR 600; *Nichols* v. *Jessup* [1986] 1 NZLR 226, *Nichols* v. *Jessup (No. 2)* [1986] 1 NZLR 237. In *Blomley* v. *Ryan* (1954–6) 99 CLR 362, 415 Kitto J said that the principle contained in *Fry* v. *Lane* is 'a well-known head of equity. It applies whenever one party to a transaction is at a special disadvantage in dealing with the other party because illness, ignorance, inexperience, impaired faculties, financial need or other circumstances affect his ability to conserve his own interests, and the other party unconscientiously takes advantage of the opportunity thus placed in his hands.'

[24] [1985] AC 1000; on appeal from New Zealand. Although the Privy Council did not refer to *Fry* v. *Lane* itself, they discussed the principles of unconscionable bargains as stemming from *Earl of Aylesford* v. *Morris*. See also pp. 215–16, below.

[25] It may seem rather surprising that a person's *incapacity* to contract should depend on the other party's knowledge (actual or constructive) of the incapacity; however, this is clearly designed to protect the innocent person dealing with someone he has no reason to know is not mentally competent. By contrast, the incapacity of a *minor* to contract does not depend upon the knowledge of the other party: it seems that the law takes a stricter view, as a matter of policy, to protect minors; see Treitel, pp. 426-35. It may also be that a person dealing with a minor can be expected more readily to realize that he is dealing with someone who is not of full age and capacity. It

avoid a contract on the ground of lack of mental capacity was similar to the jurisdiction relating to unconscionable bargains:[26]

Their Lordships have not been referred to any authority that a court of equity would restrain a suit at law where there was no victimisation, no taking advantage of another's weakness, and the sole allegation was contractual imbalance[27] with no undertones of constructive fraud.

And what is necessary, for the contract to be vitiated as an unconscionable bargain, is 'victimisation, which can consist either of the active extortion of a benefit or the passive acceptance of a benefit in unconscionable circumstances'.[28] The plea that the bargain was unconscionable failed because there was, on the facts, no such victimization:[29]

[The purchaser] acted with complete innocence throughout. He was unaware of the vendor's unsoundness of mind.[30] The vendor was ostensibly advised by his own solicitor. The [purchaser] had no means of knowing or cause to suspect that the vendor was not in receipt of and acting in accordance with the most full and careful advice. The terms of the bargain were the terms proposed by the vendor's solicitor, not terms imposed by the

---

appears that for *drunkenness* to vitiate a contract the other party must know of it: *Gore* v. *Gibson* (1845) 13 M. & W. 623, 626: 'Where the party, when he enters into the contract, is in such a state of drunkenness as not to know what he is doing, and particularly when it appears that this was known to the other party, the contract is void altogether, and he cannot be compelled to perform it. A person who takes an obligation from another under such circumstances is guilty of actual fraud' (Parke B). Again, though, a person dealing with a drunkard ought generally to realize that the drunkard is not fully capable of entering to the contract. Further, in relation to *ultra vires* contracts of a company, see Treitel, pp. 437–43; Companies Act 1989, s. 108; and for the doctrine of *non est factum*, which protects those who execute written contracts which they are incapable of understanding, see pp. 46–7, above.

[26] [1985] AC 1000, 1024.

[27] i.e. a contract unfair in its terms: see [1985] AC 1000, 1017–18, quoted at pp. 215–16, below.

[28] [1985] AC 1000, 1024. For a case where there was a passive acceptance of a manifestly one-sided transaction, see *Nichols* v. *Jessup* [1986] 1 NZLR 226; *Nichols* v. *Jessup (No. 2)* [1986] 1 NZLR 237.

[29] [1985] AC 1000, 1028.

[30] This passage appears to indicate that the absence of such knowledge was not the only bar to a remedy: if the purchaser had known of the vendor's incapacity, he could have been guilty of victimization; but even without such knowledge, other actions on the purchaser's part could have rendered the bargain unconscionable. It has been held in New Zealand that actual knowledge of the incapacity is not necessary: it is sufficient if the stronger party 'ought to have known of [the disability]; when a reasonable man would have adverted to the possibility of its existence': *Nichols* v. *Jessup* [1986] 1 NZLR 226, 235.

defendant or his solicitor. There was no equitable fraud, no victimisation, no taking advantage, no overreaching or other description of unconscionable doings which might have justified the intervention of equity.

Again, we see that the court requires more than just an unfair bargain, or a position of inequality; it is obtaining the bargain in circumstances which affect the conscience which is required—victimization, or taking advantage of the other's weakness.[31] This was emphasized by Somers J in the New Zealand case of *Nichols* v. *Jessup*:[32]

The equitable jurisdiction to set aside unconscionable bargains is not a paternal jurisdiction protecting or assisting those who repent of foolish undertakings. It is a jurisdiction protecting those under a disadvantage from those who take advantage of that fact; equity looks to the conduct of the stronger party.

The language of unconscionable bargains has also been used in other factual contexts. What must be considered is whether similar principles are being used to those described above, or whether contracts can be vitiated in some areas by virtue simply of the unfairness of the bargain, or the inequality between the parties.

(*b*) Contracts in Restraint of Trade[33]

At first sight, the law relating to contracts in restraint of trade may appear to be applying a public policy different from that contained in the *Fry* v. *Lane* line of cases. The general rule is that a contract whose terms are harsh or unconscionable will be enforced unless there is present one of the recognized vitiating factors—such as duress or undue influence. If, however, the contract is one in restraint of trade—that is, it contains terms whereby one party agrees to fetter his own earning power, for example by agreeing not to carry on a particular business for a prescribed period in a given area—the courts treat it differently, and allow it to be enforced only if it can be shown to be reasonable.[34] There is clearly a public policy at work

---

[31] See also pp. 215–16, below.
[32] [1986] 1 NZLR 226, 235.
[33] *Chitty*, §§1190 ff.
[34] *Esso Petroleum Co. Ltd.* v. *Harper's Garage (Stourport) Ltd.* [1968] AC 269, 295 (Lord Reid).

here, which seeks to protect the freedom of an individual to trade; it is, however, necessary to balance it against the policy of freedom of contract.[35] The courts have taken the position that the ability of the parties to bargain freely is relevant to their determination of whether a contract in restraint of trade is reasonable, and so enforceable.

In *A. Schroeder Music Publishing Co. Ltd.* v. *Macaulay*,[36] for example, Lord Diplock went so far as to suggest that the abuse of a superior bargaining position underlay the public policy implemented by the courts in cases of restraint of trade: it was 'not some 19th-century economic theory about the benefit to the general public of freedom of trade, but the protection of those whose bargaining power is weak against being forced by those whose bargaining power is stronger to enter into bargains that are unconscionable'.

Other judges have also said that the bargaining positions of the parties have a bearing on the reasonableness of the clause.[37] Commercial practices and the generality of contracts made freely by parties bargaining on equal terms are the bench-mark against which a contract is to be tested, to determine its reasonableness; and where there are no circumstances of oppression the courts will tread warily in substituting their own views for those of current commerce generally and the contracting parties in particular.[38] Some contracts which are restrictive of trade may have been generally adopted, and it may be presumed that such terms will have been moulded under pressures of negotiation, competition, and public opinion, so as to satisfy the test of public policy: the courts will allow such contracts to stand.[39] However, it is where there is no such general acceptance, and in particular where the bargaining position of the parties is unequal, that a court will look particularly closely at the clause to which the weaker party has ostensibly agreed.[40]

[35] Ibid., at pp. 304–6 (Lord Morris).

[36] [1974] 1 WLR 1308, 1315.

[37] In *Clifford Davis Management Ltd.* v. *WEA Records Ltd.* [1975] 1 WLR 61, 64–5, Lord Denning MR, referring to Lord Diplock's judgment in *A. Schroeder Music Publishing Co. Ltd.* v. *Macaulay*, said that restraint of trade was an example of the principle of inequality of bargaining power which he had stated in *Lloyds Bank Ltd.* v. *Bundy* [1975] QB 326; p. 218, below.

[38] *Esso Petroleum Co. Ltd.* v. *Harper's Garage (Stourport) Ltd.* [1968] AC 269, 323 (Lord Pearce).

[39] Ibid., at pp. 332–3 (Lord Wilberforce).

[40] *A. Schroeder Music Publishing Co. Ltd.* v. *Macaulay* [1974] 1 WLR 1308, 1314 (Lord Reid), 1316 (Lord Diplock).

(c) **Mortgages**

This is not the place to discuss in detail the law relating to mortgages.[41] However, one principle which must be noted is that the courts have always been keen to protect the right of the mortgagor to redeem the mortgage and recover his property.[42] Until early this century, the courts were very protective, and tended to strike down any provision in the mortgage which could affect the mortgagor's right to redeem;[43] however, more recently the courts have tended to allow bargains freely entered into to be enforced.[44] The position which the courts now take is that a provision in the mortgage, even if it tends to restrict or discourage redemption, or to give the mortgagee more than the return of his money with interest, will be upheld, as long as the provision was not *unconscionable*; and it has been made clear that this test is not simply whether the terms of the provision are unreasonable, or unfair, but whether the provision has been *obtained* unfairly. For the mortgage to be set aside, therefore, there must be an abuse by the mortgagee of his position, which led to the mortgagor agreeing to the inclusion of the relevant provision in the mortgage.

In *Multiservice Bookbinding Ltd.* v. *Marden*,[45] a mortgage included provisions that interest would be paid on the full capital sum for the whole of the mortgage period; that interest would be capitalized after twenty-one days; that the loan would not be called in or redeemed for ten years; and that the value of capital and interest would be index-linked to the Swiss franc. Because of the movement of the Swiss franc, the total capital repayment on redemption at the end of ten years was £87,588, representing an average annual rate of interest of 16.01% on an initial loan of £36,000. Browne-Wilkinson J held that the mortgage was valid. The test[46] was whether the term is 'unfair and unconscionable'; but

[41] For which, see Cheshire and Burn's *Modern Law of Real Property*, 14th edn., 1988, ch. 21.

[42] The 'equity of redemption': see ibid., at pp. 626–7.

[43] Ibid., at pp. 638–46. See in particular *Samuel* v. *Jarrah Timber and Wood Paving Co. Ltd.* [1904] AC 323; *Fairclough* v. *Swan Brewery Co. Ltd.* [1912] AC 565; *Bradley* v. *Carritt* [1903] AC 253.

[44] See particularly *Kreglinger* v. *New Patagonia Meat and Cold Storage Co. Ltd.* [1914] AC 25; *Knightsbridge Estates Trust Ltd.* v. *Byrne* [1939] Ch. 441.

[45] [1979] Ch. 84. See also *Cityland and Property (Holdings) Ltd.* v. *Dabrah* [1968] Ch. 166.

[46] [1979] Ch. 84, 110, applying *Kreglinger* v. *New Patagonia Meat and Cold Storage Co. Ltd.* [1914] AC 25, 61 (Lord Parker).

a bargain cannot be unfair and unconscionable unless one of the parties to it has imposed the objectionable terms in a morally reprehensible manner, that is to say, in a way which affects his conscience.

The classic example of an unconscionable bargain is where advantage has been taken of a young, inexperienced or ignorant person to introduce a term which no sensible well-advised person or party would have accepted. But I do not think the categories of unconscionable bargains are limited: the court can and should intervene where a bargain has been procured by unfair means.

This appears, therefore, to be an application of the same principle as underlies the *Fry* v. *Lane* line of cases.[47]

(*d*) Purchases by Trustees: 'Self-Dealing' and 'Fair-Dealing'

Equity has long taken a cautious view of contracts entered into by trustees in relation to trust property or interests in the trust:[48] 'equity is astute to prevent a trustee from abusing his position or profiting from his trust: the shepherd must not become a wolf'.[49] In consequence, two rules were developed: that a purchase of trust property by a trustee is voidable at the option of the beneficiary (the 'self-dealing' rule); and that a purchase by the trustee of the beneficial interest of a beneficiary must be justified by the trustee (the 'fair-dealing' rule). The self-dealing rule is strict, and applies irrespective of the fairness of the transaction. Its basis is that the position of the trustee is such that he should never be allowed to purchase the property of the trust unless all the beneficiaries consent: he has a conflict of interest between his desire to purchase and his obligation impartially to administer the trust.[50]

---

[47] *Fry* v. *Lane* (1888) 40 Ch. D. 312 and *Cresswell* v. *Potter* [1978] 1 WLR 255 were cited in argument, but were not referred to by Browne-Wilkinson J. See also *Alec Lobb (Garages) Ltd.* v. *Total Oil (Great Britain) Ltd.* [1985] 1 WLR 173; *Commercial Bank of Australia Ltd.* v. *Amadio* (1982–3) 151 CLR 447. Under the Consumer Credit Act 1974, ss. 137 and 138, the court has power to reopen a credit bargain which is *extortionate*: that is, it requires the debtor or a relative of his to make payments which are grossly exorbitant, or it otherwise grossly contravenes ordinary principles of fair dealing. Factors to determine whether this test is satisfied are set out in s. 138. This is, however, a quite separate jurisdiction from that applied in *Multiservice Bookbinding Ltd.* v. *Marden*. Under the Act, the test is not whether the creditor has acted in a morally reprehensible manner, but simply whether the conditions of s. 138 are fulfilled: *Davies* v. *Directloans Ltd.* [1986] 1 WLR 823, 831.

[48] Hanbury and Maudsley, *Modern Equity*, 13th edn., 1989, pp. 560–1; Goff and Jones, ch. 34.

[49] *Tito* v. *Waddell (No. 2)* [1977] Ch. 106, 241 (Megarry V-C).

[50] *Campbell* v. *Walker* (1800) 5 Ves. Jun. 678; *Ex p. Lacey* (1802) 6 Ves. Jun. 625; *Holder* v. *Holder* [1968] Ch. 353; *Re Thompson's Settlement* [1986] Ch. 99.

The fair-dealing rule is less strict, because there are genuinely two parties to the transaction—the trustee and the beneficiary.[51] However, a contract by a trustee to purchase a beneficiary's interest is voidable by the beneficiary 'unless the trustee can show that he has taken no advantage of his position and has made full disclosure to the beneficiary, and that the transaction is fair and honest'.[52] In *Coles* v. *Trecothick*[53] Lord Eldon said,

a trustee may buy from the *cestui que trust*, provided there is a distinct and clear contract, ascertained to be such after a jealous and scrupulous examination of all the circumstances, providing, that the *cestui que trust* intended, the trustee should buy; and there is no fraud, no concealment, no advantage taken, by the trustee of information, acquired by him in the character of trustee.

Here, then, we see rules developed by equity to protect beneficiaries against the advantages which could be taken of them by their trustees. Similar rules are also applied to contracts between fiduciaries and those to whom they owe their fiduciary duties, if the nature of the fiduciary relationship gives rise to a similar conflict of interest.[54]

In *Edwards* v. *Meyrick*,[55] for example, it was applied to a contract between a solicitor and his client. Wigram V-C said,[56]

the rule the Court imposes is, that inasmuch as the parties stand in a relation which gives, or may give, the solicitor an advantage over the client, the onus lies on the solicitor to prove that the transaction was fair.

However, the precise relationship between the parties and the nature of the transaction must be considered to see whether one party could have been in a position to take advantage of the other:[57]

The nature of the proof . . . which the Court requires must depend upon the circumstances of each case, according as they may have placed the attorney in a position in which his duties and his pecuniary interests were conflicting,

---

[51] *Re Thompson's Settlement* [1986] Ch. 99, 115–16.

[52] *Tito* v. *Waddell (No. 2)* [1977] Ch. 106, 241. See also *Thomson* v. *Eastwood* (1877) 2 App. Cas. 215, 236.

[53] (1804) 9 Ves. Jun. 234, 246–7.

[54] *Aberdeen Railway Co.* v. *Blaikie Brothers* (1854) 1 Macq. 461 (dealings between a director and his company). Cf. the analogous situation of a trustee making a profit out of his dealings with trust property: *Keech* v. *Sandford* (1726) Sel. Cas. t. King 61; the rule applies to other fiduciaries, but depends on the particular details of the fiduciary relationship, and especially whether there was a conflict of interest: *Boardman* v. *Phipps* [1967] 2 AC 46, 127 (Lord Upjohn).

[55] (1842) 2 Hare 60.   [56] Ibid., at p. 68.   [57] Ibid., at p. 70.

or may have given him a knowledge which his client did not possess, or some influence or ascendancy or other advantage over his client; or, notwithstanding the existence of the relationship of attorney and client, may have left the parties substantially at arm's length and on an equal footing.

On one view, this is simply an application of equity's rules designed to protect those in weak positions against trustees and fiduciaries. However, we have also seen that other consequences in the law of contract may follow from holding that the parties were in a fiduciary relationship or a relationship of trust—duties of disclosure[58] and a presumption of undue influence.[59] Although these are *separate* rules, which have developed independently and to deal with different circumstances,[60] there seems to be a consistent policy developed by equity to prevent abuse of a position of strength.

(e) Forfeiture and Penalty Clauses

It might also be argued that the rules by which the courts relieve parties against forfeiture and penalty clauses have as an underlying principle the avoidance of abuse of one party's bargaining position.[61]

(i) Forfeiture

Equity has long asserted the right to relieve against forfeiture of property—such as mortgages and leases.[62] This has been extended outside the area of real property, but it is still limited to contracts involving the transfer or creation of proprietary or possessory rights.[63] It does not, therefore, apply generally to contracts where there is a right to determine the contract on specified events of default.[64] The juridical basis of the forfeiture jurisdiction is wider

---

[58] p. 91, above.   [59] p. 180, above.

[60] See e.g. *Moody* v. *Cox* [1917] 2 Ch. 71, 78–80; *Bank of Credit and Commerce International SA* v. *Aboody* [1990] QB 923, 962–4.

[61] Waddams, 'Unconscionability in Contracts' (1976) 39 MLR 369, 370–5, who does not, however, always distinguish unfairness in the terms of a contract and unfairness in its procurement by reason of inequality of the parties.

[62] *Shiloh Spinners Ltd.* v. *Harding* [1973] AC 691, 722; Cheshire and Burn's *Modern Law of Real Property*, pp. 412–13.

[63] *Scandinavian Trading Tanker Co. AB* v. *Flota Petrolera Ecuatoriana, The Scaptrade* [1983] 2 AC 694; *BICC plc* v. *Burndy Corporation* [1985] Ch. 232.

[64] However, the distinction between contracts involving the transfer or creation of proprietary or possessory rights, and mere contractual licences, can be fine: cf. *Sport Internationaal Bussum BV* v. *Inter-Footware Ltd.* [1984] 1 WLR 776 and *BICC plc* v. *Burndy Corporation* [1985] Ch. 232; Treitel, pp. 595–6.

than simply an application of the principle of abuse of bargaining position at the time of making the contract, since relevant considerations include the parties' conduct *after* the contract has been concluded.[65] But Robert Goff LJ, giving the judgment of the Court of Appeal in *The Scaptrade*,[66] talked of both relief against forfeiture and relief against penalties in the following terms:

whatever may be the breadth of the application of these principles today, we need not be surprised at the type of case in which equity has thought it right to intervene in the past. No doubt at bottom the equitable jurisdiction:

'rests upon the idea that it is not fair that a person should use his legal rights to take advantage of another's misfortune, and still less that he should scheme to get legal rights with this object in view.'

See Holdsworth, *A History of English Law*, vol. V, 3rd. ed. (1945) p. 330. However the cases where equity has intervened are cases where parties were frequently not at arm's length; and frequently also where the relevant contract conferred an interest in land, the loss of which could have serious personal consequences.

We can see here ideas both of the fairness of the contractual terms and of the obtaining of an unfair term by a person in a position of advantage. Indeed, it is precisely because of the absence of inequality between the parties that the Court of Appeal and the House of Lords refused to extend the equitable jurisdiction to relieve against forfeiture to the commercial contract—a time charter—which was involved in *The Scaptrade*:[67]

a time charter is a commercial transaction in the sense that it is generally entered into for the purposes of trade, between commercial organisations acting at arm's length. It is for the parties to bargain about the terms of the contract . . . Parties to such contracts should be capable of looking after themselves.

(ii) Penalty Clauses

There is an equitable jurisdiction to relieve against penalty clauses. If

[65] In *Stockloser* v. *Johnson* [1954] 1 QB 476, 495 Romer LJ thought that relief against forfeiture would not be granted where the forfeiture provision had been freely negotiated with equality of bargaining power; the other judges, Somervell and Denning LJJ, thought that the jurisdiction was wider.

[66] [1983] QB 529, 538–9.

[67] Ibid., at p. 540 (CA) approved at [1983] 2 AC 694, 703–4 (HL). There is, however, no rule that relief cannot be granted against forfeiture of commercial agreements: *BICC plc* v. *Burndy Corporation* [1985] Ch. 232.

a provision in a contract for the payment of money or the transfer of property[68] on breach[69] is characterized as a liquidated damages clause, it is enforceable: the sum (or property) is payable in substitution for the damages which would otherwise be payable on such a breach. If, however, the provision is characterized as a penalty clause, the plaintiff can recover only the normal measure of damages payable on such a breach.[70]

The courts, in determining whether a provision is a liquidated damages clause or a penalty, have often used the language of unconscionability.[71] In this, they seem to be referring to the fairness of the terms of the contract, rather than its procurement. However, the procurement is relevant. Lord Dunedin in *Dunlop Pneumatic Tyre Co. Ltd.* v. *New Garage and Motor Co. Ltd.*[72] set out a test to distinguish a penalty clause from a liquidated damages clause:

1. Though the parties to a contract who use the words 'penalty' or 'liquidated damages' may prima facie be supposed to mean what they say, yet the expression used is not conclusive. . . .

2. The essence of a penalty is payment of money[73] stipulated as in terrorem of the offending party; the essence of liquidated damages is a genuine covenanted pre-estimate of damage. . . .

3. The question whether a sum stipulated is penalty or liquidated damages is a question of construction to be decided upon the terms and inherent circumstances of each particular contract, judged of as at the time of the making of the contract, not as at the time of the breach. . . .

4. To assist this task of construction various tests have been suggested, which if applicable to the case under consideration may prove helpful, or even conclusive. Such are:

(a) It will be held to be a penalty if the sum stipulated for is extravagant and unconscionable in amount in comparison with the greatest loss that could conceivably be proved to have followed from the breach. . . .

(b) It will be held to be a penalty if the breach consists only in not paying a sum of money, and the sum stipulated is a sum greater than the sum which ought to have been paid . . .

---

[68] *Jobson* v. *Johnson* [1989] 1 WLR 1026.

[69] *Export Credits Guarantee Department* v. *Universal Oil Products Co.* [1983] 1 WLR 399.

[70] The recovery may be under the clause, as limited: *Jobson* v. *Johnson* [1989] 1 WLR 1026, 1035, 1040; or at common law, the penalty clause being ignored in the contract: *The Scaptrade* [1983] 2 AC 694, 702.

[71] See e.g. *Dunlop Pneumatic Tyre Co. Ltd.* v. *New Garage and Motor Co. Ltd.* [1915] AC 79, 87, 97; *Jobson* v. *Johnson* [1989] 1 WLR 1026, 1032.

[72] [1915] AC 79, 86–8.

[73] *Jobson* v. *Johnson* [1989] 1 WLR 1026 extends this to include transfers of property.

(c) There is a presumption (but no more) that it is penalty when 'a single lump sum is made payable by way of compensation, on the occurrence of one or more or all of several events, some of which may occasion serious and others but trifling damage.'[74]

On the other hand:

(d) It is no obstacle to the sum stipulated being a genuine pre-estimate of damage, that the consequences of the breach are such as to make precise pre-estimation almost an impossibility. On the contrary, that is just the situation when it is possible that pre-estimated damage was the true bargain between the parties.

The key point is that a penalty is a provision designed to frighten the potential contract-breaker into performing, rather than breaking, his contract. By contrast, a liquidated damages clause is a '*genuine covenanted pre-estimate of damage*'. One must therefore look behind the document to see whether, at the time that the contract was entered into, there was a genuine, free agreement between the parties about the likely consequences of a breach, and therefore about the sum payable in the event of such a breach. This suggests that one relevant criterion is the inequality of bargaining power between the parties, taken in conjunction with a promise to pay an unreasonably high sum. This idea is also present in the judgment of Lord Parmoor in *Dunlop Pneumatic Tyre Co. Ltd.* v. *New Garage and Motor Co. Ltd.*:[75]

there is no question as to the competency of parties to agree beforehand the amount of damages, uncertain in their nature, payable on breach of a contract. There are cases, however, in which the Courts have interfered with the free right of contract, although the parties have specified the definite sum agreed on by them to be in the nature of liquidated damages, and not of a penalty. If the Court, after looking at the language of the contract, the character of the transaction, and the circumstances under which it was entered into, comes to the conclusion that the parties have made a mistake in calling the agreed sum liquidated damages, and that such sum is not really a pactional pre-estimate of loss within the contemplation of the parties at the time when the arrangement was made, but a penal sum inserted as a punishment on the defaulter irrespective of the amount of any loss which could at the time have been in contemplation of the parties, then such sum is a penalty, and the defaulter is only liable in respect of damages which can be proved against him.

[74] *Lord Elphinstone* v. *Monkland Iron and Coal Co.* (1886) 11 App. Cas. 332, 342.
[75] [1915] AC 79, 100–1.

The law relating to penalty clauses is a very particular area which has developed from its historical roots.[76] It is not suggested that it involves a general application of the principle of abuse of position; merely that it is yet another instance where abuse of position is a criterion taken into account as part of the underlying principle.

3. THE UNDERLYING PRINCIPLE

It becomes clear, then, that the principle which underlies the cases in this area is not simply one of public policy against inequality of bargaining power, or the unfair terms of the contract. The cases consistently refer to the advantage taken by one party of the other. Although the relative bargaining strengths of the parties and the terms of the bargain may give rise to a presumption, which must be rebutted by the person resisting the setting aside of the contract, that presumption is that there has been an *abuse* of the bargaining position. We are not here concerned with fiduciary relationships; simply with the factual ability of one party to take advantage of the other, derived from such factors as the relative knowledge, wealth, or impaired faculties of the parties. As early as 1876,[77] it was said that

if two persons—no matter whether a confidential relation exists between them or not—stand in such a relation to each other that one can take an undue advantage of the other, whether by reason of distress or recklessness or wildness or want of care, and where the facts show that one party has taken undue advantage of the other, by reason of the circumstances I have mentioned—a transaction resting upon such unconscionable dealing will not be allowed to stand.

This area bears a close resemblance to the law of presumed undue

[76] 'Historically there is a good deal of disagreement as to how it grew up': Scrutton LJ in *Widnes Foundry (1925) Ltd.* v. *Cellulose Acetate Silk Co. Ltd.* [1931] 2 KB 393, 405. See also *Jobson* v. *Johnson* [1989] 1 WLR 1026, 1032.

[77] *Slator* v. *Nolan* (1876) Ir. R. 11 Eq. 367, 386. See also *Alec Lobb (Garages) Ltd.* v. *Total Oil (Great Britain) Ltd.* [1985] 1 WLR 173, 182, where Dillon LJ said that Lord Selborne in *Earl of Aylesford* v. *Morris* (1873) 8 Ch. App. 484 was emphasizing *extortion*—'undue advantage taken of weakness, an unconscientious use of the power arising out of the inequality of the parties' circumstances, and . . . unconscientious use of power which the court might in certain circumstances be entitled to infer from a particular—and in these days notorious—relationship unless the contract is proved to have been in fact fair, just and reasonable'.

influence.[78] In both cases there is a presumption that advantage has been taken, which arises from an analysis of the relationship between the parties coupled with a transaction which is disadvantageous to the weaker party.[79] We can begin, then, to see that there may be some common principle which underlies these areas of the law which have developed separately.[80]

It must be emphasized that neither an unfair bargain, nor an inequality between the parties' bargaining positions, of themselves vitiate a contract. What is required is an abuse of that inequality, which may be shown by the existence of an unfair bargain.

(a) More than an Unfair Bargain

The courts have in recent years frequently said that merely an unfair bargain is not sufficient to vitiate the contract on the grounds of an unconscionable bargain. It was put most forcefully by Lord Brightman in *Hart* v. *O'Connor*:[81]

If a contract is stigmatised as 'unfair', it may be unfair in one of two ways. It may be unfair by reason of the unfair manner in which it was brought into existence; a contract induced by undue influence is unfair in this sense. It will be convenient to call this 'procedural unfairness.' It may also, in some contexts, be described (accurately or inaccurately) as 'unfair' by reason of the fact that the terms of the contract are more favourable to one party than to the other. In order to distinguish this 'unfairness' from procedural unfairness, it will be convenient to call it 'contractual imbalance.' The two concepts

---

[78] Lord Selborne LC in *Earl of Aylesford* v. *Morris* (1873) 8 Ch. App. 484, 491 spoke of the law relating to unconscionable bargains as being analogous to undue influence.

[79] See pp. 177 ff. (undue influence); 198–9 (unconscionable bargains).

[80] There are some statements in Australian, Canadian, and New Zealand cases that undue influence and unconscionable bargains are different, in that undue influence, like common law duress, looks to the quality of the consent of the weaker party, whose will is overborne; but the law relating to unconscionable bargains looks to the conduct of the stronger party in taking advantage of a position of weakness: see *Commercial Bank of Australia Ltd.* v. *Amadio* (1982–3) 151 CLR 447, 461, 474; *Morrison* v. *Coast Finance Ltd.* (1965) 55 DLR (2d) 710, 713; *Knupp* v. *Bell* (1968) 67 DLR (2d) 256, 259; *K* v. *K* [1976] 2 NZLR 31, 36. However, we have seen (p. 195, above) that undue influence is in fact concerned with advantage taken—or presumed to have been taken—of a person by the application of pressure on him.

[81] [1985] AC 1000, 1017–18. In *Burmah Oil Co. Ltd.* v. *The Governor and Company of the Bank of England* (reported only in *The Times*, 4 July 1981), Walton J said, 'It is clearly . . . not sufficient for a bargain to be labelled "unfair"; before equity will interfere it must be an unconscionable bargain, one whose very terms speak for themselves to the effect that somebody has been dealt with in such a way as to shock the conscience of the Court.' See also *Griffith* v. *Spratley* (1787) 1 Cox 383, 388–9.

may overlap. Contractual imbalance may be so extreme as to raise a presumption of procedural unfairness, such as undue influence or some other form of victimisation. Equity will relieve a party from a contract which he has been induced to make as a result of victimisation. Equity will not relieve a party from a contract on the ground only that there is contractual imbalance not amounting to unconscionable dealing.

This passage draws the fundamental distinction between the unfair *terms* of a contract, and a contract which has been obtained by unfair *conduct*. There is a danger, in using such a phrase as 'unconscionable bargains', that this distinction is lost, and it can come to be thought that the courts are concerned only with the fairness of the terms of the bargain.

(b) 'Inequality of bargaining power'?

An attempt was made by Lord Denning MR in *Lloyds Bank Ltd.* v. *Bundy*[82] to deduce an underlying general concept of 'inequality of bargaining power' not only in the cases relating to unconscionable bargains, but also in areas such as duress and undue influence. The case involved a guarantee and charge over property by a father in favour of the bank, to secure his son's overdraft. There had been earlier charges and guarantees, of increasing value, but on each previous occasion the bank had left the documentation with the father, who had then taken his solicitor's advice. The documents which were the subject of the action were, however, signed in different circumstances. The bank manager visited the father, in the company of the son, at home; he brought the documents already completed and did not leave them for the father to consider; the father at the meeting said that he was '100 per cent behind' the son, and signed the forms on the spot. The Court of Appeal set aside the guarantee and charge. The majority held that there was undue influence.[83] Lord Denning MR, however, took a different line as his main ground, although as a second ground he agreed that there was undue influence.

Lord Denning's starting-point[84] was that in the vast majority of cases a customer who signs a bank guarantee or charge cannot get out of it. Even if the terms of the transaction are harsh, the general rule is that the transaction stands. 'No bargain will be upset which is

---

[82] [1975] QB 326.   [83] See p. 182, above.   [84] [1975] QB 326, 336.

the result of the ordinary interplay of forces.'[85] There are, said Lord Denning, exceptions to this rule, 'in which the courts will set aside a contract, or a transfer of property, when the parties have not met on equal terms—when the one is so strong in bargaining power and the other so weak—that, as a matter of common fairness, it is not right that the strong should be allowed to push the weak to the wall.'[86] Lord Denning deduced this principle from five categories of case:[87]

(1) Duress of goods. We have considered this category above.[88] Lord Denning saw the inequality of bargaining power here as the 'urgent need of the goods' by the weaker party, as opposed to the possession of goods by the stronger.

(2) Unconscionable transactions. This was the principle of *Fry* v. *Lane*,[89] as developed into a general principle of 'unconscientious use of power by a stronger party against the weaker'.[90]

(3) Undue influence. This is said to cover both actual and presumed influence.[91]

(4) Undue pressure. This is a category which does not fit easily into the traditional analysis of vitiating factors. Lord Denning gave as examples *Williams* v. *Bayley*[92] and *Ormes* v. *Beadel*,[93] which we have seen can be characterized as cases of undue influence, and *D & C Builders Ltd.* v. *Rees*.[94]

[85] Ibid.   [86] Ibid., at pp. 336–7.

[87] In *Avon Finance Co. Ltd.* v. *Bridger* [1985] 2 All ER 281, 285–6 Lord Denning MR suggested a sixth category which involved inequality of bargaining power: where one person is influenced by another to sign a guarantee in favour of a third party; the third party cannot enforce the guarantee where it left the arrangements for execution of the document to the second party: *Chaplin & Co. Ltd.* v. *Brammall* [1908] 1 KB 233; p. 189, above. And in *Clifford Davis Management Ltd.* v. *WEA Records Ltd.* [1975] 1 WLR 61, 64–5, Lord Denning MR said that the restraint of trade doctrine was also an illustration of the principle of inequality of bargaining power: see p. 206, above.

[88] pp. 156 ff. It should be noted that, at the time when *Lloyds Bank Ltd.* v. *Bundy* was decided, the recent developments of the law of duress—in particular the development of economic duress—had not yet taken place.

[89] (1888) 40 Ch. D. 312.

[90] [1975] QB 326, 337. Lord Denning referred to 'the cases cited in *Halsbury's Laws of England*, 3rd ed., vol 17 (1956) p. 682, and, in Canada, *Morrison* v. *Coast Finance Ltd.* (1965) 55 DLR (2d) 710 and *Knupp* v. *Bell* (1968) 67 DLR (2d) 256'. See n. 80, above.

[91] See Ch. 8, above.

[92] (1866) LR 1 HL 200; p. 172, above.

[93] (1860) 2 Giff. 166, 174.

[94] [1966] 2 QB 617, 625, where pressure was put on a creditor by a debtor to accept less than the full amount of the debt, under threat of obtaining nothing at all. This could have been characterized as undue influence; and would now constitute economic duress (the threat involved the tort of intimidation, and so would be illegitimate).

(5) Salvage agreements. The rule in cases where a vessel is in distress and a rescuer obtains the agreement of the vessel's owner or captain to pay for his help is that the court will only enforce the agreement if it is fair and just.[95]

From these categories, Lord Denning deduced a general principle:[96]

They rest on 'inequality of bargaining power.' By virtue of it, the English law gives relief to one who, without independent advice, enters into a contract upon terms which are very unfair or transfers property for a consideration which is grossly inadequate, when his bargaining power is grievously impaired by reason of his own needs or desires, or by his own ignorance or infirmity, coupled with undue influences or pressures brought to bear on him by or for the benefit of the other.

Lord Denning made it clear that, by using the word 'undue', he did not imply that there must be any deliberate wrongdoing—the motive of the stronger party may be entirely self-interested, without realizing the distress caused to the weaker party. Nor need the will of the weaker party be overcome—he may know perfectly well what he is doing, although he is only agreeing to relieve the straits in which he finds himself.[97]

The principle stated by Lord Denning can be a useful tool in analysing the vitiating factors. One point must, however, be borne carefully in mind. The choice of 'inequality of bargaining power' as the catchword for the principle is unfortunate. It can suggest that the courts will give relief simply on the basis of the unequal position of the parties, rather than on an *abuse* of that position. It is clear from Lord Denning's own statement of principle that he did not intend mere inequality to give rise to a remedy: he said that there needs to be an unfairness in the bargain, and an impairment of bargaining power of the weaker party, 'coupled with undue influences or pressures brought to bear on him'. We have seen in relation to unconscionable bargains[98] that the courts have recently emphasized the need for unfair conduct, to link the inequality of position with

---

[95] *Akerblom* v. *Price, Potter, Walker, & Co.* (1881) 7 QBD 129, 133; *The Port Caledonia and the Anna* [1903] P. 184.

[96] [1975] QB 326, 339.

[97] Cf. the controversy over whether duress involves a vitiation of consent: p. 161, above.

[98] p. 208, above.

the unfairness of the bargain; Lord Denning's statement of principle appears to be entirely consistent with this.

In a sense, Lord Denning's principle gets us only a little further forward, since it still contains the concept of 'undue' influences or pressures; this begs the question of what sort of pressures should vitiate a contract. However, it is useful in its emphasis that the concept of an illegitimate advantage-taking by one party underlies a number of separate areas.[99]

Lord Denning's ideas have not, however, found universal favour. Sachs LJ in *Lloyds Bank Ltd.* v. *Bundy*,[100] whilst noting that the areas covered by Lord Denning in his judgment had not been discussed by counsel, expressed 'some sympathy' with the view that undue pressure ought to be a ground of relief. The idea of the underlying principle was, however, strongly disapproved by Lord Scarman in *National Westminster Bank plc* v. *Morgan*.[101] It will be recalled that this case involved undue influence—and sought to emphasize that undue influence requires the victimization of one party by the other; the presumption of influence being raised by a manifestly disadvantageous transaction entered into with a person in a position to dominate the other.[102] Lord Scarman said[103] that undue influence has been sufficiently developed not to need the support of the principle stated by Lord Denning; and he noted that, since undue influence can apply also in the case of gratuitous transactions,[104] which by their nature do not involve a bargain, it is inappropriate to use such language as inequality of 'bargaining power'. He even doubted whether 'inequality of bargaining power' was a useful term in the

---

[99] Curiously, Lord Denning included only duress of goods—which was a rather doubtful category of duress at the time that *Bundy* was decided; he could have included duress generally—since (as we have seen) all forms of duress, to the person, goods, and now to economic interests, involve illegitimate pressure exerted by one party against the other. In *Burmah Oil Co. Ltd.* v. *The Governor and Company of the Bank of England, The Times*, 4 July 1981, Walton J noted that Lord Denning's heads (1) and (5) 'owe nothing to equity'. This is not, however, to say that it is wrong to look for some general principles underlying the area of pressure and abuse of position—whether at common law or in equity.

[100] [1975] QB 326, 347.

[101] [1985] AC 686, 707–8. See also Lord Radcliffe in *Bridge* v. *Campbell Discount Co. Ltd.* [1962] AC 600, 625–6.

[102] See pp. 184–5, above.

[103] [1985] AC 686, 708.

[104] Such as in *Allcard* v. *Skinner* (1887) 36 Ch. D. 145; see text to n. 3, p. 171, above.

law of contract, drawing attention to certain instances where Parliament had intervened to protect such inequalities.[105]

The objections to the concept of 'inequality of bargaining power' should not be overstated. From the legislative examples which Lord Scarman cited, it appears that he was viewing the principle stated by Lord Denning as involving the vitiation of contracts simply by virtue of the inequality of position of the parties or by virtue of a bargain which is unfair to one party. But we have seen that the key element is the *link* between the unequal position of the parties and the bargain: the *abuse* of that position of inequality is required. And it may be that the language of 'bargain' is unhelpful outside the law of contract; but this is only a problem of terminology.

Moreover, in *Pao On* v. *Lau Yiu Long*[106] Lord Scarman resisted the idea that English law should adopt a general rule that a contract could be void for public policy on the basis of unfair use of a dominant bargaining position:

It is unnecessary because justice requires that men, who have negotiated at arm's length, be held to their bargains unless it can be shown that their contract was vitiated by fraud, mistake or duress. . . .

Such a rule of public policy as is now being considered would be unhelpful because it would render the law uncertain. It would become a question of fact and degree to determine in each case whether there had been, short of duress, an unfair use of a strong bargaining position.

Lord Scarman may be right that it is not possible or desirable to abandon the existing categories of vitiation of contracts in favour of a single category of inequality of bargaining, or abuse of position. But once it is realized that there is a general principle at work, underlying the several categories, which hinges upon the relative positions of the parties at the time of contracting, and the abuse of that position by one of the parties, it helps to explain the coherence of the law relating to these vitiating factors—and also to enable a more sensible examination of the ways in which the vitiating factors should—or should not—be developed.

---

[105] Supply of Goods (Implied Terms) Act 1973, Consumer Credit Act 1974, Consumer Safety Act 1978, Supply of Goods and Services Act 1982, and Insurance Companies Act 1982.
[106] [1980] AC 614, 634.

IV
CONCLUSIONS

10

Common Themes

This book has considered a number of areas of law surrounding the formation of a contract. At the beginning[1] the following questions were identified:

(1) Is there a contract?
(2) On which terms is it formed?
(3) Are there any inherent defects in the contract arising out of the circumstances of its formation?

We have now considered separately the areas of law which relate to these three questions. Part I discussed questions (1) and (2): and Parts II and III discussed question (3), by considering the various vitiating factors which may be present at the time of the formation of a contract. We are therefore now in a position to discover common themes and ideas which underlie these different areas of the law of contract.

1. *SMITH* v. *HUGHES* REVISITED

Smith v. *Hughes*[2] was discussed in detail in Part I.[3] The case is very instructive of the general approach taken by English law to the bargaining process leading up to the formation of a contract.

The Court in that case held that the purchaser of the oats would be bound under a contract to accept new oats (even though he intended to buy old oats), as long as his words or conduct had been such that the vendor reasonably could, and in fact did, believe that he was so agreeing. And if the parties did not intend the age of the oats to be a term of the contract, but the purchaser simply made a mistake about the factual quality of the oats, this would not allow him to escape

---

[1] p. xxix, above. [2] (1871) LR 6 QB 597. [3] pp. 6 ff., above.

from the contract, *even if* the vendor realized the mistake, *provided that* the vendor had done nothing to cause the purchaser's mistake:

for, whatever may be the case in a court of morals, there is no legal obligation on the vendor to inform the purchaser that he is under a mistake, not induced by the act of the vendor.[4]

This tells us two things about the general approach to contract formation. First, that the approach taken by the courts is objective, in the sense that contractual obligations are determined by what a negotiating party has by his words or conduct communicated, rather than by what he himself intended to communicate. A party cannot walk away from a contract by simply saying that he did not intend to be bound. If he has communicated inaccurately his intentions, it is the other party, who actually and reasonably thought that a particular agreement was being made, who is allowed to assert his understanding at the expense of the first party. There is therefore a responsibility on a negotiating party to ensure that he communicates accurately his intentions in relation to the obligations to be created by the contract. So it is not enough to look at what the parties intended, to determine the existence and content of a contract. There must be a close analysis of the whole circumstances surrounding the bargaining process, to see what the words and conduct of each party can be taken to have communicated to the other.

The second thing which *Smith* v. *Hughes* tells us is that, when we are looking not at the terms of the contract, but at the quality or general attributes of the subject-matter, each party must ensure that the contract gives him what he expects. Even if one party knows that the other is deluded about the benefits which the contract will confer upon him, the contract still binds.

We have seen this idea elsewhere. The courts will not generally investigate a bargain to see whether the terms are fair and equal.[5] A person must be free to conclude a bad bargain, as well as a good bargain, and this extends to the case where one party knows that the other is entering into a disadvantageous transaction.[6] There is no

---

[4] (1871) LR 6 QB 597, 607 (Blackburn J), quoted above, p. 7.

[5] Treitel, pp. 58–9; p. 184, above.

[6] See e.g. the cases on economic duress, where a disadvantageous contract is binding if entered into under only commercial pressure, rather than pressure which is sufficient to constitute duress: Ch. 7, above. The plaintiffs in *The Alev* [1989] 1 Lloyd's Rep. 138, for instance, must have known that the defendants were entering into a disadvantageous arrangement under pressure.

general rule in English law that a party has to bargain in good faith, or to comply with a principle of fair and open dealing.[7]

However, even if English law does not enforce a rule of fair dealing, it does take account of *unfair* dealing. *Smith* v. *Hughes* contains the idea that, although one party is under no obligation to disabuse the other of mistakes about the quality or general attributes of the subject-matter, he is under a duty not to induce those mistakes.[8] If one party has by a misrepresentation caused the other to misunderstand some aspect of the transaction or the subject-matter, then his misrepresentation overrides the rule that he may take advantage of a good bargain at the other's expense. And although, as we have seen,[9] the courts will not avoid a contract simply on the ground that its terms are very unfair to one party, they will look into the causes of the unfairness. If it is shown to be—or, sometimes, can be presumed in the circumstances to be—the result of unfair conduct of the party who has obtained the contract in his favour, then the courts may allow that underlying unfair conduct to vitiate the contract.

2. RESPONSIBILITY IN NEGOTIATING

Throughout this book we have seen that the words and conduct, and the relative positions of the parties, at the time of entering into the contract, are crucial to determine the scope and validity of the obligations created. Particular areas which we have seen are statements made by one party to the other; relative positions of skill or knowledge of the parties; and unfair pressure applied by one party to the other.

(a) Statements

The most obvious area in which statements made by one party to the other are relevant is in the area of misrepresentation. We saw in Part II[10] that the law relating to pre-contractual misrepresentations is complex, and has developed without any clear or coherent analysis

---

[7] *Interfoto Picture Library Ltd.* v. *Stiletto Visual Programmes Ltd.* [1989] QB 433, 439.

[8] See p. 7 n. 21, above.

[9] p. 215, above.

[10] See p. 62, above.

by the courts or the legislature of the interrelation between the
different causes of action for misrepresentation (nor between the
different remedies available).

However, we saw[11] that the remedy of rescission was available for
a misled party for even a wholly innocent misrepresentation. And
from this it appears that an underlying principle of misrepresentation is that the mere fact of having been misled by a false statement
is enough to justify the misrepresentee having a remedy.[12] The
making of the statement disturbs the balance of the parties'
bargaining positions. Even though the misrepresentor may be
wholly innocent, in the sense that he does not realize—nor even
ought to realize—that he is not telling the truth, the fact of making a
statement upon which the other negotiating party relies carries with
it a responsibility. The nature of that responsibility will vary
according to the circumstances of the misrepresentation; and we saw
that different remedies are available according to the different
circumstances. But every misrepresentation[13] will disturb the
balance between the parties, and will prima facie justify the misled
party being preferred over the party making the statement.

It is not only in relation to remedies for misrepresentation,
however, that statements between the parties are significant. In the
basic test for the formation of the contract, and the ascertainment of
the obligations created under the contract, the words used by the
parties are crucial. We saw in Chapter 1 that the basic approach of
the cases, in the absence of actual agreement between the parties, is
to follow *Smith* v. *Hughes*[14] in saying that A can assert his terms
against B if, but only if, B's words and conduct were such that a
reasonable man could, and A in fact did, believe that B was assenting
to A's terms. This appears[15] to be a rule of interpretation of the
communication between the parties; but its underlying principle is
that the fact that one party has said or done something which—
however innocently—caused the other party reasonably to misunderstand the first party's intention justifies the other party's
interpretation of the contract being preferred. This is a similar idea to

[11] p. 103, above.

[12] pp. 103–4, above.

[13] There are of course certain problems in relation to misrepresentations of law,
opinion, and intention: see pp. 74 ff., above. But this does not detract from the general
proposition relating the underlying principles of misrepresentation.

[14] (1871) LR 6 QB 597.

[15] p. 15, above.

misrepresentation, but it is being used in a quite different manner. In misrepresentation, the misled party is seeking remedies to extricate himself from the consequences of being committed to a contract to which he would not have agreed had he known the truth at the time of contracting. In *Smith* v. *Hughes*, however, the party who misunderstands the other's intentions is seeking to uphold a contract—but *his* version of the contract, rather than the other's version.[16]

(b) Relative Positions of Knowledge or Skill

A party's knowledge can be relevant in a number of situations. In relation to the terms of the contract, A's knowledge that B is not intending to agree with his terms will be fatal to A's claim that there is a contract on his terms. The 'objective' test of *Smith* v. *Hughes*[17] can be applied in A's favour only if he honestly and reasonably believes that B is agreeing with him. Therefore, actual or constructive knowledge by A that B is not agreeing will affect the terms of the contract created. Moreover, we saw that in relation to the remedy of rectification, one party's knowledge of the other's intentions is important.[18] The fact that there is a written document containing a particular set of terms may be overridden by the knowledge of the party resisting rectification that the document did not accurately reflect the other party's intentions. The knowledge must exist at the time of contracting, so that it can be said that the conduct of the party resisting rectification was at that time unfair in obtaining the contract in its written form; and here the knowledge must be actual—constructive knowledge is not sufficient.[19] But again one party's knowledge of the terms intended by the other overrides his own intentions.

Importance is attached to the relative positions of the parties in other areas. In misrepresentation, for example, we saw[20] that the force to be given to a false statement made by one party to the other often depends upon the context in which it is spoken—and in particular whether the position of the misrepresentor is such as

---

[16] See also *Curtis* v. *Chemical Cleaning and Dyeing Co.* [1951] 1 KB 805; p. 44, above.
[17] (1871) LR 6 QB 597.
[18] p. 54, above.
[19] p. 54, above. For the reason for requiring *actual* knowledge, see p. 57 n. 89, above.
[20] pp. 145–8, above.

could lead the misrepresentee to attach more weight to the statement. The remedy of rescission generally[21] requires that the misrepresentation be of fact; but we saw[22] that the circumstances of the
representation must be considered to see whether it can be
characterized as being one of fact, rather than, for example, opinion.
If the representor is in a better position to know the facts about
which he speaks, his statement is more likely to be held to have been
a representation of fact, and so to be actionable.

In this area, then, a party's responsibility for his words may be
greater simply because of his stronger position in relation to the
other party. And the same is true of other remedies for misrepresentation. For a misrepresentor to be liable in the tort of negligence, he
must owe a duty of care;[23] and the duty of care depends upon the
'special relationship' between the parties—which is, in essence, that
the representor is in a superior position of skill or knowledge as
regards the subject-matter of his statement, so that the representee
is entitled to rely upon the representation. Moreover, the terms of a
contract can also depend upon the relative positions of the parties. If
a statement is made by one party to the other during the course of
negotiations, it is more likely to be incorporated as a term of the
contract if the representor is in a superior position.[24]

Indeed, one party's position may even be so much more powerful
than the other's as to give rise to a positive obligation on him to
disclose what he knows which is relevant to the contract; or may
raise a suspicion that advantage could be taken by the stronger of the
weaker and so an obligation is imposed on the stronger to establish
that he has not taken such advantage.

The first of these—obligations of disclosure arising by virtue of the
relative positions of the parties—arises in relation to fiduciary
relationships, and under the heading of contracts *uberrimae fidei*.[25]
The latter—presumptions of advantage being taken by the stronger

---

[21] Unless the representation is fraudulent, in which case the fraud overrides the
policy rule that actionable misrepresentations are limited to representations of fact: p.
78, above.

[22] *Smith* v. *Land and House Property Corporation* (1884) 28 Ch. D. 7; *Bisset* v. *Wilkinson*
[1927] AC 177; p. 80, above.

[23] *Hedley Byrne & Co. Ltd.* v. *Heller & Partners Ltd.* [1964] AC 465; *Smith* v. *Eric S.
Bush* [1990] AC 831; p. 120, above.

[24] *Oscar Chess Ltd.* v. *Williams* [1957] 1 WLR 370; *Dick Bentley Productions Ltd.* v.
Harold Smith (Motors) Ltd. [1965] 1 WLR 623; pp. 136–7, above.

[25] pp. 91–3, above.

of the weaker—arises in cases of presumed undue influence,[26] and 'unconscionable bargains'.[27] We have seen that in these areas there are certain generic relationships which have been characterized by the courts as normally giving rise to the necessary inequality;[28] however, these are at root only applications of the general rule that the particular relationship between the parties should be considered to see whether one is in fact in a position of superiority so as to require the court to consider carefully the contract entered into to ensure that the position of superiority has not been abused. Varying terminology has been used to describe the relationship between the superior and the inferior party: fiduciary relationships;[29] special relationships;[30] relationships of confidence.[31] However, it is clear that the courts are scrutinizing the relative positions of the parties to establish whether one was in such a position that he ought to be required to be more open in his dealings with the other, or to show that he had not taken advantage of his position.

We have seen, however, that there is no general doctrine that an inequality—however great—in the position of the parties of itself vitiates the contract. There must, generally,[32] be an abuse of that inequality. In undue influence, for example, we saw that the current thinking of the courts is that the presumption of influence which arises from a consideration of the relative positions of the parties coupled with the manifestly disadvantageous transaction, is a means of establishing the advantage which one party has actively taken of the other.[33] And even in the case of unconscionable bargains, it is the advantage taken by one party of the other which is presumed from the relative positions of the parties and the terms of the bargain entered into between them.[34]

---

[26] pp. 177 ff., above.

[27] pp. 197 ff., above.

[28] For example, in contracts *uberrimae fidei*, contracts of insurance: p. 92, above; and in presumed undue influence, such relationships as parent/child, solicitor/client.

[29] Duties of disclosure: p. 91, above; undue influence: p. 180, above.

[30] Undue influence: p. 179, above; cf. *Hedley Byrne & Co. Ltd.* v. *Heller & Partners Ltd.* [1964] AC 465, p. 120, above.

[31] Undue influence: pp. 179–80, above.

[32] There are, however, certain situations where the relationship between the parties is *conclusive* of the vitiation of the contract, on the basis that the superior party can never be allowed to obtain an unimpeachable contract in such a situation, even if it appears that there has been no actual abuse of position on the facts; e.g. purchases by a trustee: see pp. 208–10, above.

[33] pp. 185; 195–6, above.

[34] pp. 214–15, above.

(c) Unfair Pressure

A particular form of abuse of a position of strength is the application of unfair pressure. The clearest case of this is, of course, duress;[35] but undue influence can also involve the application of unfair pressure. 'Actual' undue influence requires proof that the party who was in a position to exert an unfair pressure or influence did so use that position;[36] but we have seen that 'presumed' undue influence also involves the presumption, from the circumstances and the terms of the contract, that unfair pressure or influence has been applied.[37]

In relation to pressure, the general problem is to ascertain the type of pressure which is unacceptable, given that (particularly in a commercial context) some degree of persuasion and pressure is natural in the negotiations leading up to a contract. We saw that, in the case of duress, the courts are presently wrestling with the criterion of *legitimacy* of pressure;[38] and although there is no similar explicit criterion in the case of undue influence, the courts have identified certain types of case where pressure—which does not fulfil the requirements of duress at common law—is unacceptable in equity and so may vitiate the contract.[39]

3. UNFAIR BARGAINS AND UNFAIR BARGAINING

We have seen throughout this book that English law draws a clear distinction between two situations: a contract which is unfair or unequal in its terms—an unfair or unequal *bargain*; and a contract which is procured unfairly by one of the parties—a contract which is the result of unfair or unequal *bargaining*. Although there may be relief against unfair terms under certain statutes,[40] the common law does not generally allow the unfairness of the terms to vitiate the contract. What may, however, vitiate a contract is the unfair means by which the contract has been procured. This distinction was drawn explicitly by Lord Brightman in *Hart* v. *O'Connor*,[41] in relation to the

---

[35] Ch. 7, above.   [36] p. 171, above.   [37] p. 185, above.
[38] pp. 163 ff., above.   [39] p. 172, above.
[40] e.g. hire purchase and consumer protection legislation, referred to by Lord Scarman in *National Westminster Bank plc* v. *Morgan* [1985] AC 686, 708; p. 220 n. 105, above.
[41] [1985] AC 1000, 1017–18, quoted at pp. 215–16, above.

circumstances in which equity will intervene in contracts; but the same principle applies also to the common law.

The reason for this principle is clear: although English law is committed to the policy that contracts should be upheld, and parties should not be able to extricate themselves from contracts just because they have not obtained the benefit for which they hoped, this policy is overridden by unfair activity of one of the parties in obtaining the contract. Parties are free to bargain; and to bargain well or badly. But if one party, by his words or conduct, or by abusing a position of strength which he holds *vis-à-vis* the other party, disturbs the balance of the negotiations, the disadvantaged party should have appropriate remedies.

None of this is to suggest that, by identifying an underlying principle of the vitiating factors as being the unfair procurement of the contract, these areas can simply be merged into a single rule. For as soon as one says that the principle is the *unfair* procurement of the contract, this immediately raises the question: what sort of procurement is unfair? The answer given by English law is that procurement of a contract is unfair, and so vitiates the contract, if it involves misrepresentation, duress, undue influence, or the other particular areas which have been discussed in this book. But once it is realized that there are common links between these vitiating factors, and that these are themselves linked to the basic rules for the formation of the contract and the establishment of its terms, the general approach taken by English law in relation to the negotiations leading up to a contract can be seen to have a coherent basis which can be used as a guide for the future development of the law.

11

A Contrast

1. COMMON MISTAKE: A CONTRAST

In the preceding chapters of this book, we have identified as a common link between the vitiating factors in the formation of a contract the fact that one party procures the contract by some activity which the law characterizes as unfair. It may be deliberate wrongdoing, such as fraudulent misrepresentation or duress; or it may sometimes even be an innocent activity, such as making a wholly innocent misrepresentation, or failing to act in a particular way which is demanded by one's position in relation to the other party. But throughout the law of misrepresentation, duress, undue influence, and unconscionable bargains, a common link is that one party, by his actions or by the use of his superior position *vis-à-vis* the other party, has disturbed the balance of negotiations at the time of the contract: the bargaining is unequal.

Another vitiating factor is 'common' mistake,[1] where the parties are in agreement about the terms on which they wish to contract, but have both made the same mistake about the subject-matter. We shall see that an operative common mistake may render a contract either *void ab initio* or *voidable*; it may therefore be regarded as a vitiating factor which is present from the time of the formation of the contract. However, common mistake is a wholly different kind of vitiating factor from those which have so far been considered in this book. In the case of those other vitiating factors, there is something in the conduct or position of one party which disturbs the balance of the negotiations; the 'weaker' party is therefore preferred over the 'stronger'. In common mistake, however, there is no such disturbance of the balance of the negotiations by either party. There is nothing that one party has done to the other which justifies

---

[1] For the varying terminology of writers in relation to the categorization of mistake, see p. 4 nn. 3 and 4, above.

overriding the policy of upholding contracts. In consequence, the courts have been much more reluctant to allow common mistake to vitiate a contract.

2. THE RULES GOVERNING COMMON MISTAKE[2]

The doctrine of common mistake is bedevilled by its historical origins. Until 1949, it was not thought that common mistake was dealt with substantially differently at common law and in equity. There were cases decided explicitly on equitable principles;[3] but there was no separate doctrine of common mistake in equity: a contract would not be held valid under the common law rules, whilst being held voidable in equity for a common mistake. However, we shall see that, since the landmark decision of *Solle* v. *Butcher*[4] in 1949, a separate jurisdiction has been developed in equity which is liable to allow a party to escape his contract on the basis of a common mistake of fact which would not be sufficient to vitiate the contract at common law.

(a) Common Mistake at Common Law

The basic position which has been taken consistently by the common law is that a contract will be void[5] for common mistake only if it is a mistake of fact[6] which has the effect of rendering the subject-matter of the contract fundamentally different from that which both parties believed at the time when they concluded the contract. This can be illustrated from three key cases.

[2] For an earlier account of the issues surrounding the relationship of the rules of common law and equity for common mistake, see Cartwright, '*Solle* v. *Butcher* and the Doctrine of Mistake in Contract' (1987) 103 LQR 594.

[3] e.g. *Cooper* v. *Phibbs* (1867) LR 2 HL 149.

[4] [1950] 1 KB 671.

[5] Notice that, at common law, a contract is void, rather then voidable, for mistake. Under the rules of equity propounded in *Solle* v. *Butcher* [1950] 1 KB 671, the effect of an operative mistake is to render the contract voidable.

[6] This is to be contrasted with mistakes of law—a similar rule to that employed in the law relating to misrepresentation: see pp. 74 ff., above. Indeed, many of the cases referred to there were cases discussing mistakes, rather than misrepresentations, of law. In misrepresentation, fact is also contrasted with intention and opinion, but these are irrelevant in the case of mistake: there can hardly be a common mistake about the intention or opinion of one of the contracting parties.

The leading case is *Bell* v. *Lever Brothers Ltd.*,[7] where an employer paid large 'golden handshakes' to two senior employees, when they could in fact have been dismissed summarily because of breaches of duty which they had committed. The case was decided on the basis that the employees did not have in mind the breaches of duty when they entered into the contract[8]—and so the mistake was common. Their Lordships were divided on the application of the law to the facts,[9] but all the judgments clearly held that the doctrine of common mistake was narrow, and required a very serious mistake indeed before the contract was avoided. Lord Atkin[10] discussed the principles of common mistake at length, pointing out that the common law may avoid a contract if, unknown to both parties, the subject-matter of the contract has perished[11] or if, in a contract of sale, the buyer already owns that which the seller purports to sell.[12] He went on to deal with other common mistakes, and to consider the general approach taken by the common law, as follows:[13]

Mistake as to quality of the thing contracted for . . . will not affect assent unless it is the mistake of both parties and is as to the existence of some

---

[7] [1932] AC 161.

[8] This was found by the jury: [1932] AC 161, 186.

[9] Lords Blanesburgh, Atkin, and Thankerton held that the contract was valid; Viscount Hailsham and Lord Warrington of Clyffe that it was void. The trial judge, Wright J, and the unanimous Court of Appeal had held the contract void. The disagreement appears to have been a consequence of their Lordships' different interpretations of the facts surrounding the mistake. The majority in the House of Lords appear to have thought that the question addressed by the parties was: 'Is there a contract of employment to terminate?' The answer to this was: 'Yes'. There was therefore no mistake: see [1932] AC 161, 233, 236 (Lord Thankerton), 223–4 (Lord Atkin). However, the minority in the House of Lords (together with the trial judge and the Court of Appeal) thought that the question was: 'Is there a *valid* contract of employment to terminate, which requires the agreement of the employees to terminate it?' The answer to this question was: 'No', since the employees by their breaches of duty had rendered their own service contracts terminable at the will of the employer. A further fact which may have influenced the decision of the majority is that the employer received extra benefits from the employees' planned and co-operative retirement from their posts: [1932] AC 161, 181, 197; *Associated Japanese Bank (International) Ltd.* v. *Crédit du Nord SA* [1989] 1 WLR 255, 267.

[10] [1932] AC 161, 217–18.

[11] *Res extincta*: *Galloway* v. *Galloway* (1914) 30 TLR 531; *Strickland* v. *Turner* (1852) 7 Ex. 208. But it is always possible for one of the parties to have undertaken in the contract the risk that the subject-matter is in existence: *Couturier* v. *Hastie* (1856) 5 HLC 673; *McRae* v. *Commonwealth Disposals Commission* (1951) 84 CLR 377, 409–10; *Associated Japanese Bank (International) Ltd.* v. *Crédit du Nord SA* [1989] 1 WLR 255, 268.

[12] *Res sua*: *Cooper* v. *Phibbs* (1867) LR 2 HL 149. This is similar to *res extincta*, since the rights which are purported to be sold do not exist.

[13] [1932] AC 161, 218.

quality which makes the thing without the quality essentially different from the thing as it was believed to be.

And he later[14] expressed the view that common mistake might be looked at in another way: that there is implied into the contract a condition precedent—the contract will be binding only if the assumed facts are true. Even if common mistake were characterized in this way, however, the test for the existence of the implied condition would be the same as the test for an operative common mistake:[15]

We therefore get a common standard for mutual[16] mistake, and implied conditions whether as to existing or as to future[17] facts. Does the state of the new facts destroy the identity of the subject-matter as it was in the original state of facts?

Lord Thankerton also used very restrictive language. He said[18] that there will be an operative common mistake only if it relates 'to something which both must necessarily have accepted in their minds as an essential and integral element of the subject-matter'. And Lord Warrington,[19] discussing the distinction between operative and inoperative mistakes, said that the question was whether the mistake was

of such a fundamental character as to constitute an underlying assumption without which the parties would not have made the contract they in fact made, or whether it was only a common error as to a material element, but one not going to the root of the matter and not affecting the substance of the consideration.

The judgments in *Bell* v. *Lever Brothers Ltd.*[20] relied heavily on an earlier case which had emphasized how narrow is the doctrine of common mistake at common law: *Kennedy* v. *The Panama, New Zealand and Australian Royal Mail Co. Ltd.*[21]

In *Kennedy*, the defendant company had issued a prospectus inviting subscriptions for new shares, 'in order to enable the

---

[14] Ibid., at pp. 224–5.   [15] Ibid., at pp. 226–7.

[16] i.e. common. See p. 4 n. 4, above.

[17] i.e. frustration: see [1932] AC 161, 225. The 'implied condition' has in the past been regarded as the theoretical basis of the doctrine of frustration: see *National Carriers Ltd.* v. *Panalpina (Northern) Ltd.* [1981] AC 675, 687 (Lord Hailsham of St Marylebone LC); *Taylor* v. *Caldwell* (1863) 3 B. & S. 826. For the modern view of the theoretical basis, see *Davis Contractors Ltd.* v. *Fareham UDC* [1956] AC 696, 729.

[18] [1932] AC 161, 235.   [19] Ibid., at p. 208.

[20] Ibid., at pp. 207, 219, 233.   [21] (1867) LR 2 QB 580.

company to perform the contract recently entered into with the General Government of New Zealand for a monthly mail service between Sydney, New Zealand, and Panama'.[22] The plaintiff read the prospectus and subscribed for shares. In due course, and following a change of government in New Zealand, the mail contract was disputed; the new Government refused to recognize the contract, and a compromise was reached between the company and the Government on a new (but—for the company—less lucrative) contract. The plaintiff, on learning of the dispute, claimed to rescind the contract under which he became a shareholder.

The plaintiff failed in his action. He sought to rely on two separate grounds: misrepresentation and mistake. The Court of Queen's Bench held that there was no operative misrepresentation. Although there had been a material misrepresentation which induced the plaintiff to enter into the contract, it was only an honest statement; and, in 1867, the common law required *fraud* before a misrepresentation became operative.[23]

It was, however, accepted that, even if there was not an operative misrepresentation, a contract might still at common law be rescinded[24] on the ground of mistake; but only in the case of very serious mistakes. Blackburn J said,[25]

There is . . . a very important difference between cases where a contract may be rescinded on account of fraud, and those in which it may be rescinded on the ground that there is a difference in substance between the thing bargained for and that obtained. It is enough to shew that there was a fraudulent representation as to *any part* of that which induced the party to enter into the contract which he seeks to rescind; but where there has been an innocent misrepresentation or misapprehension, it does not authorize a rescission, unless it is such as to shew that there is a complete difference in substance between what was supposed to be and what was taken, so as to constitute a failure of consideration.

On the facts, however, the Court decided that there was not a 'complete difference in substance' between the shares which the plaintiff actually received and those he expected to receive under the

[22] Ibid., at p. 584.   [23] See p. 69, above.

[24] The judgment of the Court does not discuss the distinction between void and voidable contracts.

[25] (1867) LR 2 QB 580, 587, quoted at pp. 69–70, above. Blackburn J (at pp. 587–8) compared the English law rules with those relating to *error in substantia* in Roman Law: D. 18.1.9, 10, 11. However, the Roman Law was not identical to English law: see Mackintosh, *The Roman Law of Sale*, 2nd edn., 1907, pp. 32–4; Zulueta, *The Roman Law of Sale*, 1945, pp. 26–7; *Associated Japanese Bank (International) Ltd.* v. *Crédit du Nord SA* [1989] 1 WLR 255, 268.

contract. He obtained the very shares for which he had applied—it just turned out that the company had not such a profitable contract with the New Zealand Government as he had thought.

We can therefore see that the common law took a very restrictive approach to the issue of common mistake of fact. The mistake would be operative only if it was 'fundamental'[26] or 'basic'[27] or so serious that the contract as entered into was 'essentially'[28] or 'in substance'[29] or 'in identity'[30] different from that which the parties had supposed. This restrictive approach of the common law has been confirmed more recently in *Associated Japanese Bank (International) Ltd.* v. *Crédit du Nord SA*.[31] In that case, Steyn J deduced from *Kennedy* v. *The Panama, New Zealand and Australian Royal Mail Co. Ltd.* and *Bell* v. *Lever Brothers Ltd.* the following test for common mistake at common law:[32]

the mistake must render the subject matter of the contract essentially and radically[33] different from the subject matter which the parties believed to exist.

[26] *Bell* v. *Lever Brothers Ltd.* [1932] AC 161, 208 (Lord Warrington); *Norwich Union Fire Insurance Society Ltd.* v. *Wm. H. Price Ltd.* [1934] AC 455, 463 (Lord Wright).

[27] *Norwich Union Fire Insurance Society Ltd.* v. *Wm. H. Price Ltd.* [1934] AC 455, 463 (Lord Wright).

[28] *Bell* v. *Lever Brothers Ltd.* [1932] AC 161, 218 (Lord Atkin).

[29] *Kennedy* v. *The Panama, New Zealand and Australian Royal Mail Co. Ltd.* (1867) LR 2 QB 580, 587 (Blackburn J).

[30] *Bell* v. *Lever Brothers Ltd.* [1932] AC 161, 227 (Lord Atkin).

[31] [1989] 1 WLR 255, 264 ff.

[32] Ibid., at p. 268. Steyn J went on to add a restriction which was not discussed in any earlier English case: 'a party cannot be allowed to rely on a common mistake where the mistake consists of a belief which is entertained by him without any reasonable grounds for such belief: cf *McRae* v. *Commonwealth Disposals Commission* (1951) 84 CLR 377, 408. That is not because principles such as estoppel or negligence require it, but simply because policy and good sense dictate that the positive rules regarding common mistake should be so qualified.' It is not, however, clear that the judgment in *McRae* v. *Commonwealth Disposals Commission* justifies this restriction: see Cartwright, [1988] LMCLQ 300, 301. It should be noted, however, that the rules relating to *non est factum* have a similar restriction, in that the party seeking to deny that he is bound by the document which he has executed must show that he was not at fault in making the mistake: see pp. 46–7, above. And we have seen throughout this book that the relative and respective positions of the two contracting parties are crucial in determining the validity of the contract; it is therefore not altogether surprising that the notion of fault should be introduced as a further limiting factor in common mistake at common law.

[33] This word had not traditionally been used in relation to mistake; but it is a key word in the modern test for frustration: *Davis Contractors Ltd.* v. *Fareham UDC* [1956] AC 696, 729 (Lord Radcliffe). Steyn J took the view that the principles of common mistake and frustration are closely related: [1989] 1 WLR 255, 264–5; and see Cartwright, (1987) 103 LQR 594, 603–4.

(*b*) Common Mistake in Equity

Although the common law took—and continues to take[34]—a restrictive approach to the granting of relief for a common mistake of fact, the courts have developed equitable rules which are less restrictive. Originally, it appears that the Courts of Equity, whilst granting equitable remedies in response to a claim of common mistake,[35] has not gone so far as to hold voidable for mistake a contract which the common law would have held valid.[36] In *Solle* v. *Butcher*,[37] however, Denning LJ delivered a judgment which has given rise to considerable development in the scope of the equitable jurisdiction for common mistake. He expressed the view that a common mistake did not as such vitiate a contract at common law; but that there was an equitable jurisdiction to rescind a contract for mistake. Parts of Denning LJ's judgment have already been considered;[38] it is, however, worth setting out the relevant passage again in full:[39]

Let me first consider mistakes which render a contract a nullity. All previous decisions on this subject must now be read in the light of *Bell* v. *Lever Brothers Ltd.*[40] The correct interpretation of that case, to my mind, is that, once a contract has been made, that is to say, once the parties, whatever their inmost states of mind, have to all outward appearances agreed with sufficient certainty in the same terms on the same subject matter, then the contract is good unless and until it is set aside for failure of some condition on which the existence of the contract depends, or for fraud, or on some equitable ground. Neither party can rely on his own mistake to say it was a nullity from the beginning, no matter that it was a mistake which to his mind was fundamental, and no matter that the other party knew that he was under a mistake. A fortiori, if the other party did not know of the mistake, but shared it. . . .

Let me next consider mistakes which render a contract voidable, that is, liable to be set aside on some equitable ground. Whilst presupposing that a contract was good at law, or at any rate not void, the court of equity would

---

[34] *Associated Japanese Bank (International) Ltd.* v. *Crédit du Nord SA* [1989] 1 WLR 255, 266–7.

[35] *Cooper* v. *Phibbs* (1867) LR 2 HL 149.

[36] Cartwright, (1987) 103 LQR 594, 605–7.

[37] [1950] 1 KB 671.

[38] p. 22, above.

[39] [1950] 1 KB 671, 691–3.

[40] [1932] AC 161, 222, 224, 225–7, 236.

often relieve a party from the consequences of his own mistake, so long as it could do so without injustice to third parties. The court, it was said, had power to set aside the contract whenever it was of opinion that it was unconscientious for the other party to avail himself of the legal advantage which he had obtained: *Torrance* v. *Bolton*[41] per James LJ.

The court had, of course, to define what it considered to be unconscientious, but in this respect equity has shown a progressive development. It is now clear that a contract will be set aside if the mistake of the one party has been induced by a material misrepresentation of the other, even though it was not fraudulent or fundamental; or if one party, knowing that the other is mistaken about the terms of an offer, or the identity of the person by whom it is made, lets him remain under his delusion and concludes a contract on the mistaken terms instead of pointing out the mistake. . . .

A contract is also liable in equity to be set aside if the parties were under a common misapprehension either as to facts or as to their relative and respective rights, provided that the misapprehension was fundamental and that the party seeking to set it aside was not himself at fault.

Denning LJ was here saying that equity will rescind a contract on the basis of common mistake if:

(1) the mistake was fundamental; and
(2) the party seeking rescission was not 'at fault'.

The language of 'fundamental' mistakes—language which had been used by the common law—was therefore part of the test of rescission in equity for common mistake.[42] Given that Denning LJ took the view that the common law had no role to play in relation to common mistake, it might be thought that the test he set out in *Solle* v. *Butcher* was as restrictive as the approach which we have seen that the courts took at common law in *Kennedy* v. *The Panama, New Zealand and Australian Royal Mail Co. Ltd.*[43] and *Bell* v. *Lever Brothers Ltd.*[44] In effect, that equity had simply replaced the area once covered by the common law. However, when subsequent cases are considered, it is clear that the test set out by Denning LJ has been accepted by a number of judges as showing the approach to be taken by equity in

---

[41] (1872) LR 8 Ch. App. 118, 124.
[42] See also Bucknill LJ [1950] 1 KB 671, 686. The third member of the Court of Appeal, Jenkins LJ, dissented on the ground that the mistake in the case was of law, not of fact: see p. 75, above.
[43] (1867) LR 2 QB 580; p. 235, above.
[44] [1932] AC 161, p. 234, above.

relation to common mistake;[45] and that the test is to be applied more generously than the common law test.[46] The judge in the most recent case on the subject has shown that the original common law jurisdiction in relation to common mistake remains intact, and that the effect of *Solle* v. *Butcher* was to add on a wider jurisdiction in equity for those cases where the mistake is not sufficiently fundamental to satisfy the common law test. He said[47] that we now have

a narrow doctrine of common law mistake (as enunciated by *Bell* v. *Lever Brothers Ltd.*), supplemented by the more flexible doctrine of mistake in equity (as developed in *Solle* v. *Butcher* and later cases).

3. COMMON MISTAKE CONTRASTED WITH OTHER VITIATING FACTORS

The purpose of considering common mistake here is to contrast it with the other vitiating factors which we have considered in this book. We may begin with the common law rules relating to common mistake.

(a) The Common Law

We have seen that the common law took a very narrow view of operative common mistakes: they must be *fundamental*; their effect

[45] *Grist* v. *Bailey* [1967] Ch. 532; *Magee* v. *Pennine Insurance Co. Ltd.* [1969] 2 QB 507; *Laurence* v. *Lexcourt Holdings Ltd.* [1978] 1 WLR 1128; *Associated Japanese Bank (International) Ltd.* v. *Crédit du Nord SA* [1989] 1 WLR 255. The House of Lords has never had the opportunity to review the decision in *Solle* v. *Butcher*, however; and most of the approval in subsequent cases is found either in the judgments of Lord Denning himself or in judges at first instance (who are in any event bound to follow the decision of the Court of Appeal in *Solle* v. *Butcher*). It can be argued that the wide equitable jurisdiction in *Solle* v. *Butcher* is not in line with the other vitiating factors in contract: Cartwright, (1987) 103 LQR 594; p. 245, below.

[46] For example, in *Grist* v. *Bailey* [1967] Ch. 532, Goff J held that a contract for the sale of a house 'subject to the existing tenancy thereof' was not void at common law where there was in fact no protected tenant. The consequence of the mistake for the seller, who wished to avoid the contract, was that he had agreed to sell the house for £850 (the value of a house without vacant possession) when it was worth £2,250 because vacant possession could be given. Goff J concluded that this mistake, which was reflected in the value of the subject-matter of the contract, was not sufficiently fundamental at common law. It was, however, sufficiently fundamental to satisfy the test of equity set out in *Solle* v. *Butcher*; the contract was therefore set aside.

[47] *Associated Japanese Bank (International) Ltd.* v. *Crédit du Nord SA* [1989] 1 WLR 255, 267–8 (Steyn J).

must be to render the subject-matter of the contract *essentially* or *radically* different from that which both parties thought.

It is very clear from the common law cases why such a restrictive test was adopted: it is founded upon the policy of *pacta sunt servanda*—that contracts should be upheld. In *Bell* v. *Lever Brothers Ltd.*,[48] Lord Atkin gave four examples of the restrictive nature of the common law test. He said that the contract would be valid in each of the following situations:

(1) A buys B's horse, wrongly thinking that it is sound. B has made no representation or warranty that the horse is sound.

(2) A buys B's picture, both parties wrongly thinking it to be the work of an old master. B has made no representation or warranty about its authorship.

(3) A agrees to lease or buy a house from B, both parties wrongly thinking that it is fit for habitation. B has made no representation or warranty about its fitness.

(4) A buys a roadside garage business from B; B knows, but A does not, that there is to be a bypass which will divert most of the traffic from the garage.

Lord Atkin justified his conclusion in each of these examples as follows:[49]

All these cases involve hardship on A and benefit B, as most people would say, unjustly. They can be supported on the ground that it is of paramount importance that contracts should be observed, and that if parties honestly comply with the essentials of the formation of contracts—i.e., agree in the same terms on the same subject matter—they are bound, and must rely on the stipulations of the contract for protection from the effect of facts unknown to them.

The first point, then, is that Lord Atkin took a narrow view of the common law test for mistake explicitly on the basis that there is an important policy to be implemented—that of holding parties to their contracts.

However, we can see two other important aspects of the examples given by Lord Atkin. First, that in each case the mistake[50] concerns

---

[48] [1932] AC 161, 224.   [49] Ibid.

[50] Either a mistake made by both parties—as in examples (2) and (3)—or made by just one party—as in (4); Lord Atkin did not specify whether B in example (1) knew of A's mistake.

some fact external to the contract. It is in each case a fact which is very relevant to the parties' decision to enter into the contract; but it is not a mistake about any of the terms of the contract itself. Lord Atkin said that B had not *warranted* the mistaken fact. A clear line is therefore to be drawn between parties being in disagreement about the terms of the contract and their disagreement or mistake about some external fact relevant to the decision to enter into the contract. The case where the parties are at cross-purposes about the actual terms of the contract raises quite different issues, which have been considered in detail already.[51]

And there is a further crucial point which unites Lord Atkin's examples: he emphasized that B had made no *representation* about the mistaken fact. If there had been such a representation, there would of course be remedies for misrepresentation.[52] But in his emphasis that there had been no warranty or representation, Lord Atkin was showing why the common law approach to mistake is rightly narrow. The key contrast between common mistake and other vitiating factors such as misrepresentation, duress, and undue influence is that those other vitiating factors are one-sided: during the negotiations, one party so acts or uses his superior position in relation to the other party that that other party is allowed to escape the contract. Mistake, by contrast, is a vitiating factor where neither party does anything to the other during the negotiations so as to justify that other having the right to avoid the contract. Neither party disturbs the balance of the negotiations. There is no inequality of bargaining.

Of course, contracting parties may make mistakes as a result of what is said to them, either by the other contracting party or by some third party. The mistake may therefore be induced. Or the mistaken party may simply have misread the facts relevant to the contract, or have jumped to some wrong conclusion. But when a mistake alone is relied upon as a vitiating factor, it is because the other contracting party was not responsible for the mistake. If a party has been induced to make a mistake by a misrepresentation of the other party, then it is the misrepresentation, rather than the

---

[51] See generally Part I; and (in relation to misrepresentations which are incorporated into the contract) Ch. 5 s. 5.

[52] Part II, above.

mistake, which will be relied upon.[53] And of course there are then remedies available.[54] But in the case of a common mistake where neither party has caused the mistake, one party is seeking to escape the contract in spite of the fact that he cannot say that the mistake is in any way attributable to the other party. There is therefore nothing to choose between the two parties in their respective positions or conduct at the time of contracting—and if the contract is to be avoided it is simply on the basis that the facts as now discovered make the contract less favurable to one party than he had foreseen. The common law does not totally deny him a remedy; but a remedy will be granted only in exceptional cases—where the consequences of the mistake are so serious that he cannot really be said to get in substance what the parties intended.

It is not surprising that the common law takes such a narrow view of mistake. There is a similar idea in a number of areas in contract: in effect, the position taken by the common law is that a contract can be avoided or terminated by reason of the harsh effects which the terms of the contract work on the position of one of the parties—but only if those effects are so serious as to deprive the party of substantially the whole intended benefit of the contract.[55]

(b) Equity

We have seen that, since *Solle* v. *Butcher*,[56] the courts have accepted that a contract may be voidable in equity for common mistake, even in circumstances where the common law test has not been satisfied.

---

[53] This may explain why there are relatively few reported cases of mistake—in practice what must often happen is that one party misleads the other into making a mistake of fact. Of course, the mistake in such a case will be *common* only if the misrepresentation is innocent.

[54] Part II, above.

[55] Frustration: *Davis Contractors Ltd.* v. *Fareham UDC* [1956] AC 696, 729; *The Hannah Blumenthal* [1983] 1 AC 854, 918. Termination for breach: *Photo Production Ltd.* v. *Securicor Transport Ltd.* [1980] AC 827, 849; *Hongkong Fir Shipping Co. Ltd.* v. *Kawasaki Kisen Kaisha Ltd.* [1962] 2 QB 26, 66; *Afovos Shipping Co. SA* v. *Pagnan* [1983] 1 WLR 195, 203. *Non est factum*: *Saunders* v. *Anglia Building Society* [1971] AC 1004, pp. 46–7, above. This is not to suggest that in all these areas the tests of the common law are applied in identical manner; just that the common law has a core concept of releasing parties from their contracts when the effects of their contracts are—through no fault of their own—fundamentally different from that which they had contemplated.

[56] [1950] 1 KB 671.

The effect, therefore, has been to allow contracts to be avoided for less serious mistakes.[57] This has created a tension between the common law rules and the rules applied in equity:[58]

Throughout the law of contract two themes regularly recur—respect for the sanctity of contract and the need to give effect to the reasonable expectations of honest men. Usually, these themes work in the same direction. Occasionally, they point to opposite solutions. The law regarding common mistake going to the root of a contract is a case where tension arises between the two themes.

It may be that the rules of common mistake applied by equity are an adequate solution to this tension, on the basis that the rules are sufficiently flexible.[59] In support of this it could be said that the equitable remedy is discretionary (as opposed to the rigid rule of the common law); that the court has the power in equity to impose terms upon its order of rescission;[60] and that in any event a contract is only *voidable* in equity (rather than being *void* at common law) and so third parties who have obtained rights in the subject-matter of the contract are protected. However, the Court in *Solle* v. *Butcher* and in later cases did not deal squarely with the argument of the common law that the policy of upholding contracts deserves to be implemented strictly. So there might yet—at least at the highest level—be some further adjustment of the relationship between the common law and equity in relation to common mistake.[61]

One point which deserves emphasis, though, is that the rationalization of the rules of equity, set out in the judgment of Denning LJ in *Solle* v. *Butcher*[62] fails to distinguish between the vitiating factors where one party disturbs the balance of the negotiations by his conduct at or leading up to the contract, and common mistake, where there is no such conduct by either party in relation to the other. Denning LJ said that equity acts on the basis of 'unconscientiousness'; and he gave three examples of such unconscientiousness:

(1) misrepresentation;

[57] *Grist* v. *Bailey* [1967] Ch. 532; *Associated Japanese Bank (International) Ltd.* v. *Crédit du Nord SA* [1989] 1 WLR 255, 270.
[58] *Associated Japanese Bank (International) Ltd.* v. *Crédit du Nord SA* [1989] 1 WLR 255, 257 (Steyn J).
[59] Ibid., at pp. 267–8.
[60] As in *Solle* v. *Butcher* [1950] 1 KB 671 and *Grist* v. *Bailey* [1967] Ch. 532.
[61] Cartwright, (1987) 103 LQR 594.
[62] [1950] 1 KB 671, 691–3, quoted above, pp. 238–9.

(2) mistakes (about terms or identity) which are known by one party but not disclosed to the other;

(3) common mistakes.

The first category is well established;[63] and although there are considerable difficulties in holding that there is an equitable (rather than common law) jurisdiction in relation to the second category,[64] it is at least consistent with the first in that it involves one party *actively* taking advantage of the other at the time of contracting. But the third category, common mistake, is—as we have already said[65]—a vitiating factor in which neither party has said or done anything which justifies preferring the other; the remedy flows simply from the harsh consequences of holding a party to the contract in the light of the mistaken facts. And we have seen throughout this book that the courts have been reluctant to allow a contract to be vitiated simply on the basis of an unfair bargain—in addition, they generally require some unfair practice or some advantage that one party has over the other by virtue of his position.

It is therefore suggested that it was not appropriate for Denning LJ in *Solle* v. *Butcher* to categorize common mistake under the banner of 'unconscientiousness' along with misrepresentations and known mistakes. It involved using the word 'unconscientious' in two different senses. In misrepresentation and known mistakes, the unconscientiousness consists in the fact that one party has—even if only innocently, in the case of misrepresentation—taken advantage of a superior position during the bargaining process leading up to the contract. In common mistakes, however, the unconscientiousness arises only out of the harshness, for one party, of the terms of the contract. If this distinction is observed,[66] the courts might be more cautious in allowing contracts to be avoided for mistake under the equitable rules.

---

[63] Part II, above.
[64] See p. 23, above.
[65] p. 242, above.
[66] Cf. *Hart* v. *O'Connor* [1985] AC 1000, 1017–18, quoted at pp. 215–16, above.

Index